Hard labour

The sociology of parenthood

Hard labour

The sociology of parenthood

Caroline Gatrell

Open University Press

Open University Press
McGraw-Hill Education
McGraw-Hill House
Shoppenhangers Road
Maidenhead
Berkshire
England
SL6 2QL

email: enquiries@openup.co.uk
world wide web: www.openup.co.uk

and Two Penn Plaza, New York, NY 10121-2289, USA

First published 2005

A catalogue record of this book is available from the British Library

ISBN 0 335 21488 6 (pb)   0 335 21489 4 (hb)

Library of Congress Cataloguing-in-Publication Data
CIP data applied for

Typeset by RefineCatch Ltd, Bungay, Suffolk
Printed in the UK by Bell & Bain Ltd, Glasgow

For Tony,
and Anna and Emma

Contents

Acknowledgements

There are many friends and colleagues who have helped in the writing of this book. First and foremost I would like to thank my family – my husband Tony who has always been there for me and encouraged and supported me all the way, and my dear daughters Anna and Emma, without whose existence I probably would never have come to write it. Also thank you to my parents, Pam and Max, to whom I owe a great deal.

Very special thanks are due to David Brown and Rosemary Deem for all the backing they have given me both in relation to *Hard Labour* and personally. Thank you also to Jennifer Mason, David Morgan and Maureen McNeil for commenting on the proposal and encouraging me to write this book. I would also like to thank Debbie Harrison and Jennifer Flowerdew who offered valuable support at the start of this project.

For reading and commenting on the manuscript, I am very grateful to Peter Anthony, Will Medd and Valerie Stead.

I owe thanks to those who have supported me at work, especially my good friends in the women's pressure group: Sue Eccles, Carole Elliott, Sarah Gregory, Ellie Hamilton, Valerie Stead, Elaine Swan, Sharon Turnbull and Helen Woodruffe-Burton. Additionally, I would like to note my appreciation of my colleagues Sally Watson, Rick Crawley and John Mackness for all the backing they have given me. I am also indebted to Dawn McCracken and Sarah Patterson for their unstinting support and friendship.

Thanks are also due to Open University Press, especially to Mark Barratt for all his support and encouragement. I would also like to thank Malie Kluever and Richard Leigh for all their help.

Finally, I would like to say a big 'thank you' to those without whom there would be no book: the mothers and fathers who took part in the 'Hard Labour' research project, and who gave up precious time to talk to me.

Introduction

The current educational landscape, while certainly consistent with, if not inspired by, the agenda of the equality feminists, is not conducive to women's happiness [because] it creates the questing of women who feel that they should not be fulfilled in their marriages and families . . . and that they should be looking outside to the world of work for their happiness, even as they doubt they can possibly find it there. To be honest, I am not sure I would love domesticity as much as do the women I have quoted, let alone be any good at it. But this . . . brings us back to the discussion of whether . . . [housework] is equally as fulfilling for men as it is for women. Clearly, there are gender differences in the way men and women respond to domesticity. The unhappiness that many women clearly feel in being moved away from a sphere that could be the source of their fulfilment, to a sphere that is clearly not, creates the urgent need to find out what can be changed in society and what may be harder to change if biologically grounded.

(Tooley 2002: 120)

Focus on:

Lone mothers, poor mothers and the diversity of family practices
Lived experience in a socially constructed world
An overview of key arguments
    Overview of Part 1
    Overview of Part 2

Before she had children, Sarah-Jane was a hospital consultant. It had taken her until almost the age of 40 to attain this position and she had devoted herself to medical work, to the exclusion of all else, until she reached consultant status. Sarah-Jane specialized in disorders of the blood. She dedicated herself to working with sick women, often those who were dying of leukaemia or breast cancer. Sarah-Jane's medical training will have cost society around £250,000 (Pringle 1998), to say nothing of the personal price she has paid, working the long hours necessary to build up the level of expertise required in her field. When Sarah-Jane became a mother, she asked permission to return to work part-time. She was told that this was impossible, and was offered a stark choice. Either she returned to her hospital job full-time, as a consultant, or went back part-time and accepted a downgrading in her position. She was told that if she gave up her consultant status, she would never regain it. Sarah-Jane accepted the latter option and went back to work part-time as a 'staff grade' doctor, a lower-level post without the prestige or authority associated with the title 'consultant'. She continued, however, to be highly regarded, and one particular colleague (a woman) went to some lengths to facilitate a situation whereby Sarah-Jane continued to treat the same group of patients as before. Sarah-Jane believed that being a mother herself was helpful in her work because it enabled her to empathize with women who knew that they would not live to see their own children grow up. Sarah-Jane had outstanding talent, and she worked exceptionally hard to help improve and prolong the quality of life of the women she treated.

Given her age, Sarah-Jane could not afford to delay motherhood any longer. She took the decision to have more children, and to try and manage this along with her job. Her work was stressful, her journey long and her regional managers inflexible. Eventually, Sarah-Jane went to the UK Department of Health to beg for a career break as she was finding it difficult to manage her dual responsibilities towards family and patients. She asked for a four-year break. In order to practise in NHS hospitals, doctors are allocated a 'regional number'. Sarah-Jane was told clearly that, should she choose to take the four-year career break, she would lose her number and would no longer be able to work as a hospital doctor in the UK. For a further year, Sarah-Jane struggled on. Although it was difficult to manage, Sarah-Jane's husband supported her. He knew how important her vocation was to her, and felt it was key to her social identity. Sarah-Jane felt her patients needed her, and considered that being a doctor was a privilege. She also considered that she had a moral obligation to society, which had paid to train her in her specialty. In addition to this, she knew that for some women, especially those suffering from breast cancer, it was very important to be treated by a female doctor – of whom there were few available. Twelve months ago, I spoke to Sarah-Jane on the phone. She was upset. 'I'm sorry,' she said, 'but I'm worried in case I've spoilt your study. I can't go on with this any more so I've given up work. I feel so resentful. Why should I have to give up the next 25 years of working life, just because I want to have some time to bring up my children?'

Equal opportunities legislation in Europe and North America has been in place for decades. Yet after all these years, the subject of this book – professional women who combine motherhood with career, leaving small children in the care of others during the day – remains controversial, even if children are being cared for at home by their own fathers. This book is about the sociology of parenthood, but the focus is on mothers because when writers and governments talk with authority about 'parenting', they are by implication (especially in relation to very young children) talking about mothers (Marshall 1991). As Warin *et al.* (1999: 31) note, the 'benchmark of good parenting [is] centred on the ideal of mother as carer'. Fathers' parenting, by contrast, is rendered 'invisible' because it is often assumed that 'involvement' with children is an additional role, tacked on to fathers' principal purpose of economic provider (Warin *et al.* 1999).

The purpose of this book is to examine changes in family practices and employment by focusing on a group who are an important part of social change: highly qualified women who combine the mothering of pre-school children with employment. The book explores the experiences of these women and their male partners in the context of the current debate on family practices and employment, and contemporary social and political processes. The intention is to offer a picture of what 'is' as opposed to what 'ought to be'. The desirability and suitability of combining work and motherhood, especially when children are very young, is widely and regularly discussed in government, and by influential agencies. Mothers are often heavily criticized for wanting to work, on the basis that this is somehow 'unsuitable' and that women are expected to be satisfied with less than men when it comes to career success because they are assumed to be responsible for small children in a way that men are not. Men, on the other hand, are believed to be career-orientated and unlikely to want extended involvement with their own children when they are very young. The behaviour of women with children who take a job in order to 'make ends meet' is just about accepted, but working women who are ambitious or (heaven forbid) successful are often represented as uncaring, or at least misguided.

The implication is that aspiring women should *make a choice* between career and children, because they cannot or should not attempt to take on the dual role of career mother. Additionally, it is implied that women who do choose 'career' will live to regret it. For example, in his book, *The Miseducation of Women*, Tooley (2002) argues that career women are unhappy because their social identity is mistakenly embedded in their occupation rather than in motherhood, which would be more appropriate. Tooley suggests that women should forgo paid employment and aspire to being housewives and mothers, as this would make them more contented (and more attractive to heterosexual men). In her book, *Baby Hunger*, American economist Sylvia Hewlett (2002) argues that 'high achieving' women should have children early because delaying motherhood in favour of career might mean an inability to conceive, which is too high a price to pay for a successful career. Allison Pearson's (2002) novel, *I Don't Know How She Does It: The Life of Kate Reddy, Working Mother*, provides a fictional account of the problems of combining motherhood and employment, and has been a bestseller in Britain and North America. In a review of this novel, the Canadian newspaper, *The Toronto Star*, observed that 'Women everywhere see themselves in Kate. They love their jobs, but want to be good mothers too.' It is both sobering and depressing that Pearson's heroine, a brilliant financier, gives up her career because she is made to feel inadequate as a mother and because her husband – despite the fact that he is a perfectly competent principal carer – wants more attention from his wife, and therefore threatens divorce. I am not aware of any contemporary novels suggesting that male bankers who go out to work are not 'proper' fathers!

The arguments put forward by Tooley, Hewitt and Pearson (that successfully combining motherhood with career is almost impossible) are widely known because they have been reviewed and discussed at length in the media (e.g. Baxter 2002; Armistead 2002; Wishart 2002; Stoffman 2002). The level of interest in these books is unsurprising because career motherhood is currently a 'hot topic', meaning that articles in the press about whether mothers ought to go out to work or remain at home appear frequently. In this respect, despite their supposed right to equal opportunities and pay, mothers' paid work is often associated by the media with the decline of the family, and with 'taking their employers for a ride . . . women cannot expect to have it all' and should not 'want to have their employment cake and eat it' (Phillips 1999: 17).

I shall contest the views of writers such as Phillips and Tooley, which seem to have more relevance to post-war initiatives to free up jobs for men in the 1950s, than to well-educated women in the twenty-first century. In doing this, I will challenge two assumptions which are embedded in such views: the first is that well-qualified women should choose between paid work and children; and the second is that fathers are automatically more career-oriented than mothers. In order to justify my position, although the principal subjects of this book are mothers who combine child-rearing with profession, I shall also take into account the views of fathers. This is unusual because – with the exception of Hochschild's (1997) work – much recent literature on parenting and paid employment tends to examine experiences post-divorce (for example, Smart and Neale 1999; Collier 1994). Previous texts on parenting practices within a relationship have tended to confine themselves, as a matter of principle, to whichever sex they are concerned with. For example, Ribbens (1994) and Oakley (1981) focus exclusively on mothers, while Lewis (1986) considers the father's viewpoint at the expense of the mother's, stating:

> It was hoped that I could interview fathers alone so that . . . we would not be distracted from our joint task, but in some cases . . . the wives wanted to attend, if only for part of the discussion and I felt it would cause too much friction if I pressed my claim to exclude them.
>
> (Lewis 1986: 25)

Lone mothers, poor mothers and the diversity of family practices

It is important to be explicit at the outset that, in contributing to the debate on working motherhood, this book deals with a specific group of relatively well-off women, all of whom are highly educated and all of whom were in heterosexual partnerships at the time I interviewed them. As I will explain in Chapter 1, the reasons for choosing to focus on these women and their partners are founded in statistical evidence, which shows that highly qualified women in heterosexual relationships are at the vanguard of a major social change: the increasing trend for mothers of very young children to remain in employment. At the same time as recognizing this trend, however, it is important to acknowledge that (while it is hoped that there might be changes in policy and organizational behaviour to benefit *all* working mothers and their families) there are many mothers struggling under even more adverse circumstances, some of whom may not have the option of paid work at all. It is important to be aware that, as Phillips (1999) has pointed out, the debate about whether women should combine mothering with career is rarely applied to poorly paid women in deprived areas, but rather to the group under consideration in this book – well-qualified, managerial or professional women with 'careers' rather than 'jobs' who are, by implication, in heterosexual relationships and who are seen to have a 'choice' about whether or not they work. Arguably, this is also true of much of the key academic literature on working parents and family practices (for example, Etzioni 1993; Beck and Beck-Gernsheim 1995; Beck-Gernsheim 2002). The discussions in these texts tend, in the context of 'marriage', to focus on the pressures that 'training courses in different cities, weekend seminars, business trips, evening meetings' (Beck-Gernsheim 2002: xi) can place on parental relationships. Such descriptions do not exactly conjure up a picture of single mothers with low qualifications working in menial jobs, but suggest a concern with affluent heterosexual 'career couples'. Thus, before going on to consider the professional women and men who are the focus of this book, I will refer briefly to three groups who are, to a large extent, excluded from the trends discussed in Chapter 1 – lone mothers, mothers in low-paid work, and deprived mothers from non-Western backgrounds.

In the UK, many lone mothers are poor, with 60% living on incomes well below the national average. Employment rates for this group (at 44%) are much lower than those for married or cohabiting mothers (Thair and Risdon 1999: 108). Perhaps unsurprisingly, lone mothers are likely to experience greater difficulty securing appropriate childcare than professional mothers, thus making it less likely that they will combine mothering with paid work (Pullinger and Summerfield 1998: 38). Many are in receipt of state support, and the incentives to be in paid work are low, since this often fails to lift many of them above the poverty line (Millar 1998). This may be because, on average, lone mothers are reported as having lower levels of qualifications than those within marriage/partnerships.

There is also an irony, observed by Crompton (1997: 82), that the increase in women's employment at the professional level has led to an increase in private sector caring jobs such as childminding which support parents who are better off and which are 'insecure and poorly paid' (1997: 82), as well as increasing the growing polarization between 'work rich households containing two people in paid employment and "work poor" households containing none'. This was alluded to by many mothers who took part in the 'Hard Labour' project and who acknowledged that, in order to facilitate their own employment, they were reliant on other women – nursery nurses, childminders and cleaners – on low wages. It is argued by Brannen and Moss (1991) and even more forcefully by Brannen *et al.* (1994) that social deprivation 'may be intensified by rising female employment among women of middle and upper-middle class origins in high status jobs who have partners of similar origins at similar occupational levels' (Brannen *et al.* 1994: 23). This hypothesis is confirmed by Burghes *et al.*:

> When both parents work full-time they are all but guaranteed a family income above the lowest quartile [and] . . . dual-earner families with full-time fathers and part-time mothers are just as likely to be in the top . . . income quartile, reflecting the range of male and female earning these families command (but just as the dual-earner family has become increasingly common, so has the 'no-earner' family).
> (Burghes *et al.* 1997: 51)

Furthermore, although their situation is not the focus of this book, it seems important to acknowledge that the picture is different for mothers from non-Western countries, in poor economic situations. Many women who do not have the advantages of a higher education are obliged to make a stark choice between motherhood and paid work. As Ehrenreich and Hochschild (2003) are keen to point out, for women from Third World countries, undertaking paid work might even imply being separated from their birth children altogether, as they seek jobs as nannies or domestic workers, particularly in the USA.

Finally, it is important to explain that, although I have focused on career women in heterosexual partnerships in the context of this book, this does *not* imply a belief that there is any one 'best' way in which family practices should be defined or performed, but quite the reverse. Although this research has focused on a particular social group, my view is that family practices are, and should be, diverse and that 'good' parenting can be defined in many ways, none of which is related to sexual orientation, wealth, or the popular notion of pre-divorce 'stability' (Smart and Neale 1999: 29). This view is supported by recent research. Many employed mothers may be single and low-paid, and women from deprived or ethnic minority backgrounds might find their choices in relation to paid work to be sharply circumscribed, but – as Bostock (1998) has demonstrated – most mothers are determined to provide love, security and excellent care for their children no matter how adverse their circumstances. Recent research has also confirmed that children with gay or lesbian parents, and who are brought up by single-sex couples, thrive and do well at school – what is important is the love of their parents, not the latter's gender, or sexual orientation (Ananova 2004).

Lived experience in a socially constructed world

The research discussed in this book is based upon a belief that the social world in which research participants are living, is constructed by human beliefs and attitudes about social roles, which in turn shape practices – because social constructions can be very powerful. Thus, in the context of this book, social or human reality is regarded as a concept with multiple dimensions which might look very different depending on the perspective of the individual or group under consideration. In my view, the social world can only be understood through human interpretations and mental constructions. This is not to claim that the lived experiences of those who took part in this research are in some way imaginary. The beliefs underpinning this research accord with those of Stanley and Wise – that there are multiple 'realities' and that individuals understand 'social reality' through lived experience, which is 'daily constructed by us in routine and mundane ways, as we go about the ordinary and everyday business of living' (Stanley and Wise 1993: 116). Stanley and Wise also argue that social realities are constructed through human perceptions and state that: 'We believe that there are many (often competing) versions of truth ... even if such a thing as "truth" exists, this is undemonstrable. This is because "truth" is a belief which people construct out of what they recognize as facts.' (1993: 113). The belief that the social world is interpreted and constructed does not deny the importance or the validity of agency, and lived experience. As Stanley and Wise (1993: 114) suggest, it is important to 'take other people's truths seriously' and accord respect to the everyday lives of research participants, for whom experiences are 'valid and true'. They note that: 'We, as well as other people, base our lives on our belief that "social facts" exist.' This is important because it will be argued that everyday lives and behavioural practices of career mothers and their partners are influenced by others' attitudes to their behaviour, as well as by traditional social practice. This would include both the attitudes of close family and kin (as explored in Ribbens 1994) and the perceived 'public attitudes' of a wider society (Scott 1999). Scott believes attitudes to be important because they can shape individual behaviour. She argues that

> The reason attitudes are important is not because they are good indicators of behaviour, but rather because they help constitute the climate of opinion against which behaviour is judged. For example, acute strain can result if mothers work while holding attitudes (or being exposed to attitudes) that take the view that their action is harmful to children. Thus, shifts in public attitudes . . . are likely to inhibit or facilitate social change.
>
> (Scott 1999: 75)

In my view, therefore, social practices and attitudes are important determinants of social behaviour. They may feel very 'real' to those individuals or groups experiencing them and are likely to influence the decisions that people make about their lives. At the same time, however, I would argue that external constraints do not necessarily prevent people from trying to initiate change. Dryden (1999: 146) noted that despite the difficulties this posed for them, wives and mothers in her study of marriage were 'actively engaged in challenging the legitimacy of perceived gender power imbalances with their husbands'.

The tension between individual agency and external social structure is considered by Anthony Giddens (1979) in his work on the theory of structuration. Structuration is a complex theory which I do not intend to explore in detail here. However, it comprises two key elements which are close to my own set of beliefs. Giddens, who is sympathetic to the interpretive approach to sociology, argues that social structure and human agency are interdependent and that social theory must allow for the importance of both. Giddens therefore contends that human beings may be living their lives in the context of wider social structures and institutionalized roles. However, he also argues that existing social traditions, while they may be constraining, can also be challenged, with the possible outcome that social practice and attitudes will change. He states: 'all action exists in continuity with the past . . . *structure is not to be conceptualised as a barrier to action but as essentially involved in its production*' (Giddens 1979: 70; emphasis in original). In their work on family practices and daily lives, Janet Finch (1989) and Isabel Dyck (1999) have already demonstrated that structuration theory can be effectively applied to personal and everyday lives within a wider social setting. Giddens's arguments are also relevant to the research participants for this study, who are operating in a social context where experience, upbringing and tradition may inform their behaviour. However, they also possess agency, and may choose not to conform to what they believe is expected of them by friends and family, or by the society in which they are living.

An overview of key arguments

As I have already noted, my objective is to explore the lived experiences of a group of parents where mothers are pursuing careers, and to understand their situation as they believe it actually 'is' – as opposed to what others think it 'should be'. I believe that these issues can best be explored if the empirical work is theoretically driven, and if the arguments are developed in relation to the established literature on parenting, employment and family practices. This book is therefore presented in two parts. Part 1 provides an up-to-date, comprehensive and (I hope) readable overview of key literature on women's employment, family practices, motherhood, fatherhood, and mothers' commitment to paid work. Drawing on a qualitative study of the lives of 20 mothers and their male partners, Part 2 then offers a new analysis of how men and women in relationships are managing commitments to work and family, situating these discussions in the context of the literature discussed in Part 1. Topics such as 'motherhood' and 'fatherhood' are presented as discretely as possible for the convenience of readers, which means that they can choose whether to read the book from beginning to end, or to dip in and out in any order, moving between Parts 1 and 2 with ease because the topics in which they are most interested are clearly identified under the heading 'Focus on' at the beginning of each chapter. This should be useful for students working in particular areas and, I hope, will make it simple to pick out the sections that they require. It also means, however, that for those who do not need all the 'background' in Part 1 (either because they are already familiar with it, or because they are practitioners who are 'living' the areas of concern), there is an option to focus on the research outcomes described in Part 2.

The research participants who took part in the 'Hard Labour' project were all based in the UK. However, Scott and Duncombe (1991) have argued that there are parallels between the UK and USA with regard to parenting practices and social attitudes. While differences between the two countries (such as the less generous arrangements for maternity leave in the USA) are recognized, it is also acknowledged that important research in America (for example, Hochschild 1997; Padavic and Reskin 2002) has focused on issues which were also key to the parents who took part in this research. Thus, while the research sample was drawn from the UK, discussions of motherhood, fatherhood and family practices are set in a wider geographical context, and cross-national comparisons are made where appropriate.

Overview of Part 1

Part 1 provides a review and analysis of significant literature in five main areas:

- the employment of career mothers, including the analysis of large-scale data;
- the sociology of motherhood (and the distribution of domestic labour);
- the sociology of family practices;
- the sociology of fatherhood;
- a discussion of the motivation of mothers to undertake paid work, including a discussion relating to social identity and the power of paid employment.

The first topic introduced in this section, the employment of career mothers, is different from the others as it is mainly descriptive (as opposed to analytical) in content. However, this is important because it provides a detailed explanation as to why the group of mothers and fathers considered here are significant in research terms. Chapter 2 opens with a discussion of Talcott Parsons' influence on the social construction of family practices. Parsons' work on families and roles is threaded throughout the book to help explain the impact of institutionalized family roles upon contemporary heterosexual relationships where there are children, and where the mother undertakes paid work. More recent texts which have been central in the redefining of family practices and intimate relationships as a 'mainstream' area of academic study are then considered. In Chapter 3, I examine the concepts of the 'institution of motherhood' and the 'Domestic Goddess', and the social construction of how motherhood 'should' be performed is a key theme throughout the book. I explore women's responsibility for domestic labour and discuss women's health following childbirth. Chapter 4 considers fatherhood and occupation both within a relationship and post-divorce. I argue that the law provides a particular construction of fatherhood and the way it 'should' be performed, fathers being judged by their ability (or lack of it) to make economic provision for their children. In Chapter 5 the motivation of professional mothers in heterosexual relationships to undertake paid work is explored. Here, I will contend that mothers' commitment to paid work is multi-faceted and difficult to separate from gender relations. I then engage in a theoretical discussion about power and social identity. These concepts, against which the empirical findings from the 'Hard Labour' research project are compared in Part 2, assist in explaining why the professional mothers of pre-school children are motivated to continue their careers.

Overview of Part 2

Part 2 analyses the research project which explores what life is like, at the turn of the twenty-first century, for professional mothers of babies and pre-school children in the UK, and for the fathers of these children. The study considers questions in five strategic areas which have been identified as important in Part 1:

- How do mothers and fathers cope with the transition to parenthood?
- How do both mothers and fathers manage to combine paid work with the responsibilities of parenting small children and managing a household?
- How do mothers and fathers construct the concept of 'commitment' towards children and paid work?
- What is the experience of mothers and fathers in relation to equal opportunities laws and policies?
- How do the experiences of the research sample fit into the context of the wider debate and the broader social setting, and what are the recommendations for policy?

In order to try and shed light on these issues, I interviewed, in depth, 20 women and 18 men from the UK who are married or cohabiting, each of whom (except in the case of three couples) was interviewed separately. All the women held professional or managerial posts, were qualified to degree level or higher, were mothering at least one baby or pre-school child, and were living with the father of the child. Because the research sample is small, the study does not claim to be representative of a wider population of men and women in the same situation. However, Part 2 does present the detailed findings from the research in the context of the literature considered in Part 1. This enables an explicit comparison to be made between the experiences of participants and previous research in order to identify similarities and departures, and to theorize from these. It is therefore possible to hypothesize about social change: what the needs and attitudes of a wider population might be.

Throughout Part 2 the experiences of the research sample and the decisions they make are set against the background of the wider social and economic contexts: the demographic shifts described in Chapter 1, and the general debate on career motherhood. In comparing the fieldwork with the literature described in Part I, the book demonstrates some areas where research participants revealed much in common with existing literature: the conflict between love for children and the low social capital associated with motherhood; and women's continuing responsibility for domestic labour. However, some significant departures from the literature are also indicated, including the unexpectedly high level of practical involvement by fathers in caring for their children, and the recognition by fathers that care of children may be an important source of power in relationships. A further departure from the literature was the strong commitment demonstrated by the mothers towards their paid work. This is in contrast to assumptions by writers such as Hakim (1995) and Gaillie *et al.* (1998) who claim that the principal motivation for mothers to undertake paid work is financial. I assert that mothers' professional orientation must be high if they continue working in spite of the pressures they face. I also contend that career mothers' commitment to paid work is concerned more with their sense of identity and the need to maintain equality in their marriages than with the desire for money (though earned income, like education, is seen as a key to independence). In addition, this research demonstrates how, despite legal and policy initiatives aimed at enhancing the rights of working mothers (such as the Sex Discrimination Act 1975 and the government's National Childcare Strategy of 1998), the women taking part in this research (and in some cases their partners) experienced direct discrimination on returning to work after maternity leave. They received no proactive support from either employers or government agencies, and found themselves constrained by the social expectation that, within a heterosexual partnership, roles should be 'institutionalized', with fathers taking responsibility for wage earning and mothers acting as principal childcarers. In the closing chapter, the implications for family practices are considered, as are recommendations for policy which would benefit both families and employers. As well as practical steps, recommendations for change include the need to examine the attitudes of a society that still seems to cherish a 1950s model of family life which no longer exists, and which acts to constrain those who wish to live their lives differently. It is concluded that single-sex couples, who have been excluded from traditional institutions such as marriage, and therefore have to devise their own way of doing things, might be at the vanguard of social change (as argued by Giddens, 1992). This may be of benefit to heterosexual, married/cohabiting mothers with a strong work orientation, who wish to combine career with child-rearing, since it could begin to shift cultural perceptions about the way things 'should be' done. The rejection of the 'institution of motherhood' by both mothers and fathers provides an important explanation as to why mothers in this research were motivated to continue paid work, since they did not wish to be associated with this role. It will also be shown that research participants were frustrated and surprised by the attempts made by a wider society (friends, colleagues, relatives and government agencies) to impose upon them what they regarded as '1950s style' institutionalized and gendered roles.

This book has important implications for society in general and for employers who wish to support career mothers. The issues are highly relevant to organizations, professional bodies and policy makers who 'need to keep pace with a changing world' (Dex *et al.* 1998: 79). In this respect, I hope that the book will make a contribution – however small – towards improving the situation for career mothers and their families in the UK.

PART 1
The Sociology of Parenting and Paid Work

For most new mothers, life means exhausting days and nights of broken sleep as we try to earn a living, be 'good' mothers and maintain some semblance of an adult relationship with our partners. Women can work *and* be mothers, but only if our work culture shifts enough to accommodate family life.

(Figes 1998b; emphasis in original)

Women, particularly those with young children, have increased their labour market participation over the last decade. The increase has been concentrated among women with higher qualifications and in professional and managerial occupations.

(Thair and Risdon 1999: 113)

1 'The impossible dream?'
Motherhood and employment

The image of the mother in the home, however unrealistic, has haunted and reproached the lives of wage-earning mothers.

(Rich 1977: 51)

Focus on:
Motherhood and paid work
Career motherhood – an increasing trend
  Labour Force Survey
  National Child Development Study
  National Survey of Health and Development
  The reasons for change – cause or effect?
Motherhood, employment and policy
  The social relations of gender in the workplace
  'Flexible' and part-time employment
  Policy and practice
  Paternity leave

Introduction

Over the past ten years, research has demonstrated that professional mothers of pre-school children are at the vanguard of a major social change in the UK: the sharp increase in the numbers of employed women with dependent children. This change, which has occurred over the past two decades, centres on the fact that highly qualified career women are increasingly combining motherhood with paid work. These trends are important, because they provided the impetus for this research, which sets the experiences of a small sample of men and women within the context of a wider debate. The main aim of this chapter is to outline this change by summarizing the contemporary quantitative work which describes it. Analyses confirm that the most significant shift is among women in professional or managerial careers who have at least one pre-school child and who are married to, or living with, the father of the child. The best current estimate is that there are 452,000 such women economically active within the labour market in the UK (Thair and Risdon 1999). The women most likely to combine mothering with career are highly qualified (to degree level and beyond) and will have probably gained several years of experience in the workplace before having children. They often delay motherhood until their thirties or forties.

Motherhood and paid work

> Women's increasing participation in the labour force since the 1950s means knowledge about their labour supply needs to keep pace with a changing world. A key change has been among mothers with small children.
>
> (Dex et al. 1998: 79)

In general, the participation of women in the labour force in the UK has risen sharply since the 1970s and this is due, in the main, to the numbers of women with dependent children who go out to work (as opposed to remaining in the home full-time). The most sharply increasing trend has been for women with babies or pre-school children (under 5 years) to return to paid employment within less than one year of the birth of their children. In the UK, it is significant that in 1979 the number of women who returned to work within 11 months of the birth of their child was 24%. By 1988, this number had doubled to 45%; by 1996, 67% of new mothers returned to work within a year of giving birth (Pullinger and Summerfield 1998: 38–9). This sharply increasing trend mirrors a similar situation in the USA, where the number of dual-earner families has risen by 40% since the Second World War, with 59% of women with children under 1 year participating in the labour force in 1998 (Padavic and Reskin 2002).

By far the highest percentage of British women undertaking paid work while their children are still pre-schoolers, are those with higher (degree-level) qualifications, in professional or managerial positions. 71% of these women are living with or married to the father of their child (Thair and Risdon 1999) and they will probably have established their careers before having children. This is similar to the situation in the USA, where, of those with a higher or professional qualification, almost 74% of women with children under 1 year are in paid work (Padavic and Reskin 2002). As little as 25 years ago, it would have been usual for well-educated women in heterosexual relationships in Britain and America to relinquish employment once they had children

(Oakley 1981; Rich 1977). Recently, however, the picture has changed. Table 1 summarizes the characteristics associated with mothers most likely to remain in work after childbirth. It is argued by Macran *et al.* (1996) that these women are also likely to return to work after the birth of second children, and to remain in the same employment without suffering occupational downgrading (an assertion which I will challenge in Chapter 9).

Table 1   Characteristics of women most likely to continue their career after childbirth

---

Cohabiting with/married to a heterosexual partner

Highly qualified (to degree level and beyond)

Career established before having children

Motherhood delayed beyond age 30

Working for employers with established benefits for those taking maternity leave – described as 'the higher occupations' (Macran *et al.* 1996: 275)

Likely to remain in the same employment without suffering occupational downgrading

---

Career motherhood – an increasing trend

There is a growing body of literature which explores what is happening to large numbers of women over a period of time, and which has identified the demographic trend for highly educated mothers with small children to return to work. These studies confine themselves to analysing trends, and do not attempt to understand in depth the reasons why career women combine mothering with employment, or the impact that this has on family practices. However, the studies are important because they provide the context for my own later discussions about mothers' commitment to paid work and my assertion that, in relation to mothers' employment, the attitudes of society may lag behind, and fail to acknowledge, important social changes. In order to provide the background for the 'Hard Labour' project, therefore, three key studies are described below which underline the significance to the professional labour force of the group of mothers under consideration.

Labour Force Survey

The Labour Force Survey is a quarterly survey of approximately 60,000 households covering a wide range of demographic and employment-related information. Results from the survey are 'grossed up' to reflect activities in the wider population (Thair and Risdon 1999: 115). The increase in participation of women with dependent children in the labour market is noted by Thair and Risdon (1999: 105), who focus on mothers with very young children and note the 'dramatic' increase in the number of women with small children who continue their paid employment. The authors observe that the women most likely to return to work were those who were older, in high-income families and 'in higher level occupations. They were also more likely to be married (or co-habiting), and working for employers in the public sector or which were operating "family-friendly policies"'. It is also noted by Thair and Risdon (1999: 106) that: 'the highest economic activity rates are for women with higher qualifications . . . . In Spring 1998, 86% of highly qualified women were economically active, compared with 50% of those without qualifications'. They go on to say that: 'The effect of qualifications is most marked among women with pre-school children, where only 27% of unqualified women were economically active compared with 76% of highly-qualified women. This effect of qualifications is consistent with the increase over the decade in the participation rate of women with young children' (1999: 107).

The correlation between high economic activity rates, higher education and the mothering of pre-school children is illustrated in Figure 1 and given in numerical form in Table 2. There are nearly half a million (452,000) economically active women in the UK whose youngest dependent child is under 5 years of age and who have a 'higher' qualification. Notably, for these women, the likelihood of their remaining in work is far greater than for those women with 'other' or no qualifications. Furthermore, only 10% of highly qualified women give up their jobs on becoming mothers, the percentage of those in paid work dropping from 86.3% to 76.2%. Of women with 'other' or no qualifications, 16% and 23% respectively will leave the workforce following the birth of their children.

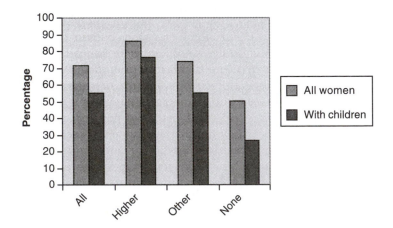

Figure 1 Economic activity status by highest qualification and age of youngest dependent child: UK, spring 1998 (Thair and Risdon 1999: 122).

Table 2 Economic status by highest qualification and age of youngest dependent child: UK, spring 1998[1]

| | Level of highest qualification held | | | | | | | |
| | All | | Higher | | Other[2] | | None | |
	No.	%	No.	%	No.	%	No.	%
All women aged 16–59	17,068,000	100	3,445,000	100	9,949,000	100	3,547,000	100
Economically active	12,206,000	71.5	2,972,000	86.3	7,362,000	74.0	1,782,000	50.2
Women aged 16–59 with youngest dependent child aged 0–4	3,095,000	100	593,000	100	2,022,000	100	460,000	100
Economically active	1,702,000	55.0	452,000	76.2	1,118,000	55.3	124,000	26.9

1. These figures include women who returned to work within 11 months of the birth of the most recent child; these women are not 'separated out' in the Labour Force Survey and would be counted as still in employment.
2. 'Other' qualifications include A Level or lower.

Source: Thair and Risdon (1999: 122)

In addition, it is noted that marriage (taken in the Labour Force Survey to include cohabitation) has a marked effect on the likelihood of women with dependent children being economically active, with 71% of those who are economically active likely to be living with a male partner. This reflects a trend noted as early as 1991, Brannen *et al.* (1991) observing that most well-qualified mothers returning to high-status jobs were also likely to be living with the fathers of their children, and that the fathers would probably also be in paid work: the 'dual-earner' couple.

National Child Development Study

Using data from the National Child Development Study (NCDS), Dex *et al.* (1998) drew their sampling frame from a survey of 11,407 individuals born in the first week of March 1958, who were aged 33 at the time of the survey. The authors focused on a sample of 5799 women. However, they reduced this number to 3889 after dropping some cases with 'missing values' (such as not having had a first baby!). Dex *et al.* (1998: 95) state that: 'Women who exhibit the most continuity in employment across childbirth were the highly educated, and by implication the high-wage group.' They note that, while highly waged women are likely to have delayed the birth of their first child, it is not merely the age of the women but their qualifications which were most important in securing job continuity. Like Thair and Risdon (1999), the authors conclude that their analysis of mothers' employment 'found evidence of polarisation in the labour force between highly educated and high-wage mothers and less educated and low-wage mothers. High-wage women, having delayed their first child, were more likely to be employed while the child is still young' (Dex *et al.* 1998: 95).

National Survey of Health and Development

According to Macran *et al.* (1996: 291):

> The secret of success is being highly educated, delaying the birth of [the] first child, taking maternity leave, returning to full-time work before having any more children and paying for childcare. The times have been favourable to the strategies adopted by these women. [But] they still appear to shoulder the double burden of childbearing and domestic duties alongside their employment.

Macran *et al.* compared the NCDS data for women born in 1958 with data relating to women born in 1946 taken from the National Survey of Health and Development (NSHD). A sample of 3894 from the NCDS was used, with a smaller sample (1543 mothers) from the NSHD. All women included in these samples were mothers of at least one child. Macran *et al.* deduce that the trend to continue career when children are little is most pronounced among highly educated women who are working in 'the higher occupations' (1996: 275) for employers with established benefits for those taking maternity leave. Among the group of women born in 1958, 65% of those with a degree had returned to paid work one year after their first birth (compared with 28% of unqualified women). This marks a highly significant difference from the women born in 1946, for whom the equivalent figures were almost identical to one another, 18% and 19% respectively, demonstrating the dramatic and recent increase in the trend for highly qualified women to return to work: 'The trend to more employment among mothers with young children is thus not a uniform experience but socially selective. As higher education became more common so did combining it with both motherhood and employment' (Macran *et al.* 1996: 285).

The reasons for change – cause or effect?

It would be interesting to understand more fully the causes of this trend, as the leap from 19% to 65% over such a short time period is striking. Macran *et al.* (1996) speculate as to what the reasons for rising female participation rates in the labour market might be. They suggest that changing 'social norms' regarding the acceptability of mothers engaging in paid work may have encouraged more women to maintain careers after giving birth. This argument is supported by Pullinger and Summerfield (1998) who nevertheless sound a note of caution to the effect that attitudes regarding working mothers are far more likely to be positive among women who are employed (86%) than among women who were not working (44%) (Pullinger and Summerfield 1998: 40). The inference, therefore, is that changing attitudes could be an effect of women's increased participation in the labour market, rather than the cause of this. Dex *et al.* (1998) also consider what motivates highly educated mothers to maintain paid employment, and argue that this might relate to increased owner-occupancy and shared responsibility for mortgage payments. Macran *et al.* (1996) also argue that, in response to rising demands for women's labour, employers may introduce policies that encourage women to retain their career status. They point out that, of those women considering a return to work after maternity leave, the highly qualified professional group are likely to be offered the most advantageous conditions, this explaining their motivation to remain economically active.

> These mothers, who have delayed their childbearing, are more likely to be better educated and to be working in higher level occupations and are thus better placed to take advantage of changes in employer provisions for working mothers. In addition, they are also more likely

to have adequate incomes to pay for childcare, more flexible working arrangements and be highly motivated to be in employment.

(Macran *et al.* 1996: 290)

Questions about motivation are relevant to this book, as the issue of whether women choose to remain in paid work for purely financial reasons has fuelled the debate about women's commitment (or lack of it!) to their career. However, those working from large quantitative data sets can only speculate about the reasons, because while they are helpful in establishing the increasing trend for professional mothers of pre-school children to work, such data sets do not offer the kind of qualitative information which would be required to understand the feelings and attitudes of the women concerned towards employment. This gap has motivated the qualitative 'Hard Labour' project.

Motherhood, employment and policy

> Over and over again ... what is problematized is *women's relation to the domestic sphere*. The way women do, or do not, fit into the scheme of paid employment and organisational life is seen primarily as a correlate of their marital status and, more important still, whether they do or do not have children. This is what women *are* to most men (and to most women): people who have domestic ties. Even if the woman in question is celibate or childless she is seen and represented as one of the maternal sex. Much of the argument surrounding Equal Opportunities at work circles about the question: can women *ever* be equal, given their different relation to reproduction?
>
> (Cockburn 2002: 180; emphasis in original)

Grint (1998) relates the rise in the economic activity of professional women to changes in the law such as the Sex Discrimination Act of 1975. In spite of these changes, however, in 1995 a UK survey across a wide range of occupations, ranging from machine operatives to teaching professionals, demonstrated that in every instance men were likely to earn more than women, no matter what the nature of the work or the level of qualifications required (Grint 1998: 202). Women are likely to earn around 67% of male earnings (Grint 1998: 205). This figure could be regarded as surprising given that in theory, in the UK, employed women have the legal right to be treated on equal terms with men, and should not experience discrimination in relation to pay or conditions on grounds of their gender. This policy has been law since the 1970s, through the Equal Pay Act 1970 (in effect 1975) and the Sex Discrimination Act 1975 (Grint 1998). (In the USA, despite vigorous opposition, the

Equal Rights Amendment was passed by the Senate in 1972.) Women did not always have the right to equal pay. Both in the UK and the USA, women who had undertaken paid employment during the Second World War were encouraged, post-1945, to leave the labour market and return to household duties so as to free up jobs for men (Oakley 1981; Dryden 1999). Rowbotham (1997) observes that the war had offered American women – especially those from privileged backgrounds – the chance both to enter the workplace and to engage in higher education because colleges with places left vacant by absent men were keen to welcome women; the numbers of women doing degrees in medicine and law doubled during the war years.

However, when the war ended and men were seeking jobs, attitudes changed. Women were 'pressured to move back out of the labour force and new emphasis was placed on women's role in the home as housewife and mother' (Dryden 1999: 10). As Rowbotham (1997: 268) explains: 'When the men came . . . home, most Americans assumed that women were going to return to being housewives. Indeed, a substantial number of people thought women with husbands who could afford to support them should not be allowed to work.' American mothers who were in paid work were therefore 'accused of neglecting their families and told that children who felt abandoned could become the juvenile delinquents of tomorrow' (Rowbotham 1997: 321). During the 1950s and 1960s, therefore, with no legal guidance on equality of pay, employers and policy makers could justify discrimination against women on grounds of expediency, affordability or simply the notion that 'men – but not women – needed to be paid a "family wage" ' (Joshi and Paci 1998: 9). For example in 1946, in Britain, a Royal Commission rejected the concept of equal pay for women and men, and this was not introduced into the Civil Service until 1961. And even though the 'marriage bar' (which forced women to leave their jobs on marriage) was removed from teaching in 1944 and the Civil Service in 1946, women still found themselves unofficially (but firmly) eased out of their positions if they married (Summerfield 1998). During the 1950s and 1960s, however, despite these disincentives, in both Britain and the USA, the number of women in employment began to rise, and the women's rights movement was growing. The first women's liberation demonstration in the UK took place in London in 1971 (Rowbotham, 1997), and moves to protect women's rights in law were spearheaded by UK parliamentarian Barbara Castle as part of a campaign to tackle women's needs in relation to wider social issues. Rowbotham (1997: 341) quotes Castle's statement that women needed 'to find out what they are, what they want to be and whether they are given the backing of society to lead the lives they want to lead. Real equality must go down to the mundane things, like . . . do I or do I not have children, who will help me to bring them up?' As well as the Sex Discrimination and Equal Pay Acts, Castle also secured the right to employment protection for women while on maternity leave (Joshi and Paci 1998), and the Equal

Opportunities Commission was set up in 1975 to oversee the enforcement of the new laws.

The establishment of new laws did not, however, automatically outlaw discrimination for women. 'Exemptions and loopholes' in the new Acts, such as the exclusion of part-time workers from maternity provisions, were soon discovered by employers who wished to take advantage of these (Rowbotham 1997). Notably, for example, in America between 1977 and 1979, female bank workers were still not receiving equal pay or promotion, in contravention of the Equal Rights Amendment (Rowbotham 1997). In the UK, the Conservative government elected in 1979 showed little interest in equal opportunities, and although new laws were forced upon Britain via the European Community, progress was slow and it was not until 1994 that 'maternity leave rights were extended to all workers regardless of tenure in the job or part-time status' (Joshi and Paci 1998: 11). The Equal Opportunities Commission still exists, in the UK, to monitor cases of discrimination, but the process of making an individual claim remains lengthy, cumbersome and stressful, just as it was in the 1970s (Rowbotham 1997: 405; Joshi and Paci 1998). Perhaps this is why, despite all the legislation, the average pay gap between men and women narrowed by only 5% between 1975 and 1995 (Grint 1998: 205). In the light of the difficulties associated with enforcing equal opportunities policies and legislation, it is perhaps unsurprising that women still experience discrimination in the workplace, both in terms of pay and other prospects. Joshi *et al.* (1999) have demonstrated that women who maintained employment continuity following childbirth and continued to work full-time were likely to earn as much money as childless women, but that, in general, neither were as well remunerated as men. Davies *et al.* (2000) have also shown that motherhood has an immediate and detrimental effect on employment and longer-term earning power. This is particularly likely to be the case where mothers return to work on a part-time basis (Joshi *et al.* 1999). In 1999, the average pay for full-time male workers in Great Britain was £23,412, whereas for women it was only £16,481 (Davies *et al.* 2000: 49). In relation to this research, however, it is notable that the drop in gross lifetime earnings of highly qualified women with children will be substantially less, in percentage terms, than the gross lifetime earnings of unqualified women with children. An unqualified childless woman is estimated to earn around £534,000 during her working life, whereas her married counterpart with two children will earn only £249,000, a gap of 53%. By comparison, a highly qualified childless woman will earn approximately £1,190,000 during her working life, her married counterpart with two children expecting to earn £1,171,000, a gap of less than 2% (Davies *et al.* 2000). Thus, the earnings gap is widest for those women with few qualifications, suggesting that, while professional women may still earn less than their male counterparts, the greatest wage differentials are between qualified and unqualified women.

The social relations of gender in the workplace

Discrimination is related not only to pay and conditions, but extends much more widely. Halford *et al.* (1997) take the stance that the social relations of gender are historically and deeply embedded in complex ways in both the formal and informal workings of organizations. They argue that this is often 'hidden' beneath apparently non-gendered policies relating to targets and performance: 'The gendered substructure [of an organisation] is hidden under a shell of rationality and neutrality' (1997: 15). (This is a contention which I shall question in Chapter 8, given that the discrimination experienced by participants in the 'Hard Labour' project was quite explicit.) On examining a selection of traditionally hierarchical and bureaucratic organizations (banks, hospitals and local government), Halford *et al.* conclude that although the 'traditional masculine hegemony' is breaking down, this is being replaced by

> a new form of male dominance based around images of the competitive, performative, skill-based manager who is not over-burdened by domestic responsibilities. Women can enter the new management culture, but only by accepting these key tenets and abandoning many orthodox claims to femininity, notably mother-hood. This is something which only a minority of women were prepared to do.
>
> (Halford *et al.* 1997: 267)

These findings are mirrored in the work of Kvande and Rasmussen (1995), whose study of opportunities for female managers in Norway indicates that although opportunities for women are greater in 'dynamic', 'flexible' private sector companies than in 'static', traditional bureaucratic organizations,

> The pressure upon deregulation of the normal working day and on flexibilization of working hours may not encourage women's partici-pation on an equal footing with men . . . although dehierarchization is an appropriate measure in order to increase women's opportunities, we might also be facing lesser representation of women in manage-ment because of the intensification of work which is an important effect of the same development.
>
> (Kvande & Rasmussen 1995: 129)

Pringle (1998) provides further examples of gendered policies and practices which disadvantage women in her exploration of issues of gender and the medical profession in Australia and the UK. She observes that although 'lip-service' is paid to supporting women doctors (Pringle 1998: 9), those who wish to combine motherhood with medicine will find themselves continually undermined by a determination on the part of the male medical establishment to adhere to traditional ways of working which force women to 'work harder and longer than men and take off extraordinarily little time for the birth of their children' (Pringle 1998: 12). She notes that 'Medical resistance to women doctors now centres on the issue of part-time work. It is argued that part-time work interferes with the continuity of care ... women's demands for a restructuring of medical time strike at the heart of the medical sublime' (Pringle 1998: 10). While the male medical 'establishment' has accepted a small number of part-time doctors on the 'fringes' of general practice, they fear any serious incorporation of part-time work (or mothers!) into the medical profession. A study of career advancement for women in the pharmaceutical industry in the USA (Yudovin *et al.* 1999) offers no more encouragement than Pringle's work. This study demonstrated that, no matter where in the world women managers worked, and despite the fact that they are employed in increasing numbers, women were still poorly represented at senior levels. A remarkable 77% of women surveyed felt they had not achieved equality with men in their companies. This is important because, as we shall see in Chapter 8, discrimination among research participants was not only widespread but also overt, especially if they sought to change working practices by, for example, asking to work part-time.

'Flexible' and part-time employment

Gallie *et al.* (1998) note that part-time work has played an important part in encouraging mothers back to the workplace, and demonstrate a rise in part-time work for women in the UK (1998: 123), though, like Joshi *et al.* (1999), they also observe that part-time female workers are disadvantaged in terms of pay, opportunities and career prospects. Like Hakim, whose work I discuss in detail in Chapter 5, they argue that part-time workers (for which read 'women'!) 'attach a lower importance to employment' than full-timers (1998: 171). They construct women who work part-time as unenthusiastic about their paid work:

> arguably, women's commitment to employment is rather different from men's ... It is possible that women's primary identity has remained with their roles as mothers or wives, and that employment is viewed very much as of secondary importance.

However, they do qualify this statement, pointing out that:

> Alternatively, if the increase in female labour market participation was a reflection of deeper changes in women's values ... then there may have been a marked change over time in women's attitudes to

work, with the result that there would be no tendency for a decline in employment commitment in the workforce.

(Gaillie *et al*. 1998: 187)

The assumption that women who work part-time are uncommitted to their paid work is exacerbated if they are also mothers. Cockburn (2002), in her study of men's resistance to gender equality in the workplace, noted that many senior men questioned the commitment of mothers. She found them to be angry about women's maternity rights and disbelieving that women were capable of managing responsibilities to both children and employment. Cockburn reports that, especially in relation to senior and professional women,

> increased maternity provision that arrives in the name of equality of opportunity for women is a bit like a blow to the funny bone, leaving [male managers] midway between pain and mirth. On the one hand it is a severe nuisance. It makes practical difficulties for managers, increases the proportion of women in the labour force and brings an unwelcome domestic odour, a whiff of the kitchen and nursery into the workplace.

(Cockburn 2002: 185)

Cockburn argues that some senior men regard all women as *'problematic'* because of the possibility that they may at some point bear children. Cockburn's view is borne out by the views of some members of the Institute of Directors (Malthouse 1998). Ironically, given that mothers are portrayed as uncommitted and inefficient in relation to their paid employment because of their maternal status, it would also appear that they are unwelcome in the workforce because 'they are a growing source of competition for men in the workplace' (Cockburn 2002: 187).

Policy and practice

Had I discovered that career mothers of babies/pre-school children were ambivalent about their commitment to the workplace, this would have been unsurprising given the limitations of UK policies and benefits regarding their position. Despite firm evidence that organizations providing good 'family-friendly' benefits will 'enjoy more loyalty, motivation and skills retention among staff, particularly senior female managers' (Welch 1997; Lawlor 1998), few employers are, in reality, prepared to invest in these. In theory, even although there is evidence that three-quarters of employers believe there to be a good business case for providing benefits such as a workplace nursery, only 5% of UK employers provide this and only 5% make any contribution towards nursery costs (Finn 1998: 33). UK government policy has recently extended maternity leave from 18 to 26 weeks and has also introduced a policy entitling parents who have responsibility for a young child to three months' leave. Significantly, however, this leave is unpaid unless employers wish to fund it, and while it is supposed to be available to either mothers or fathers, it appears to be assumed that it will be 'the mother' who takes it (Malthouse 1998: 1). This implies a view among policy makers that parental units still consist of a male and a female partner with fathers undertaking the economic provider role to the extent that mothers can afford to take substantial amounts of unpaid leave. There are many groups who might find it difficult to take up childcare leave which was unpaid. These might include lone parents, couples where 'the mother' is the main earner, or men who are bringing up children in a single-sex relationship (since neither partner would find it easy to claim to be 'the mother'). Additionally, the government has introduced a new right to a 'a reasonable amount of time off during working hours to deal with a "domestic incident" ' (McMullen 1999) but there is no clear definition as to what 'reasonable' might mean – presumably it is left to the individual to negotiate this with their employer. Unfortunately, the view that only women will avail themselves of these rights means that mothers are more likely than ever to experience discrimination. Having undertaken a survey in relation to maternal rights, the Institute of Directors (IoD) found that even though the understanding of employers on regulations was 'hazy' (Malthouse 1998: 2), nevertheless '45% [of members of the IoD] believed that the laws made women of childbearing age (up to 45) less attractive to employ' than men (Malthouse 1998: 2), and almost 30% would support total abolition of laws regarding maternity rights. The views of this group (and presumably the IoD) are summed up by one respondent who states that 'maternity rights are a disincentive to hiring women'. Dishearteningly, the literature on maternity rights indicates that women who turn to the law in the hopes of safeguarding their employment may be very vulnerable. Winston (1998) argues that UK laws in general are 'extremely hazy' in relation to maternity rights. Lewis (2000) also notes that policies which theoretically seek to provide protection for pregnant women have proved to be complicated and uncertain. This would certainly seem to be attested to by the number of queries and lawsuits relating to UK laws on maternity leave and the rights of women employees, which are reported in the management press (for example, Howlings 1997; Aiken 1998), an area where even the Equal Opportunities Commission is not beyond criticism (Walsh 1998).

Paternity leave

Paternity leave provision in the UK is very limited. Men do not have the right to take long periods of leave from work (either paid or unpaid) to care for newborn children, although they have the same right as mothers to take short periods of unpaid parental leave while children are under 13 – though in theory they are supposed to give 21 days' notice of this to their employers, which may be difficult if children are unexpectedly ill (Department of Trade and Industry 2002: 1). A new right to 2 weeks' paid paternity leave following a child's birth was established in April 2003, and this can be taken either as a block of 2 weeks or as two non-consecutive single weeks (Department of Trade and Industry 2002: 2). Although this new right brings with it the advantage that all fathers will be able to spend time with newborn children, it leaves any additional benefits to the discretion of the employer and precludes employed fathers from sharing the home-based responsibilities of maternity leave (even if this is unpaid) with their female partners, unless they happen to be working for highly supportive employers. The consequence of this is to perpetuate the social expectation that mothers should raise children while fathers go to work – even if some couples might like to do things differently.

Summary

Chapter 1 began by outlining the broad economic picture for well-educated women with very small children (particularly in the UK), and continued with a discussion of the recent history of motherhood, employment and policy. Having described these significant demographic changes, it examined the challenges faced by professional mothers in relation to legal reforms and attitudes. The recent history of equal pay and employment rights for women in the UK was summarized, and gendered approaches in the workplace discussed. I noted that, despite changes in the law, workplace discrimination still exists, though this is often regarded as 'hidden'. I also observed that the attitudes of some senior men may disadvantage women in the workplace, such men believing that women are *a problem in the workplace* because of their potential to bear children. The limitations of UK equal opportunities policies were discussed, and the chapter concluded with a brief section on paternity leave.

2 Parents, children and family lives

[The baby or child is] superior to other liaisons in our barter and throw-away culture. At least as long as it is young, a child permits one to invest all one's love and involvement without risk of disappointment, of being hurt and abandoned.

(Beck and Beck-Gernsheim 1995: 76)

Focus on:

Family lives and the work of Talcott Parsons
    Criticisms of Parsons – an over-socialized vision of (wo)man?
Feminism and the invisibility of research on family lives
Family practices, family lives and mainstream sociology
Family practices and intimate relationships
    Serial monogamy and the 'pure relationship'
    The Normal Chaos of Love
    The Time Bind
    Parenting post-divorce
    The New Family?

Introduction

This chapter provides an overview of the key literature on family practices, which is important because of the rapid changes that have occurred in the past twenty years and also because the existing literature on family practices forms further context and background for Part 2 of this book. Although this may be controversial, it is my view that Talcott Parsons, in spite of the fact that his work dates from the 1950s and 1960s, remains one of the most influential writers on family practices since the Second World War. This is because his work was instrumental in establishing the image of the 'family unit' that pervaded social policy throughout Britain and America for the following fifty years. To this day, the standard against which governments, the media and policy makers measure 'normal' and 'appropriate' family behaviour is based on a 'Parsonian' ideal. In Chapter 2, therefore, although I shall go on to examine some of the key writings on family practices and to consider the concept of the 'pure relationship', parenting post-divorce, and the position of work on family practices within mainstream sociology, I shall begin by considering Parsons' work on families in some detail.

Family lives and the work of Talcott Parsons

Earlier, I began to argue that, although demographics are changing rapidly, social attitudes and policies may lag behind, and the concept of mothers as principal childcarers and fathers as economic providers remains very much in place. It has already been noted that in the post-war years pressure to encourage women out of the workplace and back into the home was prominent in both American and British culture. In relation to this, although he may not have intended it himself, Parsons' descriptions of family lives in affluent parts of post-war America not only provided policy makers (in both the USA and UK) with a vision of how people were behaving at the time, but also offered a seductive and patriarchal template for how people *should* behave in the future. Thus, while Parsons himself may have recognized the 'potential for strain' which segregated gender roles might place on families (Somerville 2000: 80), his work has nevertheless helped to ensure that the 1950s images of mother/homemaker and father/provider became the ideals to which families were encouraged by governments and advertisers to aspire. Of course, as Bernardes points out, not all family lives in America fitted into the stereotypical images that Parsons described which were, by implication, those from white, well-educated backgrounds:

> In a society with widespread poverty, a large range of ethnic minorities and a large working class, [it seems remarkable that] Parson [(1971: 53)] claimed: 'It is of course a commonplace that the American family is predominantly and in a sense increasingly an urban middle-class family . . . there has emerged a remarkably uniform, basic type of family . . . the nuclear family'.
>
> (Bernardes 1997: 5)

Throughout this book, one of the key arguments will be that motherhood has become an 'institutionalized' role, meaning that society holds particular expectations about how mothers (and consequently fathers) should behave. In this context, Parsons' views on family practices are very important because of the stereotypical social images they have created and perpetuated over the past fifty years. Talcott Parsons emphasized the importance of social position and social roles, which he believed were automatically accompanied by the allocation of specific duties. He argued that roles such as 'mother', 'professional' and 'child' were learned, and that the people playing them were influenced by what they believed to be expected of them by friends, family and society at large. Parsons' philosophy of human systems is summarized very neatly by Sam Porter, who writes that, in Parsons' view,

> a role is a combination of normative expectations relating to the rights and duties of an individual in a given social position ... it involves expectations of how we should interact with others. *When particular roles are generally accepted by large numbers of people, they become institutionalized* ... Societies in which roles are highly institutionalized enjoy a great deal of consensus among their members. Conversely, where roles are not generally accepted, society is characterized by anomie.
>
> (Porter 1998: 23, emphasis added)

Writing on families during the 1950s, Parsons laid down very clear and distinct roles and social standards for men and women, in which heterosexuality and coupledom were presented as the 'norm'. Masculinity was associated with marriage, fatherhood, and paid employment, while women were expected to become wives, produce children, and stay at home to look after them, as well as doing the cleaning and shopping. Parsons stated that: 'In our society we can unequivocally designate the husband–father as the "instrumental leader" of the family as a system' (Parsons and Bales 1956: 13). He automatically allocated to the wife and mother the 'integrative-supportive role' in which she was 'expected to develop the skills in human relations which are central to making the home harmonious' (Parsons and Bales 1956: 314). Using statistics to illustrate his point, Parsons described the roles and responsibilities of men and women as follows: 'The role of "housewife" is still the overwhelmingly predominant one for the married woman with small children.' He added that:

> It seems quite safe in general to say that the adult feminine role [is] anchored primarily in the internal affairs of the family as wife, mother and manager of the household, while the role of the adult male is primarily anchored in the occupational world, in his job and through it by his status-giving and income-earning functions for the family. Even if, as seems possible, it should come about that the average married woman had some kind of job, it seems most unlikely that this relative balance would be upset.
>
> (Parsons and Bales 1956: 14–15)

Parsons indicated that change was likely to be slow (and possibly undesirable) due to the complexity of social structures. He believed that individual human beings were part of an overall system, of which there were many subsystems, from immediate family to the wider social system:

> [Parents] are themselves integrated in the cultural value system . . . both in that they constitute, with the children, an institutionalized social system, and that the patterns have previously been internalized in the relevant ways in their own personalities. The family is . . . an institutionalized system.
>
> (Parsons and Bales 1956: 17)

Criticisms of Parsons – an over-socialized vision of (wo)man?

Although some may disagree with the philosophy underlying his approach (Oakley 2000: 129 and 333; Finch 1989), many writers on family practices would acknowledge that Talcott Parsons was a key writer on the importance of social roles during his era. Recently, however, Parsons' work has gone out of favour. This is for a number of reasons. Firstly, it is argued by some writers (Porter 1998) that Parsons' work is irrelevant in the face of contextual changes in society such as equal opportunities legislation in the USA and UK. It is certainly true that Parsons was writing at a time when 'The number [of women] in the labour force who have small children is still quite small and has not shown a marked tendency to increase' (Parsons and Bales 1956: 14), which is no longer the case (as described in Chapter 1). However, recent debates in the media suggest that changing demographics do not necessarily engender changes in attitudes, and it is argued that mothers will probably be allocated the role of principal childcarer (by, for example, school and health services) whether or not they work, and might be heavily criticized for trying to combine motherhood with career (Scott 1999). Furthermore, while we might have hoped that Parsons' views on women's roles in relation to domestic labour would be outdated, recent evidence suggests that many working mothers still carry the burden of domestic labour (e.g. Delphy and Leonard 1992; Maushart 2002), meaning that Parsons' assumption that mothers are responsible for cleaning and shopping remains as relevant today as it was fifty years ago. Finally, it is apparent from the literature discussed later (e.g. Potuchek 1997) that the contemporary father is often still assumed to be 'primarily anchored in the occupational world, in his job and through it by his status-giving and income-earning functions for the family' (Parsons and Bales 1956: 15), even where this is not the case. Thus, although statistics demonstrate that work-force patterns have changed, families who are part of this transformation may be operating in an environment where social expectations have altered very little. Parents who do not 'fit in' with the Parsonian notion of what 'the family' should look like and how its members ought to behave might find things very difficult, because the lifestyles he described are still held up by many sectors of society as the 'ideal' and parents who do not follow these patterns are seen to threaten an idealized view of 'family stability' (Morgan 1999).

Some key writers and influencers are very disapproving of changes in family practices, and mothers (either by implication or directly) are the main butt of their criticisms. For example, Malthouse (1997), writing policy documents for the Institute of Directors in Britain and referring to the work of Catherine Hakim (whose research is discussed in Chapters 3 and 5), expresses doubts about the acceptability of combining paid work with motherhood. She infers that employed mothers are responsible for unfortunate 'changes in traditional roles in Western Society' and portrays her deep reservations about career motherhood as follows:

> Many women have now been subliminally programmed to accept that their value and status are diminished by not 'having a career'. It is therefore for discussion whether Government should do anything further to increase the number of women in the workforce; or [to] create a better climate for childcare and the future of the next generation; or to address the proposition that the alleged moral degeneration of large sections of youth, and increases in truancy and crime, may be related to the absence of working parents [for which, presumably, read 'mothers'!] from the home.
>
> (Malthouse 1997: 2)

In the same vein, Patricia Morgan, examining family breakdown in Britain and the USA, criticizes lone and/or financially independent mothers and blames 'feminist demonology' for the breakdown of 'traditional families'. She argues that 'we seem to be on the verge of an unprecedented social experiment, considering that there has been no known human society built upon the mother/child unit'. This argument is interesting, as it conveniently disregards periods in recent history, such as the Second World War, during which time many women in Britain and America were expected to raise children by themselves, and indeed were encouraged to combine this with paid work, as 'wartime recruitment campaigns proclaimed that it was women's patriotic duty to release men from industry and from military offices and workshops in order to fight' (Summerfield 1998: 200). Morgan implies that wage-earning mothers are culpable for undermining masculinity and makes a link between the father/provider figure and 'family stability'. She argues that women's paid work makes no significant contribution to the economy and asserts that:

> Since the decline in intact families cannot be separated from the labour market tribulations of men, there is a need for employment

opportunities that are as considerate and 'friendly' to men as family providers, as they are ... towards parents [for which once again, presumably, read 'mothers'] as carers and mothers as providers.

(Patricia Morgan 1999: 189)

Thus, although Parsons' writing may be outdated in terms of demographics, the 'ostrich position' adopted by some key commentators in relation to social change suggests that it is highly relevant in terms of social attitudes.

Parsons was also writing at a time when divorce rates were low and he was able to identify a high proportion of families living as a 'nuclear' unit, comprising mother, father and children, because 'once they settle down to have children there is a relatively high probability that they will stay together' (Parsons and Bales 1956: 4). Although Parsons' descriptions of the 'nuclear family' and divorce rates are outdated, and there is a lot of publicity about divorce, it is notable that 71% of UK women who are managing professional careers at the same time as raising small children are doing this within a heterosexual relationship. In terms of a study about motherhood and professional career, therefore (although some couples may be cohabiting and not married), Parsons' work is relevant. Arguably, even had this particular study been considering family practices from a different angle – for instance, the experiences of divorced or lone parents, or parents in a single-sex relationship – Parsons' work would still have been important, because in constructing the 'nuclear' family as the norm, he has validated the tendency for society to define anyone who does not fit into that pattern as marginal or 'other' and to construct them as responsible for declining social standards; see, for example, Patricia Morgan's (1999) disparaging attacks on lone mothers in Britain and America.

A final criticism of Parsons' work is that his study of the social system led to a subjugation of the importance of individual personality and a denial of the concept of agency to the point where his thesis presented 'an over-socialized conception of man' [sic] (Robertson and Turner 1991: 8). This aspect of Parsons' work is very unfashionable in a sociological climate where great emphasis is placed by writers such as Ulrich Beck and Anthony Giddens on the significance of individuality. Giddens (1984: 257), for example, argues that 'Parsons' concentration on normative consensus as the foundation of the integration of societies leads him seriously to underestimate the significance of contestation of norms'. Robertson and Turner (1991: 8–9), however, argue that 'Parsons did not work with . . . fixed notions of "self and society" ', and defend Parsons' own argument that he was trying to understand the individual in sociological terms as an 'institutionalized individual'. Whether or not his view of the individual is considered to be overly bound up with the socialization process, Parsons' work on family practices remains particularly relevant, because it enables a comparison between public attitudes towards the role of 'mother' and the lived experiences of the women under consideration here. It is thus threaded through Part 2 of this book to illustrate how socially con-structed but powerful ideas about family practices and institutionalized roles produce the dilemmas faced by contemporary career parents, and it is con-sidered below in relation to other writers' work on social roles and expectation.

Feminism and the invisibility of research on family lives

As the work of Talcott Parsons waned in popularity, so did the study of family practices as a mainstream sociological approach. Significantly, in 1996, David Morgan, the well-known British writer on family practices, observed that, during the 1970s and 1980s, 'Family sociology was certainly not sexy and might have been more than a little politically suspect' (Morgan 1996: 3). Per-haps this reflects the fact that family studies in the post-Parsonian era came to be associated primarily with feminism and women's issues. As early as 1963, the American feminist Betty Friedan launched an attack on Talcott Parsons and his contemporaries, accusing them of wishing to trap women into domestic roles in order to 'keep the social structure as it is, which seems to be the functionalist's primary concern' (Friedan 1965: 117). A few years later, Germaine Greer (1970) railed against the socialization of women into sub-ordinate domestic roles, arguing for equality with men. In the late 1970s and early 1980s, a growing number of feminist writers, such as Adrienne Rich and Ann Oakley, accepted the definition of motherhood as an 'institutionalized' role, but challenged strongly the moral and logical rationale behind this. As I will observe in Chapter 3, feminist writers on motherhood and family lives focused during the 1970s and 1980s on what society *expects* from mothers, and contrasted this with their own and others' experiences. These second-wave feminist activists challenged the *status quo*, and wrote with the specific and political purpose of freeing women from the domestic roles which constrained them. Suggestions that families were not all configured like those described by Talcott Parsons, and that mothers may not wish to fit in with the roles defined for them by sociologists and post-war governments, were regarded as threaten-ing and inconvenient (Summerfield 1999). Arguably, this factor would immediately have placed research on family lives into a less significant cat-egory than research with a 'malestream' focus. As Dale Spender (1982: 24) stated: 'Women have been kept off the record in most, if not all branches of knowledge by the simple process of men naming the world as it appears to them. [Men] have taken themselves as a starting point, defined themselves as central, and then proceeded to describe the rest of the world in relation to themselves.'

Family practices, family lives and mainstream sociology

During the 1970s and 1980s, therefore, research on relationships and 'the family' held relatively lowly status in academia and was almost exclusively the province of writers concerned with feminist issues (Morgan 1975, 1985; Finch 1989; Oakley 1976, 1981). In the early 1990s, however, two publications on relationships and family lives by 'mainstream' sociologists changed all this (Giddens 1992; Beck and Beck-Gernsheim 1995). These texts are identified by Smart and Neale (1999: 4–5) as having transformed the academic view of 'the family' from 'an institution which reacts to other social changes in a passive fashion', to an entity which 'gives rise to other social changes'. While regretting the fact that it was necessary for 'malestream' sociologists to give status to work on relationships and the family (when feminists had been researching this area for years), Smart and Neale nevertheless argue that Giddens and Beck have shifted the focus of family practices from marginal to 'mainstream' in sociology. This shift has provided key writers on families (such as Morgan 1975, 1985) with greater opportunities to argue that 'the family' should not be regarded as an 'undifferentiated' unit but that it is important to 'examine what actually takes place between individuals within households' (Morgan 1996: 25). In accordance with this view, Morgan has suggested the use of the term 'family practices' to describe research on families, in the hope that this will facilitate a move away from the stereotypical 'nuclear family' with an employed father and a stay-at-home mother. Morgan (1996: 11) argues that 'This strategy should serve to underline the argument that "family" is not a thing, without denying that notions of "family" are important parts of the ways in which people understand and structure their lives.' Smart and Neale (1999:21) also like the term 'family practices' because it 'allow[s] us to imagine the social actor[s] who engage in [family] practices and who may choose to modify them'. Thus, the need to reconceptualize 'families' as diverse entities (as opposed to imposing upon them certain characteristics to make them 'fit in' with a particular ideal) has become acceptable in 'mainstream' sociology. Given their importance, I will summarize the texts by Giddens (1992) and Beck and Beck-Gernsheim (1995), as do Smart and Neale (1999), and follow this with a discussion of some recent and important work on family practices (Smart and Neale 1999; Silva and Smart 1999; Morgan 1996; Hochschild 1997).

Family practices and intimate relationships

Serial monogamy and the 'pure relationship'

In his seminal text, *The Transformation of Intimacy*, Anthony Giddens (1992) reflected on a changing society in which the traditional notion of marriage as a permanent arrangement between heterosexuals had undergone a profound transformation. Giddens saw this as part of the process of the individualization of society, in which personal fulfilment has become a legitimate goal for which to strive. 'Personal life has become an open project, creating new demands and anxieties. Our interpersonal existence is being thoroughly transformed, involving us all in what I call *everyday social experiments*' (1992: 8; emphasis in original). Giddens sees relationships as the key to social change and argues that people regard sexual and emotional fulfilment as paramount. If they cease to find fulfilment within their 'intimate relationships', people will move on and search for new intimacy, with another partner. Giddens asserts that this model of serial monogamy, which he describes as the 'pure relationship', is becoming more commonplace than the idea of a lifetime partnership. He predicts that 'pure relationships' will increasingly occur outside the confines of 'marriage'. Importantly, Giddens argues that since those in single-sex partnerships have had to 'get along without traditionally established frameworks of marriage, in conditions of relative equality between partners' (1992: 15), they are likely to be at the vanguard of the trend towards 'pure relationships'. In this respect, he also considers that lesbian and gay relationships could be an important catalyst for social change because they may be based on agreements between individuals rather than on compliance with social expectations, this in itself serving to change existing social norms. In spite of these social changes, Giddens fears that equality will be difficult for women to achieve because men are reluctant to give up their higher social status in order to be 'equal' in society. 'Men declare that they want equality, but many also make statements suggesting that they also reject, or are nervous about, what it means for them' (1992: 11). The area that Giddens does not explore in depth, which raises questions about the validity of his thesis, is that of parenting. As Smart and Neale (1999) point out, while there *is* evidence for the trend towards the 'pure relationship', there is also evidence that adults (especially women) do stay in unsatisfactory relationships when children are involved, and that children remain a key focus and responsibility once adult intimate relationships have ended. In this context, it is notable that Giddens indicates that the importance of the 'pure' relationship takes precedence over all other aspects of life, an option which many married/cohabiting mothers and fathers with children do not feel is open to them (Smart and Neale 1999). Regardless of whether this is the case, however, Giddens's emphasis on the importance of individual agency within a wider social context, and the possibility that human actors can challenge social conventions, is relevant to this book and has already been noted in the

The Normal Chaos of Love

As Smart and Neale (1999) observe, *The Normal Chaos of Love* (Beck and Beck-Gernsheim 1995) follows on from Beck's earlier work, *Risk Society* (1992), in which Beck notes that 'the lives of women are pulled back and forth by this contradiction between liberation from and reconnection to the old ascribed roles . . . they flee from housework to a career and back again and attempt . . . to hold together the diverging conditions of their life "somehow" ' (1992: 111–12). Beck and Beck-Gernsheim analyse the complexities of trying to manage career and family at the end of the twentieth century. Some of their beliefs are similar to those of Giddens; for example, their hypothesis that, historically, marriage was more of an economic partnership than a love match, meaning that expectations were lower and disappointments less. Nowadays, the search for 'love' in society is so all-consuming that it has taken on religious tones; 'love' has become a 'holy grail'. Couples now expect an emotionally fulfilling relationship, and individuals may be prepared to move on if this is not the case. 'People marry for the sake of love and get divorced for the sake of love. Relationships are lived as if they were interchangeable, not because we want to cast off our burden of love but because true love demands it' (Beck and Beck-Gernsheim 1995: 11). It is argued, however, that intimate love is doomed to fail because of the late twentieth-century trend towards individualization. If each partner is striving for personal fulfilment, it can be difficult to make the relationship work: 'If freedom is everything, restricting someone else's freedom must be the goal even if love keeps enthusing about doing quite the opposite' (Beck and Beck-Gernsheim 1995: 196). At the same time, it is argued that both men and women are responsible for this social change, urged on by popular self-help manuals which are divisive: 'To what extent is it possible to share one's life if social circumstances compel one to concentrate on one's own interest?' (Beck 1992: 52). Like Ribbens (1994), whose work is discussed in Chapter 3, Beck and Beck-Gernsheim reflect that family cohesion often stays intact at the expense of women's individual needs, and express concern that 'women are . . . making their own plans which are not necessarily focused on the family but on their own personalities. The more women come to regard themselves as people with wishes of their own [the more likely they are] to demand satisfaction and, if all else fails, to take the ultimate consequence, divorce' (Beck and Beck-Gernsheim 1995: 62). Beck and Beck-Gernsheim are concerned that 'The fact that work and family are incompatible remained concealed as long as marriage was synonymous with woman at home and man at work; it has surfaced with great turbulence now that each couple has to work out its own division of labour' (1995: 144). They conclude that society, and the workplace, should take some responsibility for the raising of children now that mothers may also be career women. They predict that new generations may force this change, as young women are reluctant to be financially dependent on their partners and young men are unwilling or unable to take on the role of sole breadwinner.

Where Beck and Beck-Gernsheim depart from Giddens' view is in their belief that, in modern adulthood, children are central to the concept of personal fulfilment. They suggest that the child–parent relationship may last longer than marriage or other intimate relationships between adults and, as a result of this, parents (both men and women) are investing a great deal in relationships with their children:

> the love between men and women has . . . proved vulnerable and prone to failure. What remains is the child. It promises a tie which is more elemental, profound and durable than any other in society. The more other relationships become interchangeable and revocable, the more a child can become . . . the ultimate guarantee of permanence, providing an anchor for one's life.
>
> (1995: 73)

Beck and Beck-Gernsheim argue that this new focus on the child is leading to a trend in which men are challenging women's traditional role as mediator and emotional manager of the family, particularly after divorce or relationship breakdown. They contend that children impact on the balance of power between mother and father and predict that men will increasingly seek residency of children following divorce. This suggestion is reflected in contemporary cases reported in the media (Waters 1999), by the emergence of activist groups such as Families Need Fathers (2002) and publications such as *Achilles Heel* (1994). All this is significant to a book that examines how women manage careers as well as their responsibilities to small children and 'the family', because it indicates a power shift in the management and division of emotional labour, an area which has traditionally been mothers' responsibility.

If Beck and Beck-Gernsheim could be criticized, it is in the following respects. Firstly, perhaps without meaning to, they imply that women bear the responsibility for social changes which have led to the increasing divorce rate – if only the mother were prepared to 'devote herself completely to the family' instead of wishing to 'work outside the home' (1995: 55), then relationship breakdown could perhaps be avoided. So while the writers are clear that it is reasonable for educated women to want to work, they imply that this may be at the expense of the family unit. Secondly, although less well-off families are referred to, the implication here (as in Giddens 1992) is that the social group really under consideration are professionals working in the 'higher occupations': 'Better educated and informed young women expect to be treated as partners in professional and private life but come up against the opposite tendencies in the labour market and their male colleagues' (Beck and Beck-Gernsheim 1995: 14). This focus on the experiences of those who are well educated and relatively affluent could be an area for criticism in texts which claim to make generalizations about society. However, in relation to the present book, which deals specifically with professional women and their partners, it happens to be convenient. Finally, it could be suggested that Beck and Beck-Gernsheim hold an idealized view of children as 'providers of permanent unconditional love' (Smart and Neale 1999: 18), when the actuality of parent–child relationships can be rather different! As Charlotte Perkins Gilman (2002) wrote in 1903 (quoted in Oakley 1993: 85), the care of small children involves 'the running of commissary and dormitory departments of life with elaborate lavatory processes' – in other words, a lot of hard work, without necessarily an immediate reward! Despite these criticisms, however, it is recognized that Giddens (1992) and Beck and Beck-Gernshem (1995) are important texts because they have paved the way for new research on family life.

The Time Bind

A further text which is essential to the understanding of family practices among heterosexual parents where mothers and fathers both work is *The Time Bind: When Work Becomes Home and Home Becomes Work*. Arlie Hochschild (1997) undertakes research in a major American company, 'Amerco', which purports to value 'family-friendly' working practices. Hochschild (who studies workers at all levels) finds that the utilization of flexible working policies, especially among senior staff, is unexpectedly low. She provides two explanations for this phenomenon. The first lies in the context of promotion and commitment to work. Although family-friendly policies exist on paper, Hochschild observes that staff are aware of an unwritten set of rules: that employees who seek part-time work will be disadvantaged in terms of their long-term career prospects. She notes that even the director responsible for implementing Amerco's work–life balance programme associates the concept of commitment (and promotion!) less with ability than with long hours at work, stating that: 'The members of the management committee . . . aren't the smartest people in the company. We're the hardest working. We work like dogs. We out-work the others . . . what counts is work and commitment' (Hochschild 1997: 56). Additionally, Hochschild argues that workers (especially women) reject family-friendly policies because they find the workplace more relaxing than their home. She observes that some working mothers found their return to the household stressful and exhausting, with meals to be cooked and chores to be undertaken while fractious children (and sometimes husbands) demanded attention. Work, by comparison, offered a more convivial environment where tasks could be tackled in order, success was easier to define and mothers felt a greater sense of control over their activities. One criticism of Hochschild's work (a view which is shared by Chira 1998) is her (perhaps unintentional) inference that the responsibility for any parenting deficit resulting from combining parenthood with career lies at the mother's door, the implication being that mothers 'do' childcare, with fathers undertaking the role of helpmate:

Is it being a 'good mother' to bake a child's birthday cake (alone or together with one's partner)? Or can we gratefully save time by ordering it and be a good mother by planning the party? Or can we save more time by hiring a planning service and be a good mother by watching one's child ... As the idea of the 'good mother' retreats before the time pressures of work and the expansion of 'motherly' services, actual mothers must continually reinvent themselves.

(Hochschild 1997: 233)

The end of Hochschild's book is depressing, because Amerco abandons its commitment to family-friendly practices and dismisses the woman responsible for implementing them.

Parenting post-divorce

Carol Smart and Bren Neale speak of 'rethinking family life' in *Family Fragments?* (1999), which argues that family practices and lifestyles are inextricably linked to social change. Smart and Neale's text focuses on parenting after divorce, and is significant because it explores major changes in social attitudes and behaviour. The authors chart changes in the divorce laws in the UK, and note how the Children Act of 1989 shifted the focus from marriage to parenthood and gave children rights and agency of their own. It is significant that, historically, women were often financially disadvantaged following divorce, but, before the Children Act, retained a strong power base in relation to the children, of whom the mother was usually awarded custody. From 1989, while it was accepted that one parent may carry the burden of childcare, it was the objective of the Act that parents (not the court) should make their own arrangements for raising their children; the implication being that fathers should play a greater part in their children's lives even after the end of a marriage. The effect of this has been that couples who divorce have to renegotiate parenthood, but without the material and emotional 'foundation to the parenting project which is on-going during a marriage' (1999: 32). Smart and Neale provide evidence that, before divorce, many fathers allowed the emotional management of their relationship with their children to be mediated by the mother, and did relatively little of the physical care of children during the marriage. They 'were one step removed from their children and their relationship was sustained via their relationship with their mother' (1999: 48). All except one man in their sample had been unwilling to sacrifice his career prospects in order to take more responsibility for the children while they were married. However, following divorce, 9 of the 29 fathers interviewed 'were willing either to abandon their identities as earners and workers, or to reduce their commitment to their careers in order to assume an identity as caring parent on divorce or separation' (1999: 53). These men were obliged to renegotiate relationships with their children, and sometimes met resistance from the mothers, who did not wish to give up their powerful role of mediator between the two parties. It is also significant that some mothers and fathers were prepared to sacrifice new intimate relationships if these threatened their relationships with their children. This is at odds with Giddens's argument that adults will put intimate relationships before all else, including the needs of their children. Smart and Neale's work is relevant to the present book, because if professional mothers of pre-school children are seeking satisfaction through employment as well as in motherhood, this may have an impact on fathers' relationships with the children – but within, rather than outside of the marriage/relationship – an issue which is discussed in Chapters 7 and 8.

The New Family?

Changes in law, policy and attitudes with regard to family practices are discussed in *The New Family?* edited by Silva and Smart (1999), in which key writers on family practices analyse significant social trends in relation to changing contexts. This is consistent with Morgan's (1996: 186) argument that family practices should 'be seen as a dimension in all or most other areas of social inquiry'. Silva and Smart describe their book as focusing on the 'lack of congruence between policies based on how families *should* be and how they *actually* operate' (emphasis added). It is argued that

> The family is still supposed to stand outside and above economic restructuring, market forces and financial, legal and technological change, as a pillar of supposed stability. This political mantra on the family is not peculiar to Conservative governments but has also become a theme of New Labour in Britain.
>
> (Silva & Smart 1999: 2–3)

This accords with Morgan's warning that it may be

> misleading, or possibly even dangerous, to talk of 'the family' in the face of an observable diversity of modern family practices and domestic living arrangements and in the context of a vigorous ideological debate about the importance of family life ... To talk about 'the family' might not only obscure the rich diversity of practices to be found in a modern society but might also lend support to right-wing political agendas.
>
> (Morgan 1996: 186–7)

Significantly, in the light of Morgan's concerns, Silva and Smart (1999: 3) accuse governments in the UK of trying to engender social change while at the same time 'striving to hold fast to a model of family life which is associated with a particular cultural and economic moment in British history'. It is surprising, given the alarmist political rhetoric about the demise of the family and the urge to cling to an image portrayed by the Good Housekeeping Institute in the 1950s (Appleyard 2000), that in 1996, 73% of British households were composed of heterosexual couples, 90% of whom were married and 50% of whom had children under 16 (Silva and Smart 1999). Nevertheless, Silva and Smart indicate that there are changes in social behaviour which will force policy makers to take seriously fluidity and changes in family arrangements, so that in the future we may see 'policy frameworks which enhance autonomous choices in living arrangements' (1999: 2). Like Beck and Beck-Gernsheim, Silva and Smart warn:

> statistical indicators show that, although most people still marry and have children at some point in their lives, the average age has increased and people have fewer children and become parents later in life. Women are now better educated, have greater control of their fertility and may be becoming less enamoured of the triple burden of paid work, housework and childcare. The number of families living solely on a man's wage has dropped significantly in the late 1990s with fewer people thinking that a wife's job is solely to look after the home and the family. [For governments] it may be changes in attitudes, rather than in household composition, that are seen as so alarming and destabilising.
>
> (Silva & Smart 1999: 4)

Summary

In this chapter I began to argue that social policy and attitudes lag a long way behind demographic change. Like Beck and Beck-Gernsheim and others who write about the problems facing career women (e.g. Franks 1999; Buxton 1998), I advocated changes in policy in order to acknowledge changes in family practices. I argued that employment and family policies should cease to be rooted in the 1950s 'Parsonian' model of 'a male breadwinner with dependent wife and children' (Silva and Smart 1999: 11), and should move forward to accommodate the practicalities of lives of mothers and their families at the turn of the millennium.

3   Domestic goddesses?

Women's position in the family is founded in their maternity, now and for all time.

(Oakley 1976: 186)

Focus on:

The sociology of motherhood
   The institution of motherhood – a feminist view
   Radical feminism
   The institution of motherhood
**The transition to motherhood – 'a whole new definition
   of "normal"'**
   The medicalization of reproduction and childbirth
   Public attitudes to pregnancy and mothers
The aftermath of birth – coping with life and motherhood
   Working mothers and the 'public interest'
Social expectations and the 'good mother'
Managing a household – the ideal of the 'domestic goddess'
Emotional labour and the 'domestic goddess'

Introduction

This chapter offers insights into what the needs and dilemmas might be for professional women who are integrating motherhood with their working lives, by considering a range of views on the following important questions about motherhood. How far should the physical bearing of children automatically bring with it the responsibility for all aspects of their upbringing? How does the transition to motherhood affect mothers' sense of self? What are the far-reaching physical and emotional consequences of giving birth (including mental and physical health)? What are the values of mothers and the commitment they feel to their children and other aspects of life? What are the connections between motherhood and domestic labour? What impact does motherhood have on health? How important are social attitudes in relation to career motherhood? I will consider these questions in the context of a chronological understanding of how motherhood has been viewed by feminist researchers and writers over the past 30 years. This will set the theoretical scene for discussions in Part 2 (Chapter 6) where I will argue that the 'institution of motherhood' – the idealized notion of a heterosexual 'stay-at-home' mother for whom homemaking *is* a career – remains important in the context of mothers' decisions about their paid work.

The sociology of motherhood

> The word 'motherhood' emerged as a concept in Victorian times when it was reified as being motherliness, of mothering . . . Motherhood is now usually considered to be an essential task or stage of women's development as well as a crucial part of their identity, often from childhood . . . . In addition to establishing women's credentials as women, it also provides women with an occupational and structural identity and can be a substitute for involvement in other activities such as employment.
>
> (Phoenix *et al.* 1991: 6)

The question of how far the bond between mother and child is biological and unavoidable, and how far 'motherhood' is a socially constructed, institutionalized role, designed to keep women in the home, has long been an issue of dispute among feminist and other writers. In Chapter 1, I touched upon the political history of women's labour and noted that in both the UK and the USA, at the end of the Second World War, 'maternal employment became . . . a thorn in the national conscience, a symbol of women's inhumanity; a sign of failing morality and decaying family life' (Oakley 1981: 13). The pressure to conform to 'the notion of woman as home maker and carer' therefore became the 'ideal to aspire to' in the post-war years (Dryden 1999: 10), and some women challenged this, fighting for legislation that would put them on an equal footing with men (Rowbotham 1997). Unsurprisingly, at the same time as politicians such as Barbara Castle pressed for changes in employment policy and law on behalf of women, female academics were considering women's labour from a sociological perspective. The sociology of motherhood was a central focus of feminist research during the 1970s and 1980s, when writers explored the issues of childbearing, child-rearing, and mothers' work (both paid and unpaid). These issues had previously been excluded from the sociological agenda, but now became a legitimate area of academic concern, albeit on the fringes of 'mainstream' sociology (Smart and Neale 1999: 3). American feminists such as Shulamith Firestone (1970) and Adrienne Rich (1977) broke new ground in their reflections on the biological and social consequences of becoming a mother, and the relative responsibilities of the individual and society. And in the UK, Oakley (1981) and Graham (1983) developed feminist ideas on motherhood by undertaking research into the everyday lives of women. Since the mid-1980s, however, many feminist writers have 'turned their backs on materialist analyses of such things as housework . . . in favour of [other issues]' (Jackson and Jones 1998: 21). This may be because writers on motherhood during the 1970s and 1980s were often considering issues relevant to highly educated women in privileged circumstances, and it is a factor for which they have been criticized (Jackson and Jones 1998). However, it makes their work very pertinent to this book. Many writers during the 1970s and 1980s who explored women's desire to combine motherhood and profession did so from a theoretical, as opposed to an empirical, standpoint. This was inevitable because, at the time, most well-qualified middle-class women gave up work following the birth of their first child. As Oakley (1981: 12) noted: 'Thirty years ago women gave up their jobs on marriage: now the occasion is impending motherhood.' Nevertheless, Oakley's work is still relevant because it expresses poignantly the feelings of women who, while they loved their children dearly, also found the experience of being at home full-time with a baby deeply frustrating. It could be argued, therefore, that writers like Oakley (1981) and Rich (1977), who experienced this dissatisfaction themselves, explain better than anyone else why some women find that the ideal of motherhood does not meet their expectations and why women may be motivated to combine parenting with career.

The institution of motherhood – a feminist view

During the 1950s and 1960s, the image of the white, middle-class, stay-at-home mother was promoted both by governments and by advertising companies in Britain and America. Images of women focused predominantly on their identity as housewives and mothers. As noted in the previous chapter, Talcott Parsons, writing in the post-war decades, constructed 'motherhood' as a role within the family setting which encompassed childcare, shopping, cleaning and husband care, but which did not include paid work. In this section, the concept of the 'institution of motherhood' (Rich, 1977) is considered from the points of view of a number of important British and American feminists, including Shulamith Firestone, Ann Oakley, Adrienne Rich and Mary O'Brien. The work of these authors is relevant to the empirical research discussed in Part 2 of this book, as well as later discussions about how the institutionalized role of motherhood and the expectations of a wider society place pressure on individual mothers and fathers. While it is not intended to 'straitjacket' these writers by wrapping them up and 'labelling' them, each (with the possible exception of Firestone) could be broadly described as 'radical feminists' at the time they were writing the works under discussion here. (Oakley's views have changed significantly since her early writings on motherhood: see Oakley 2000.) Before discussing the institution of motherhood, therefore, I will provide a brief description of radical feminism in so far as it relates to children and childbearing.

Radical feminism

Radical feminism differentiates itself from histories or theories based on the previous development of 'malestream' thought (such as Marxism), and takes the view that 'it is gender relations rather than class relations that generate fundamental inequalities in the social world' (Porter 1998: 186). Radical feminism is also a departure from liberal feminism, a long-standing movement which links back to Mary Wollstonecraft's *A Vindication of the Rights of Woman* (1792). Liberal feminism asserts women as intellectual and autonomous beings who should work towards equality with men through incremental changes in the education and legal systems. Radical feminists, however, 'give a positive value to womanhood rather than supporting a notion of assimilating women into areas of activity associated with men' (Beasley 1999: 54). Radical feminism regards women's oppression as 'the oldest, most widespread, the most obdurate and the most extreme form of oppression that exists between humans' (Porter 1998: 186). As Beasley (1999: 54) explains: 'the distinguishing character of women's oppression is their oppression as women, not as members of other groups such as their social class'. Rather than trying to be the same as men, therefore, radical feminists celebrate the concepts of womanhood and sisterhood. While it is acknowledged by recent writers that 'women' are not a homogeneous group, radical feminists nevertheless focus on 'women's similarities and the pleasures of forming . . . bonds between women in a world where such bonds are marginalized or dismissed' (Beasley 1999: 54). Thus, special groups of women, such as lesbians and mothers, are celebrated by radical feminists on the basis that they have exceptional characteristics that men cannot share. Some of the key early writers on motherhood, such as Rich and Oakley, embraced the politics of radical feminism, celebrating womanhood and motherhood, and challenging patriarchy. Firestone is also categorized (e.g. by Porter 1998) as a radical feminist; however, in comparison with Oakley, Rich and O'Brien, her work is very different as she denies the importance of childbearing and motherhood as an intrinsic and valuable part of womanhood.

While I would wish to dissociate myself completely from some of the arguments put forward by Shulamith Firestone in *The Dialectic of Sex*

(1970) – in particular, her construction of children as sexual beings – it must nevertheless be acknowledged that Firestone's work was key to the early second-wave feminist movement. Writing long before the advent of the new reproductive technologies, Firestone (1970: 270) envisioned a time when artificial reproduction might be developed to free women 'from the tyranny of their biology by any means available, and the diffusion of the childbearing and child-rearing role to society as a whole'. Firestone concluded that children should not be regarded as a biological extension of their mother but should be autonomous beings, entitled to full legal, economic and sexual rights. She argued that children should be raised within flexible households, where various adults (not necessarily the biological parents) who wished for community-style living would take responsibility. Mothers would not be obligated towards their own children but would be able to pursue their careers as a priority. Valeska (1984) shared a similar view and suggested that 'A well-developed industrial system changes children from an advantage to a deficit. Under other economic systems, children materially contribute to a family's wealth and well-being, and eventually the young take care of the old. Not so today . . . they are a pain in the ass and cost a lot of money' (1984: 77). Valeska, who explains that she gave up custody of her own three children in the face of a disapproving society, argued that the mothering of children should be a societal responsibility, with 'child-free' people taking responsibility for others' children: 'Childraising must move from the private to the public sphere, from the individual to the local and national community. *My* children must become *our* children' (1984: 77; emphasis in original). The implication of the work of Firestone and Valeska is that if women could abrogate responsibility for the reproduction and nurture of children, they would share the same biological status as men, and therefore be equal in society. In contrast to Firestone, later feminist writers such as Mary O'Brien (a midwife by background) regarded motherhood as an essential female characteristic and were unable to accept the concept that women should cease to bear and bring up their own children. O'Brien (1981) supported a 'refocusing of the central female experience, the experience of motherhood' and argued that a successful feminist agenda 'cannot emerge from the devaluation of the intimate . . . and proud relations of women and children. The feminism of the pseudo-man is passé' (1981: 91). O'Brien dismisses Firestone's vision with the words: 'Shulamith's [theoretical] baby is . . . a theoretical waif, programmed for the theatre of a disturbingly mechanistic future' (1981: 82).

The institution of motherhood

Adrienne Rich (1977) and Ann Oakley (1981) also celebrated the uniqueness and importance of motherhood, in addition to considering the constraints placed upon mothers by society. Following the death of her husband in 1970,

Rich became involved in the American feminist movement. She identified two theoretical meanings of the concept of motherhood, one biological and the other socially constructed. In her influential text *Of Woman Born: Motherhood as Experience and Institution*, which set her own experiences in the context of a theoretical debate, Rich introduced the 'institution of motherhood' as a purely social construction established by a patriarchal society to undermine the social identity of women. She challenged 'Unexamined assumptions: that a "natural" mother is a person without further identity, one who can find her chief gratification in being all day with small children [and] that maternal love is, and should be, quite literally selfless'. She was 'haunted by the stereotype of the mother whose love is "unconditional" and by the . . . images of motherhood as a single minded identity' (1977: 23). For her, *'institutionalised motherhood demands of women maternal "instinct" rather than intelligence; selflessness rather than self-realisation; relation to others rather than the creating of self'* (p. 42 emphasis added). Rich was angered by the concept of *'the institution [of motherhood]*, which aims at ensuring that . . . all women shall remain under male control' (1977: 13; emphasis added). Despite her dissatisfaction with the social construction of motherhood, however, Rich also believed that a unique and powerful bond existed between mothers and their children. She used the metaphor of the 'invisible strand' (1977: 36) to describe the strong tie between mother and child and celebrated 'the potential relationship of any woman to her powers of reproduction and to children' (1977: 13). Referring to the deep and unexpected love that many new mothers feel towards their children, Rich (1977: 36) acknowledged 'the attraction – which can be as single minded and overwhelming as the early days of a love affair – to a being so tiny, so dependent, so folded-in to itself – who is, and yet is not, part of oneself'. Rich's observations are remarkably similar to those made by mothers and fathers who took part in the research for the present book, and provide an interesting background to the discussion in Chapter 6.

Ann Oakley explored similar issues in her work in the 1980s, and her early writings on the importance of women's everyday lives remain very influential among feminist researchers. In her empirical work on the transition to motherhood among middle-class women in *From Here to Maternity*, Oakley (1981) develops arguments relating to the needs of new mothers. Relating her own experiences, Oakley (1981: 14) stated that 'To hold the child that you grew as part of yourself seems a miracle'. However, she confronted the *'challenge'* that *'women can't have professional jobs and babies at the same time – only one or the other'* (1981: 3). Like Rich, Oakley was angered by the socially constructed concept of the 'institution of motherhood', and the image of the perfect and selfless mother (1981: 12). She explains how she became a sociologist, in spite of the social expectations at the time, because of her need to be and do 'something else' as well as being a housewife and mother (1981: 12). On becoming a feminist, Oakley explains how she began to understand that her 'private conflicts were nothing more or less than the legacy that all women in modern industrial society inherit'. However, she disagrees with earlier feminist writers (such as Firestone) because of their 'distinctly anti-natalist' views and she accuses them of unconsciously echoing 'the patriarchal view of women, women as sexual objects or subjects condemned by their biology to motherhood' (1981: 23). Like Rich, Oakley underlines how women's ability to 'grow and breastfeed babies and give birth to them in pain but with satisfaction is only now beginning to be seen by feminists as a valid and valuable aspect of being a woman, a resource to be drawn on rather than a burden to be disposed of' (1981: 23).

Of the more recent research on the sociology of motherhood, a considerable proportion deals with issues of motherhood and hardship, which are of tangential relevance to this book, although they demonstrate that mothers are determined and efficient managers, however difficult the circumstances (Graham 1993). There are also some important texts which consider the demands of motherhood in the context of career. However, these either tend to be focused on a particular profession such as medicine or banking (Pringle 1998; Halford *et al.* 1997) or may be based on research undertaken over a decade ago (e.g. Brannen and Moss 1991). In addition, there is a growing body of recent popular material which explores the experience of career mothers and speculates on their commitment to the workplace and their children (e.g. Buxton 1998; Cusk 2001; Franks 1999; Figes 1998a; Freely 2000; Pearson 2002). These writers are still arguing for a balance between mothering and paid work, believing that the early feminists were wrong to deny the 'primal pull towards motherhood' (Buxton 1998: 31) yet arguing at the same time that 'Contrary to what we are told by the Earthmother's myths, not all women can find happiness for themselves and their children by staying home full-time' (Buxton 1998: 17). In relation to this argument, Buxton (1998) and Hochschild (1997) have identified a tension between career mothers and those who choose to stay at home (Buxton terms this 'the mother war'). This view is borne out by articles in the press and media where employed and stay-at-home mothers appear to be pitched against one another in a bitter battle, with motherhood and career once a gain presented as an 'either/or choice'.

The transition to motherhood – 'a whole new definition of "normal" '

The experience of pregnancy and of giving birth, especially in respect of a first baby, is a transitional experience for women both personally and in a wider context. The birth of their first child was seen as a defining moment by all of the men and women I interviewed, as will be seen in Chapters 6 and 8. For this reason, I now focus on the beginning of motherhood – on being pregnant and giving birth – and on discovering how social attitudes towards women change once they become mothers.

Tess Cosslett (1994: 17) explains how women's values and their personal and social identity change dramatically on giving birth:

> the bodily experience of giving birth . . . raises the question of . . . role and status. Being pregnant . . . challenges our usual notion of identity and individuality: two people are in one body. Birth further disrupts our categories and 'one' individual literally 'divides' into two . . . motherhood puts into question a woman's sense of identity . . . and a new social role is thrust upon her.

Ann Oakley (1981: 24) describes first childbirth as

> a turning point, a transition, a life crisis: a first baby turns a woman into a mother, and the mothers' lives are incurably affected by their motherhood; in one way or another the child will be a theme for ever.

Kate Figes (1998a: 1), recalling her own experiences, writes poignantly:

> The . . . months after childbirth were riddled with confusion, exhaustion and unhappiness . . . I was unprepared for the great land-slide of physical, sensory, emotional and psychological upheaval . . . I considered childbirth to be the greatest hurdle to the physical process of reproduction, after which life would quickly settle back to normal. I didn't realise that the birth of a child brings with it a whole new definition of normal.

Rachel Cusk (2001: 7) observes:

> I did not understand what a challenge to the concept of sexual equality the experience of pregnancy and childbirth is. Birth is not merely what divides women from men: it also divides women from themselves so that a woman's understanding of what it is to exist is profoundly changed. Another person has existed in her, and after birth they live within the jurisdiction of her consciousness.

Joyce Davidson (2001: 286) argues that:

> The embodied experience of pregnancy will not leave the shape of the self unaltered . . . [a woman] may experience [first] birth as a transition to a new self. . . . She fears a loss of identity, as though on the other side of the birth she became a transformed person, such

that she would 'never be the same again'. Pregnancy can . . . be a phenomenally intense and transformative experience, affecting . . . one's identity in previously unimagined ways.

These writings demonstrate that, when women bear children they experience powerful emotional and physical changes, which may be long-term. They are also likely to experience changes in the way they are treated by others, which may be characterized by a lack of respect – and this starts from the minute they become pregnant.

The medicalization of reproduction and childbirth

Writers on motherhood see pregnancy and the birth process as a key influence on the experience of motherhood as a whole. They regard the process of bearing children as having an impact on mothers' self-esteem and sense of identity: 'the *beginning* of motherhood could be immensely important and the way in which a birth is managed could influence a woman's whole experience of being a mother' (Oakley 1981: 2; emphasis in original). In the context of the present book, which considers how women were managing to combine their new identity as 'mother' with their familiar role as 'career woman', it was important to examine the 'physical rite of passage of giving birth' (Figes 1998a: 4), and the impact that this had on women both physically and emotionally. It seems ironic that in both Britain and America, at the same time as organizations such as the Women's Liberation Front were campaigning for women's rights, childbirth (which had historically been the province of women) became elevated as a technological and high-status medical occurrence and, as such, rapidly came under the control of male doctors (Oakley 1984). The medical profession took control of the childbirth process in the nineteenth century (Poovey 1986), and in Britain midwives came under state and medical control in 1902. From the 1960s onwards, there was a serious drive, in both the UK and the USA, to technicalize and medicalize childbirth and reproduction. During the 1970s it became common for technologically assisted/monitored births to be directed by an obstetrician, and in Britain, by 1974, the hospital confinement rate had risen to 96% (from 15% in 1927). By 1977, 99% of all first babies were born in hospital (Oakley 1981, 1984). In New York during the 1970s Barbara Katz Rothman (1982) had to fight for the right to give birth in her own home, and was seen as irresponsible for wishing to do this. Oakley (1981: 3) considered herself fortunate to have 'caught the last lap of the home confinement tide and produced a girl in 1968'. Rothman and Oakley both use a 'machine' metaphor to describe the effect on women of the medicalization of childbirth: 'The body is a machine, the doctor a mechanic' (Rothman 1982: 163). 'To put the matter crudely, obstetrics treats a body like a complex machine and uses a series of interventionist techniques to repair faults that may develop in the machine' (Oakley 1993: 21). Central to the justification of the medicalization of childbirth was the concept that every pregnant woman and her baby were at risk until it was proved otherwise (Oakley 1993: 135). Thus, over the last 30 years, it has become accepted that 'from the day a women's pregnancy is announced until after delivery, [everything she does] becomes the concern of the health professionals' (Miles 1992: 192).

Like Rich, with whose work she sympathized, Oakley (1981: 10–11) viewed the medical management of childbirth as symbolic of modernity and patriarchy. Both writers looked upon the experience of giving birth, and the medicalization of childbirth, as central to women's own self-image and the way mothers were regarded by society. Through the work of Rich and Oakley, the medicalization and technicalization of reproduction and childbirth has come to be seen as a metaphor for the control of women by men. Rich (1977) described this as follows: 'No more devastating image could be invented for the bondage of woman: . . . drugged . . . and her legs in stirrups at the very moment when she is bringing new life into the world' (1977: 171). 'As long as birth – metaphorically or literally – remains an experience of passively handing over our minds and our bodies to male authority and technology, no other kinds of social change can change our relationship to ourselves, to power and to the world outside our bodies' (1977: 185). Oakley (1981: 3) believes that her own experience of childbirth robbed her of self-esteem for a long time afterwards. As a result of this, she challenges the idea that 'the wombs of women are containers to be captured by the ideologies and practices of those who . . . do not believe that women are able to take care of themselves' and argues for greater control of the birth process by the women concerned (Oakley 1984: 292). Although women's groups have campaigned for a return to a more woman-centred model of childbirth, it would appear that change is slow. Writing over 15 years later, Cosslett (1994: 47) argued that 'Adrienne Rich is not alone in seeing the way birthing women are treated by the medical institution as emblematic of their oppression in society at large', and more recently Cusk (2001: 25) expressed her resentment that no one 'was ever ruled with so iron a rod as [are] pregnant women in the English-speaking world. I have been tagged, as if electronically, by pregnancy'. Oakley (1984: 276) has argued that medicalization of pregnancy and childbirth 're-defines control of birth . . . as the property of . . . doctors' – who even now, 20 years after Oakley wrote, are still likely, in the field of obstetrics, to be male (see Pringle 1998). Oakley (1984: 275) does accept that the medicalization of childbirth is partly associated with the medicalization of life in general, and appreciates that there are links between decreasing infant mortality rates and improved medical care. She argues, however, that improved living conditions – better nutrition and sanitation, as well as the decline in popularity of high-parity births (Oakley 1993: 117) – have also contributed to this. Sheila Kitzinger (1992a: 73) argues that male obstetricians use the suggestion of 'risk' to enable them to retain control of childbirth. Kitzinger suggests that women who fail to comply with medical advice relating to the birth of their baby are seen as irresponsible, and subject to 'emotional blackmail ... In childbirth [mothers] may be warned that they must accept hospital protocols and obstetric decisions for the baby's sake. By threatening mothers with the baby's death, obstetric power is legitimised.' However, the issue of who is in control during pregnancy and at the moment of birth – the medical professional or the mother – is seen by Oakley and Kitzinger to have serious consequences for the mother's self-esteem and social identity if she feels powerless during the birth. Oakley (1981: 3) states: 'I was delivered of my identity [when my baby was born because I was] prevented from being the central figure in the central drama of my life'. Kitzinger (1992a: 68) reports: 'For many women, childbirth is an ordeal in which they are disempowered. Control of their bodies is torn from them ... [In one woman's words]: 'The professional team was very efficient and the baby is lovely, but I don't feel a whole person [any more].' As I shall contend, this argument is relevant to the group of women I interviewed, some of whom found it difficult to return to demanding jobs because they felt that their identity and self-esteem had been eroded by a lack of control during the birth process. By raising awareness of the issues related to lack of control during childbirth, writers such as Kitzinger and Oakley, as well as campaigning groups in the UK such as the National Childbirth Trust, have made some impact upon the way that childbirth is managed and, in theory at least, have helped to establish the principle that mothers should share in the decision about how they give birth. In 1993, in the UK, in the government document *Changing Childbirth* (Department of Health 1993), it was stated that women should be given greater autonomy in the childbirth process. Mothers should be able to exercise choice and take decisions: 'the policy of encouraging all women to give birth in hospitals cannot be justified on grounds of safety' (Department of Health 1993: 1). However, it would seem that this standard only applies where the woman is in agreement with the views of her doctors. As recently as 1997, a woman was forced by the courts to undergo a Caesarean section against her will because the 'doctors' perceived ethical duty to rescue a threatened fetus came into conflict with the mother's wishes' (Goldbeck-Wood 1997). Even Goldbeck-Wood, a female doctor who writes of 'our duty ... to respect a woman's autonomy', has presented pregnant women who refuse prescribed medical interventions as 'too comfortably unaware of the dangers faced in childbirth by their great-grandmothers' and argues that 'Sometimes the best obstetric care will be declined, with disastrous consequences' (1997). This does not seem a very great improvement from Kitzinger's observation that once a woman becomes pregnant, even if she is an intelligent adult, she becomes 'relatively powerless' and it is commonplace 'for the medical system to take over the production of babies, and [to] treat women as feckless, stupid, egotistical and dangerous for their babies' (Kitzinger 1992: 63).

This issue of the management of childbirth and labour is relevant to this book because although some writers (e.g. Cosslett 1994) disagree quite strongly with Kitzinger's (1984) views about 'natural' childbirth, there is clear evidence in the literature to show that the experience of pregnancy and childbirth can affect women's mental and physical well-being for months and years after the event, with potentially significant consequences for any subsequent return to employment (Kitzinger 1992a). This provides important background and context for the discussion in Part 2 (and particularly Chapter 6) of this book. Significantly, the medicalization of childbirth is not the only area where pregnant women and mothers are considered to be legitimate targets for public scrutiny.

Public attitudes to pregnancy and mothers

The issue of others' attitudes to mothers (and the assumption by many writers and agencies that they have a 'right' to 'judge' women's mothering abilities because this is in the public interest) extends beyond the medical profession and into the realms of popular literature and others' behaviour. This is seen by writers such as Joyce Davidson as an invasion of women's private space. Davidson (2001) has explored the impact of public attitudes on mothers and their identity. She suggests that women's sense of self and independence is undermined from the moment pregnancy and impending motherhood are publicly visible. She argues that other people deprive pregnant women of the right to determine how they behave in public because

> it appears that pregnant women are somehow 'answerable' to public concerns about their appearance and behaviour. They are expected to conform to 'normative' standards of 'decency' to an even greater extent than non-pregnant women ... The female subject's usual sense of accountability is intensified as she is *reduced* to her role as expectant mother. This places added limitations upon her (already socially restricted) behaviour.
>
> (Davidson 2001: 289; emphasis in original)

This sense that complete strangers have the right to 'police' the behaviour of pregnant women extends to an invasion of their personal space which, Davidson argues, has a profound impact on women's confidence and social identity. In relation to this, one of Davidson's research participants stated:

> I feel as though being pregnant automatically deprives me of my individual identity and personal space – I've become public property. Visibly pregnant women forfeit ... their right to privacy, to keep

strangers at a respectful distance and their sense of independence diminishes at the hands of others, sometimes . . . literally. Pregnant women's 'condition' . . . confers rights on the public to take an active . . . interest in their bodies not only by looking but also by commenting on and even touching, behaviour that would not normally be sanctioned.

(Davidson 2001: 290)

Davidson's viewpoint is shared by Rachel Cusk (2001: 34–5), who noted of her own pregnancy: 'It is the population of my privacy . . . that I find hard to endure . . . It is not, I am sure, the baby who exerts this watchful pressure; it is the baby's meaning for other people, the world's sense of ownership stating its claim'.

The aftermath of birth – coping with life and motherhood

It seems a supreme irony that mothers, who are expected to hand over so much of the decision making about the birth of their babies, and who are judged so severely by their critics (e.g. Yates 2001), are left to cope in relative isolation after their babies are born, with most of the support from health services being withdrawn within days after the birth, apart from (in the UK) an occasional visit from the health visitor. Oakley (1981, 1993), Kitzinger (1992a) and Graham and McKee (1980) all note that women can feel lonely, and sometimes depressed, for months after the birth of their children. Mothers of very young children may experience frustration and ambivalence in their relationships with their babies, and some suffer severe post-natal depression, especially if the mother felt out of control during the birth experience (Oakley 1993: 86; Kitzinger 1992a). Even women who believe themselves to be 'nurturant' may suffer from feelings of hopeless inadequacy in relation to their mothering skills (Kaplan 1992: 68). Kitzinger (1992a: 66) points out, however, that women are unlikely to seek or find support at such times because unless 'a woman's unhappiness . . . interferes with other people's lives' it is unlikely to be taken seriously. As will be seen in Chapter 6, this observation was borne out by the experiences of the research sample, some of whom experienced depression following childbirth but only one of whom contacted her doctor about this. Kitzinger notes that the response from general practitioners (GPs), if help is sought, is likely to be the prescription of anti-depressants. Evidence also shows that women are likely to experience poor physical health after birth. Graham and McKee (1980: 23) note that, five months after the birth of their babies, only 36% of mothers in their sample reported that they were free from illness. Drawing upon research conducted in 1991, Figes (1998a: 13) notes that many women are still experiencing health problems (such as tiredness and haemorrhoids) between one and nine years after giving birth. Most of them come to accept these problems as 'normal' and do not seek medical advice. Jennie Popay (1992) reports that 39% of mothers with children under 5 years old are likely to feel tired to the point of exhaustion most of the time. She demonstrates that this is gendered – tiredness and ill health are twice as likely to be experienced by mothers of pre-school children as by fathers (though this suggests that 20% of fathers of pre-school children also feel tired all the time – a sizeable minority). Graham (1993: 171) suggests that 'mothers try to ignore their tiredness, like the other symptoms they experience, in order to keep going. Mothers are frequently aware of this accommodation, recognising that their caring responsibilities leave them little time to be ill [and this] can blunt their sensitivity to their own needs'. The evidence in the literature, therefore, indicates that many mothers who return to work within a short time of the birth of their babies may be feeling 'under par', both emotionally and physically. This suggests that the health of career women should be an area of concern for health services and policy makers, since the well-being or otherwise of mothers, whether they struggle to 'keep going' (Graham 1993: 171) or are absent from work, is key to both mothers and their families and to employers. Significantly, in her research on men's resistance to gender equality in employment, Cockburn (2002: 185) notes that some male managers were 'fed up to the back teeth with the continual absences of women for one thing or another' (especially if these women were of senior status). One manager stated: 'Now it's the clinic, now the baby's due, now her youngest has measles . . . men were embittered by the disturbance caused [to their routine]'. Given these attitudes, it would be unsurprising if women decided to 'keep going' even if they were not really well enough to be at work.

Working mothers and the 'public interest'

Although post-natal support from health and other agencies is very limited, the 'public interest' in motherhood does not cease once the baby is born. As well as on lone mothers (who are often criticized for not working), the spotlight is often focused on working mothers (who are criticized for choosing to work). As noted in Chapter 1, the public debate about whether mothers should be allowed to pursue careers while leaving children in the care of others, and whether they are of value in the workplace, is ongoing. This is often focused on women with similar characteristics to those interviewed for this book: well-qualified mothers in well-paid jobs. The subject of working motherhood is discussed endlessly in the press and media, where the same questions are revisited many times in the light of new research or government statements. Should mothers be obliged to make a choice between having children and continuing their career? If they choose to try and combine the two, are they risking damage to their children, and opprobrium from a wider society? Stories about successful women who sacrifice their careers due to the stress of combining paid work with mothering are popular, and are reported smugly in the press: 'No more Mrs Superwoman . . . When this Rothschild director asked her daughter what she'd like for her birthday, she said: "A stay at home mummy". That remark changed her life for ever' (Cottee 2001: 34–5). Several strands of research claiming to demonstrate the dangers to children when mothers choose to work have been well publicized (Carvel 2001; Taylor 2001). Some writers claim that motherhood makes women unfit for work, and argue that women with children are a drain on their colleagues and employers (Boase 2001; Hughes and Dean 2001). Members of the public are encouraged to join in this discussion through the national press. For example, it is significant that Jackson was awarded a £400 weekend break by the British *Mail on Sunday* for the views expressed in this letter:

> When will someone be brave enough to tell career women that you cannot have it all? . . . You cannot call yourself a mother if you think one hour of 'quality time' before bed is all your child needs. Quality time is *any* time your child needs attention, ... Children also need to wake at a normal time, [and] . . . not be dragged out of bed while it's still dark and driven miles to a childminder . . . I am aware that many women need to work to survive . . . [and would] choose to stay at home and look after their own children . . . . Those who do not should stop moaning about stress. Come on ladies, it's self-inflicted so stop asking for our sympathy.
>
> (Jackson 2002: 80)

Influential bodies such as the Institute of Directors (UK) are not afraid of suggesting that mothers of young children should stay at home: 'It is a biological fact that it is women who give birth to children and are best equipped to look after them, especially in the early years' (Malthouse 1997: 1). The most recent policy document produced by this body vilifies employed mothers who lobby for better rights, constructing their requests as unreasonable and 'insatiable' (Lea 2001: 40). The Institute of Directors appears to endorse the opinion of Melanie Phillips, whom it quotes at some length:

> Increasingly, [women] are refusing to make choices [between career and children,] insisting that they must have it all, loading the consequences on to employers instead. The government is encouraging this selfish and irresponsible attitude . . . [by] cavalierly brush[ing] aside the impact on job performance of working fewer hours and expect[ing] employers to make good any deficiencies . . . How this tarnishes those many working women who have not lost sight of the reasonable limits to self advancement [of combining] work and family.
>
> (Lea 2001: 40)

Views of this nature are openly supported by other agencies which are reluctant to look for ways in which mothers can be supported through the (often relatively short) period while children are very small, enabling them to combine mothering with profession. This can be the case even in fields where there are shortages such as general practice in the UK. For example, Holden, a member of the GP committee of the British Medical Association, is reported as having stated that:

> Medical Schools should discriminate against women to help tackle the shortage of GPs because women take more career breaks than men and work part-time more often . . . positive discrimination towards men . . . would help solve the staffing crisis. This is not about misogyny, it's about the future of the medical workforce.
>
> (Eastham 2002: 30)

This suggests a concern that women's success at work and their financial independence from men might be a catalyst for social change, and this is seen as a threat by those who have much to gain from retaining the traditional social order of things as described by Parsons in the 1950s and 1960s. Significantly, the Institute of Directors argues that 'feminist enthusiasm for women's/mothers' independence of men/fathers and their denial of marriage as the bedrock for raising their children can damage their children' (Lea 2001: 40). Even writers who are supportive of women's wish to combine profession with mothering (such as the American writer Sylvia Hewlett) appear to accept that occupational success and motherhood present women with an 'either/or' choice. Despite her evident support of career mothers, Hewlett nevertheless presents the case that women must choose a career on the basis of how well it lends itself to child-rearing and a suitable man. She asserts that women should concentrate on acquiring a male partner and giving birth early, otherwise they might suffer from 'baby hunger': 'Give urgent priority to finding a partner. This project is extremely time-sensitive and deserves special attention in your twenties . . . have your first child before 35 . . . [and] choose a career that will give you the "gift of time" ' (Hewlett 2002: 261). Other writers, however, strongly challenge the expectation that women must choose between home and work, arguing that it is unreasonable, in the twenty-first century, to expect career women to relinquish their professional identities once they become mothers (Figes 1998b, 2001; Freely 2000). Nevertheless, the social pressures on women who combine motherhood with career are intense, and one of the key issues which the research for this book has explored is the impact of the attitudes of others on the behaviour and decisions of research participants.

Social expectations and the 'good mother'

Despite the fact that increasing numbers of professional women are returning to work while their children are still babies, the standards by which these women are measured (and by which they measure themselves) in relation to 'good' mothering are higher than ever before. In 1995, Beck and Beck-Gernsheim (1995) identified a new 'virus', 'parenting mania', in which 'expert advice' is thrust at (and taken seriously by) women who do not live close to their own mothers. Beck and Beck-Gernsheim (1995: 117–18) argue that the group of women most 'highly susceptible' to the influence of 'expert' parenting texts 'are middle-class women who are well-educated city-dwellers, expecting their first child at a fairly advanced age', a description which would fit many of the women who took part in the research for the present book. It is certainly the case that the range and quantity of texts and monthly magazines likely to appeal to an educated readership has increased dramatically over the past 10–20 years, with newsagents' shelves now full of glossy (and often expensive) publications such as, in the UK, *Practical Parenting, Mother and Baby, Prima Baby* and *Junior*, all of which offer 'free' booklets and videos (provided by manufacturers marketing baby products) about 'necessary' products relating to the education and health of children. The advent of the internet has greatly increased the amount of advice available – keying in the words 'baby' and 'advice' will bring up a plethora of sites giving information on babies and their upbringing. In August 2002 these ranged from pre-conception advice (http://www.b4baby.co.uk), to advice on premature babies (http://www.bliss.org.uk) and advertisements for baby and childcare products (http://www.babyworld.co.uk). A brief visit to Amazon.com will illustrate the wide variety of books available to parents. Harriet Marshall (1991) argues that, in theory, the 'expert' publications offer advice to both parents but that the directives given are addressed specifically to women, and contain prescriptive messages about how 'good' mothers should behave. This would seem to be true of the majority of publications and websites and would, for example, apply to Babycentre (http://www.babycentre.co.uk/537546html, accessed August 2002), which, in its site on advice for 'working parents', states that: 'Babycentre will give you all the information and support you need from the moment in your pregnancy when you start deciding whether or not to return to work, or finding out about your rights and benefits during pregnancy and early motherhood'. Marshall (1991: 69–70) argues that parenting texts construct 'instant love' as an automatic, 'natural' and 'key ingredient' of motherhood which should be regarded by women as 'ultimate fulfilment'. Those mothers who fall short of this are seen as 'abnormal' or 'faulty', and the texts 'allow only minor deviations from a positive account' of motherhood. In order to be 'good' mothers, 'women are told [by experts on parenting] to put aside their intellectual and sexual identity, in fact to lay aside any identities other than mother and wife [because] a mother's interests are said to be identical to her child's: the two merge in a role for which she is supposed to be biologically adapted' (Marshall 1991: 76). 'Good' mothers are also required to be emotionally strong and well balanced: 'Temporary mood swings are permissible shortly following birth but "real" depression renders women "unnatural" mothers' (Marshall 1991: 70). As will be seen in Chapter 6, this puts pressure on mothers who do feel depressed and are reluctant to admit this, or to seek help.

A further implication underlying many parenting manuals is that, in order to fulfil the criteria of 'good child-rearing', mothers must devote most, if not all, of their time to bringing up their children:

> The mother is to be a good role model, presenting . . . ideals and moral values . . . The suggestion is that if the child grows up 'abnormally' in any respect, or has not attained certain goals at the right time, then . . . the mother has obviously not given enough attention to [the child] and her . . . bad parenting results in amoral, maladjusted delinquents, which in the final count is to the detriment of society. Social ills can thus be blamed on the individual mother.
>
> (Marshall 1991: 81)

In the light of all this, it is unsurprising that Ribbens (1994: 6), in her work on how mothers raise their children, found that: 'expert theories of appropriate child-rearing can be a source of oppression to women'. This was relevant to the mothers who took part in the 'Hard Labour' research project who, if Beck and Beck Gernsheim are correct, were among the most likely to take seriously the 'professionalization' of the institution of motherhood, as well as maintaining a demanding professional career. These women were also likely to have access to the internet and to be able to afford to buy glossy magazines. Marshall points out that most of the 'expert' manuals assume the presence of a father, and instruct the mother on what his role should be, indicating that it is her job to mediate his relationship with the new baby – in other words, mothers are responsible for the emotional management of the family. Ribbens concurs with this view, arguing that it is a mother's role to mediate with others (including fathers) on behalf of their children. In addition, Ribbens found that women were responsible for balancing the individual needs of each member of the family against the requirements of 'the family' as a unit, this leading to the belief that 'if *mothers* have lives of their own, "the family" is under threat as a social unit' (Ribbens 1994: 164; emphasis added). It is significant that in Ribbens's book (regardless of working status), most women pictured themselves at the centre of their family structure.

Scott (1999: 74) stresses the importance of considering social attitudes as well as behavioural practices, because attitudes 'give some indication of how people are predisposed to respond to the opportunities and constraints that life poses'. It would appear from the literature discussed thus far that the everyday lives and behavioural practices of career mothers and their partners are influenced by others' attitudes to their behaviour, as well as by traditional social practice. This would include both the attitudes of close family and kin (as explored in Ribbens 1994) and the perceived 'public attitudes' of a wider society (Scott 1999; Marshall 1991). Scott (1999) argues that

> the reason attitudes are important is not because they are good indicators of behaviour, but rather because they help constitute the climate of opinion against which behaviour is judged. For example, acute strain can result if mothers work while holding attitudes (or being exposed to attitudes) that take the view that their action is harmful to children. Thus, shifts in public attitudes . . . are likely to inhibit or facilitate social change.
>
> (Scott 1999: 75)

This argument would seem to be supported by the literature discussed earlier, in which it is seen that the attitudes of agencies representing employers, such as the Institute of Directors, can be very unsupportive of employed mothers. It is, however, clear that external constraints do not necessarily prevent people from trying to change attitudes. Dryden (1999: 146) notes that despite the difficulties this posed for them, wives and mothers in her study of marriage were 'actively engaged in challenging the legitimacy of perceived gender power imbalances with their husbands'. Scott notes that, although male writers such as Giddens (1992) and Beck (1992) may claim that a 'new individualism' presents people with the opportunity to actively construct their lives, this choice is gendered. The main beneficiaries are men, followed by (presumably childless) women, while mothers are still constrained by 'traditional' attitudes regarding the consequences of their undertaking paid work (i.e. 'the children suffer'). Although Scott sees some shift in this attitude among younger males, she notes that men nevertheless 'remain considerably more traditional than women in endorsing the view that children suffer if the mother works' (Scott 1999: 86).

Managing a household – the ideal of the 'domestic goddess'

> As a natural consequence of our division of labour on sex lines, giving to woman the home and to man the world in which to work, we have come to a dense prejudice in favour of the essential womanliness of the home duties . . . we have assumed that the preparation and serving of food and the

removal of dirt, the nutritive and excretive processes of the family are feminine functions.

(Gilman 1998: 111)

The literature on motherhood and the domestic division of labour indicates that it is usually the mother, even if she is working and has a partner, who will bear the main burden of household work. At the end of the nineteenth century, Charlotte Perkins Gilman (2002) made the connection between the increase in women's domestic burdens and the arrival of children. In 1981, Ann Oakley observed: 'Motherhood entails a great deal of domestic work – servicing the child, keeping its clothes and its body clean, preparing food. The demarcation lines between this and house-or-husband work blur. It is a crisis in the life of a woman, a point of no return' (Oakley 1981: 1). Even though it is far more likely now than it was in 1981 that professional women will be carrying the responsibilities of paid employment, as well as looking after children and the household, the evidence in the literature indicates that very little has changed in relation to domestic labour. Dryden's (1999: 32) research led her to conclude that 'whether women were working full-time, part-time or were full-time care givers and whether men were working full-time or were unemployed, it was in every case the women who had major responsibility for the home and for the children'. Crompton (1997) and other writers (Brannen and Moss 1991) have argued that, in general, working mothers in heterosexual relationships (no matter what their social situation) carry a far greater domestic burden than their male partners, especially if the women work part-time. Scott (1999: 73) notes that even where men and women in dual-earner households devote the same amount of time to their paid work, women undertake around 9 hours per week more housework than men. This is similar to the trend reflected in research in North America by Hochschild (1997) and by the HRM Guide Network in Canada, which notes that 'While the share of paid work done by young women is high, their share of unpaid work is even higher' (HRM Guide 2004). Delphy and Leonard (1992) observe, wryly, that 'even though nowadays husbands are said to "help" with the housework' when wives have paid employment 'what [male partners do] is still clearly defined as "helping"'. The wife always has overall responsibility. These authors argue that, often, men deal only with the non-routine aspects of childcare, while mothers are left to do the housework and 'routine childcare (feeding, dressing and washing . . .) while men play with children and take them out. Employed women therefore generally end up working very long days, at the least favoured aspects of household work . . . even when they have "good" husbands' (Delphy and Leonard 1992: 240). Sullivan concludes that the free time remaining for women with small children who are also in employment is less than that available to their husbands/partners and notes that 'women's time is . . . more pressured in terms of intensity' (Sullivan 1997: 235) and that the stress induced by the pressure on time has serious implications for the quality of women's lives. This is in accordance with Chira's (1998: 248) study of working mothers in the USA, in which she observes that most mothers carry the 'double load' of paid work and housework, even if male partners 'help'.

Furthermore, Delphy and Leonard (1992) argue that in a heterosexual relationship where both partners are working, women undertake a further burden (not shared by men) of supporting their partner's/husband's career, and that this is in part due to the social expectations of employers that male employees will be assisted in their working lives by a female partner. It is suggested that 'employers benefit from their (male) employees' wives' labour because they can assume that none of their workers has responsibility for the physical care of any dependents or needs to do much domestic work for themselves' (Delphy and Leonard 1992: 235). Delphy and Leonard note that there are unlikely to be reciprocal expectations from either husbands or employers – a career woman is expected, by both her partner and his employer, to offer practical and emotional support, but to cope with the demands of her own job and the household by herself. It is further asserted that 'The social position of a woman's husband not only influences the actual tasks she performs, but also her rhythm, pattern and place of living' (Delphy and Leonard 1992: 241), this observation linking with Parsons and Bales's (1956) observation that a woman's 'place' in the community is decided by her husband's occupation. Arguably, if women are under a social obligation to manage the household and childcare, as well as supporting their partner's career, it is more likely that they will choose employment enabling them to do this (e.g. not involving extensive travel) – which might damage their own long-term career prospects. It is suggested that employed women are under a social obligation to demonstrate that, in spite of their paid work, 'husbands and children "do not suffer"' (Delphy and Leonard 1992: 247).

Susan Maushart (2002) describes this kind of responsibility as 'wifework'. Like Delphy and Leonard, Maushart argues that wives perform an overwhelming percentage of the domestic and childcare labour within a marriage because it is their job to support their husband's career and this is done by absolving him from household/childcare duties. 'Wives' paid work was regarded as a . . . privilege . . . The price of that privilege was continuing to accept full responsibility for what we have now learned to call the "second shift" at home. Those who baulked at this deal . . . were branded as selfish' (Maushart 2002:101). Maushart continues: 'Marriage . . . exploit[s] the willingness of wives to perform roughly three times the unpaid domestic labour of husbands. Intellectually we rejected the concept of wifework a long time ago. Emotionally and behaviourally we remain stalled within the old patriarchal paradigm' (Maushart 2002: 115). Maushart's description of wifework accords with Van Every's (1995: 262) characterization of the role of the 'wife' as an unpaid drudge who 'is defined by the appropriation of her paid and unpaid labour, financial dependence . . . and the characteristics (like submissiveness) which accompany these material factors. Wifehood is gendered feminine'. The ironing of men's shirts – perhaps because it is associated with the female enhancement of male careers – stands out from other domestic duties as symbolic of wifework. Maushart (2002) recounts a story in which a working mother is seen as 'selfish' because she fails to iron her husband's golf shirt, and in Van Every's study, which focused on couples who were practising anti-sexist living, 'Ironing stood out . . . as a task which seemed central to defining anti-sexism, but [this] statement contrasts sharply with the research evidence about the division of housework. Laundry (including ironing) . . . [is] most likely to be done exclusively by women' (Van Every 1995: 265). Maushart further argues that even the most loving father takes little responsibility for childcare: 'His parental responsibilities, relative to those of his wife, will remain largely abstract, centring on his role as financial provider' (Maushart 2002: 123). Popular women's magazines and radio programmes echo these arguments. *Woman's Hour* (BBC Radio 4, 11 January 2002) outlined the theory of heterosexual 'Quiche man', who can 'speak the language of equality' and impress guests by baking quiche Lorraine, but who does not see the overall responsibility for the household as his, offering to 'help' and undertake domestic tasks only when these are pointed out to him by his female partner.

Some writers, however, do not see the picture in quite such bleak terms, especially where professional women are concerned. Doucet (1995) argues that previous work on the domestic division of labour may fail to take into account gender differences in labour – women may be tied into the 'routine' domestic chores, but men may spend time on repair and maintenance of the car or the house and should be given some credit for this. This gendered division of labour is confirmed by Crompton (1997: 85), who concurs with Doucet's view that mothers of very young children carry out high levels of domestic work. Conversely, however, it is also argued (by Chira 1998) that the outdoor household jobs which are often associated with fatherhood (such as mowing lawns or chopping logs) may involve a level of freedom not offered to mothers, since women usually deal with indoor tasks and look after children simultaneously, whereas men mowing the lawn would be exempted from the care of small children on safety grounds. Crompton, however, suggests that a woman's job status can have a positive effect on the amount of domestic work done by her partner, arguing that 'couples from higher social classes are more likely to have egalitarian attitudes to gender and gender roles', while admitting, however, 'that equality ideals may be frustrated by the demands of the husband's job' (1997: 87).

Deem (1996: 12) also points out that 'for women in middle class occupations there was a greater likelihood that they would be able to afford domestic help'. This is reflected in Gregson and Lowe's (1994) study of the rise of hired domestic help in middle-class households. Deem (1996: 9) also suggests that women in paid work might feel more entitled to claim some formal 'leisure time' for themselves than women who were full-time house-workers: 'The salaries such women earned . . . provided them with economic resources which enabled them to engage in out-of-home leisure, and their jobs conferred the legitimacy with which to claim a right to leisure'. However, even if they are able to fund domestic help from their salaries, it is argued that 'the value of women's time counts only in so far as it enables them to buy replacement domestic service' (Silva 1999: 51). It also appears that the management of paid domestic assistance in the home, particularly in respect of paid childcare, is the woman's responsibility, 'because childcare is called women's work' (Gregson and Lowe 1994: 187). As Delphy and Leonard (1992: 236) point out, this involves more unrecognized work for women, because employees (whether part-time cleaners or paid childcarers) 'have to be hired, trained and managed . . . they also require emotional work: helpers have to be listened to, praised, made to feel important and to have their anxieties soothed, etc.'. (It also raises questions about the ethics of women paying other women to undertake domestic and family labour, an issue which is not dealt with here, but which is explored in depth by Ehrenreich and Hochschild 2003.) If mothers are required to pay for childcare in order to be able to work, it should be noted that, in financial terms, this requires a significant amount of expenditure. The Daycare Trust (2002) noted that the average cost of a nursery place in the UK ranges from £6200 to £7500 per annum, with some areas in London costing considerably more (up to £15,000 per annum): 'Not much cheaper than sending a child to Winchester, Britain's most expensive public school' (Driscoll and Waterhouse 2002).

The experiences of women in lesbian partnerships 'appear to turn upside down many of the assumptions which shape heterosexual practices' (Dunne 1999: 72). Dunne notes that women in lesbian relationships are careful to share out household tasks as fairly as possible, especially if they have previously been in heterosexual relationships: 'freedom from gender assumptions around the allocation of household tasks was key [in lesbian relationships] . . . they felt greatly advantaged by the absence of "gender scripts" to guide their relationships with women [and] contrasted the ease with which domestic arrangements emerged in their partnership with women', as opposed to men (Dunne 1999: 73). Additionally, lesbian partnerships 'provide insights into a more egalitarian social world where gender seems to have lost much of its power to structure relationships along lines of difference and inequality' (Dunne 1999: 76). This may be because, as Dunne suggests, if they have previously been in heterosexual relationships, women know how unpleasant it is to bear the brunt of household work and are therefore willing to share this out evenly. However, it may also be, as indicated by Delphy and Leonard (1992), Giddens (1992) and Eichler (1997), because those in single-sex relationships do not have the option of defining their relationships through the traditional, legal route of marriage (which would be open to cohabiting heterosexual couples). Single-sex couples have therefore negotiated new ways of living together, which appear to include a fairer allocation of domestic labour.

Emotional labour and the 'domestic goddess'

Traditionally, women are associated with responsibility for emotional labour both in the workplace and within a marriage or partnership. Some of the best-known texts on emotional labour have focused on the exploitation of women's labour in the workplace (e.g. Hochschild 1983; Adkins 1995). These texts are relevant, in that they provide a definition of 'emotional labour', emphasizing the requirement for women to manage their own emotions effectively so that they can concentrate on the emotional needs of others. However, in this book the principal focus on emotional labour will be in the context of motherhood and family practices. As noted by Oakley (1999, 2002), the original ideal of the perfect wife and mother was described in a popular Victorian poem, *The Angel in the House* (Patmore 1856), the metaphorical 'angel' characterizing the 'ideal woman' as a self-sacrificing person devoted to the physical and emotional well-being of others:

> Be man's hard virtues highly wrought,
> But let my gentle mistress be,
> In every look, word, deed and thought
> Nothing but sweet and womanly
> Her virtues please my virtuous mood
>   (Patmore 1856: 169)

Oakley (1993: 15) observes that the 'The Angel in the House was the ideal woman – intensely sympathetic, immensely charming, completely unselfish'. From Victorian times onwards, 'The angel in the house' became symbolic of unselfish femininity. Oakley (1993) notes the work of Virginia Woolf, who singled out this poem for criticism. Woolf (1979) regarded the angel in the house as an idealized 'phantom' which has haunted women ever since – especially if they wished to focus on their careers. Both Oakley (1993, 2002) and Woolf believe the Victorian metaphor of women as 'selfless angels' to have been emblematic of the exploitation of women, since it has validated an image of wives and mothers whose role was purely to please others. This has induced feelings of guilt and failure in women for decades and made it difficult for them to take their own needs seriously. Many years after *The Angel in the House* was written, Parsons and Bales (1956: 163) identified emotional labour (which they defined as selflessness and the creation of harmony within the home) as one of the key duties of wives and mothers. Almost half a century on, some contemporary writers attempt to put women firmly back in their place (the home!) by emphasizing the value of the 'traditional roles of wife and mother' (Tooley 2002: 95) and the importance of women supporting husbands' careers at the expense of their own (Appleyard 2003). Popular writers on home-making and cookery present mothers with high ideals to live up to, centred on the preparing of delicious meals for children and husbands, apparently effort-lessly, whilst looking beautiful and being elegantly dressed. In her book of household hints Quigg (2001: 7), who identifies herself as 'a busy country housewife and mother', constructs women as selfless beings who are respon-sible for the happiness of others, a mother's principal obligation being to ensure that her home 'runs happily and smoothly' (Quigg 2001: 7). Nigella Lawson's (2000) book, in which the 'angel' has transformed herself into the fantasy of a 'domestic goddess', seems to epitomize this genre, the elegant and talented writer urging other women with children to celebrate their femininity by elevating domestic chores (like cooking!) to heavenly status, dressed in a 'pink cashmere cardigan and fetching gingham pinny' (Lawson 2000: vii). Lawson 'hang[s] around the kitchen with the children . . . baking fairy cakes' (2000: 209) and provides comfort – and comfort food – to all the family by making the kitchen the centre of the home. Lawson exemplifies the 'perfect' mother, who keeps family traditions alive through recipes for favourite foods (e.g. 'my mother-in-law's Madeira cake') and thus constructs the 'domestic goddess' as responsible for 'putting down roots' on behalf of the family, 'laying down a part of the foundation for living' (Lawson 2000: 336). Lawson states:

> I do think that many of us have become alienated from the domestic sphere, and that it can actually make us feel better to claim back some of that space . . . a way of reclaiming our lost Eden. [Perhaps] . . . we don't want to feel like a post-modern, post-feminist, overstretched woman but, rather, a domestic goddess, trailing nutmeggy fumes of baking pie in our languorous wake.
>
> (Lawson 2000: vii)

The idea that mothers are responsible for the emotional management of the household, for balancing and ordering the emotional needs of the family, accords with the findings of Jane Ribbens (1994). Women's responsibilities included both the intimate relationship between mother and father (see also Duncombe and Marsden 1993, 2002) and the mediation of relationships between fathers and children. Morgan (1996: 105) gives a broad definition of emotional labour, in line with the ideas explored in the analysis of emotion and employment, as work which

> involves a multiplicity of skills designed to control or to handle the emotions of others, to smooth tensions and strains between other family members as well as providing a refuge from or a counter-balance to the tensions of the public sphere.

More specifically, he extends this definition to the home and applies it to the physical task of caring for small children, noting that:

> What the woman gives in this work is emotion as much as any kind of physical labour [– for example,] caring for a sick child involves . . . physical care and monitoring, handling the fears and frustrations experienced by the sick child, handling the adjustments required on behalf of other members of the family who may be resentful of the attention being accorded the sick child, and drawing upon one's own emotional resources and exercising emotional control while doing all of this. Even this very simple example can highlight some of the complexities of emotional labour when applied to work in the home.
>
> (Morgan 1996: 105)

Morgan's definition is helpful because it pins down what it means to perform emotional labour, because this is not merely an abstract concept but one which entails demanding and time-consuming tasks. The implication from the work of the above writers is that, within marriages/partnerships, emotional labour is more usually associated with women than with men. In the light of this (as readers will discover in Part 2), the findings from the 'Hard Labour' research project are unexpected because, while many men were happy to leave domestic chores to their partners, some fathers became deeply involved in their children's lives and regarded the care of sick children as just as much part of a father's role as it was a mother's. This will be explored at length in Chapter 7.

Summary

In this chapter, I argued that the management of pregnancy and childbirth is closely linked to mothers' self-esteem in the following months. Examining the work of writers on motherhood, I argued that the birth of (particularly first) babies is a defining moment in women's lives. I contended that 'public interest' in and opprobrium of mothers' behaviour can be intrusive, and that (conversely) support for new mothers is lacking. I argued that the 'institution of motherhood' raises expectations of how motherhood should be performed and puts pressures on women to be 'perfect'. The challenges faced by professional mothers are closely intertwined with responsibilities towards husbands/partners, children and the household. Mothers may be seen as inadequate if they do not spend their time exclusively with the children and do not personally perform domestic duties to perfection. (Men are excluded from this requirement!) Despite the demographic trends indicating that women are increasingly joining the labour market, images of 'angels in the house' and 'domestic goddesses' continue to haunt mothers and make it hard for them to prioritize their own needs.

4 Moneybags and the invisible father

> Despite women's massive entry into the paid labour force, social discourse about the good provider role for men still seems deeply entrenched.
>
> (Dienhart 1998: 23)

Focus on:

Fatherhood within a marriage/relationship
Fatherhood post-divorce/separation
Fatherhood and occupation versus 'invisible' fatherhood

Introduction

Following on from Charlie Lewis's work in the 1980s and David Morgan's (1992) influential text on *Discovering Men*, there has been a surge of interest in research on men and masculinities. This has reached the point where two books with exactly the same title (*Men and Masculinities*) have recently been published almost simultaneously in the UK (Whitehead 2002; Haywood and Mac an Ghaill 2003). The writers of these texts indicate that they are not, through their consideration of men's issues, trying to deny the existence of patriarchy or reject feminism. Whitehead, in particular, claims that in his investigation of masculinity he writes as a 'pro-feminist' (Whitehead 2002: 2). It is certainly the case that both texts draw upon feminist theory to enhance the understanding of masculinity. The question of how far any male writer can be considered feminist has already been considered (Harding 1987), and while one might question the appropriateness of applying to masculinity a methodology developed to 'shatter the silence' of women's voices (Graham 1983: 135), it is nevertheless recognized that both texts offer a comprehensive and accessible introduction towards a sociology of masculinity. Although they are primarily concerned with a broader consideration of what it means to be a man in contemporary society, each of the two books includes a chapter on fatherhood. Both texts make the point that social policies about fathers often fail to reflect the diversity of meaning of fatherhood in modern society – for example, the legal rights to guardianship of their children by non-biological fathers and men in single-sex relationships (Haywood and Mac an Ghaill 2003).

However, a further range of recent texts on masculinities focus specifically on the meaning of fatherhood, both within marriage/partnerships, but particularly post-divorce. The image of the father following relationship breakdown will be the focus of this chapter because, as I will demonstrate, recent laws in Britain and America have served to confirm the social construction of fathers as economic providers *before all else*. It is my view that the legal interpretation of 'the post-divorce father' has perpetuated the institutionalized role of 'father as main breadwinner'. As I will argue in Part 2, this causes problems for both men and women when fathers wish to extend their involvement with childcare at the expense of career and paid work.

Fatherhood within a marriage/relationship

One of the most influential writers on fatherhood, masculinity and the legal system is Richard Collier, whose recent work I will discuss later in this chapter. Collier has observed a 'massive growth in the study of fatherhood over the past twenty years' (2001: 526), and he argues that this is partly a reaction to the feminist studies on motherhood during the late 1970s and 1980s and a consequent desire on the part of men to 'redress the balance' (Collier 2001: 526). This premise seems reasonable given the approach espoused by some writers such as Lewis, who set out explicitly to 'examine fathering from the man's point of view' (Lewis 1986: 11). Lewis, who interviewed 100 fathers during the first year of fatherhood, relates his research to Oakley's work on new mothers and explains that, 'like Oakley, I wanted to report the accounts of fathers in detail to consider just why they appear to experience their role with "perplexed bewilderment" ' (Lewis 1986: 12).

Lewis's (1986) work emphasizes the attachment between father and child, but nevertheless acknowledges the continued existence of the link between 'the division made by Parsons and Bales (1956) between the "instrumental" male, who links the family with the outside world, and the "expressive female", who maintains the emotional stability of the family' (Lewis 1986: 125). Lewis also notes, however, that at the time of his research (in the early 1980s, since when, as noted in Chapter 1, many more mothers have joined the workforce) only 15 of the wives in his sample worked more than 15 hours per week, with 67 not in paid work at all. He indicates that one of the main reasons for the greater involvement of mothers than fathers in childcare responsibilities was that wives did not undertake paid work but were with children all day, whereas most of the fathers were out of the house during weekdays, fulfilling the traditional role of male breadwinner: 'The longer a man worked outside the home during the day, the less childcare he reported doing' (Lewis 1986: 107). However, even though the number of employed women in his sample was small, Lewis analysed the amounts of paternal involvement in childcare in relation to the mothers' employment status. He observed: 'There was a positive, linear relationship between the wife's employment status and her husband's involvement . . . [with childcare] . . . the father's involvement appears to be influenced by the couple's working arrangements outside the home' (Lewis 1986: 109). Lewis notes that four fathers who 'arranged their work to fit in with their wives' employment . . . stood out as taking a highly involved role' (Lewis 1986: 107).

Despite the widening participation of women in the labour market (especially at professional level), the relationship between fathers and the provider role, and mothers and the carer role, continues to be emphasized by more recent writers such as Lupton and Barclay (1997) and Warin *et al.* (1999). Lupton and Barclay consider the experiences of 16 Australian new fathers in the context of contemporary discourses on fatherhood and note that although some of the men in their research sample aspired to be 'involved' fathers, several found this adjustment difficult, especially if it extended to the responsibility for domestic chores! The writers imply that lack of fatherly involvement may in part be due to a culture of long working hours in Western society (Lupton and Barclay 1997: 132). However, Lupton and Barclay also construct the child as an instrument of power to which mothers cling, trying to 'position themselves' as principal carer, at the expense of fathers' rights to be a nurturer. These writers argue that low involvement by fathers of children under 1 year is often not the father's fault but the mother's, because women find it difficult to relinquish childcare to their partner. According to Lupton and Barclay, therefore, it is not merely the institutionalization of roles which prevents fathers from sharing in the care of their small children, but the determination of mothers to retain the role of principal carer. Citing as an example the situation of one of their research participants, who worked long hours while his partner was at home with the baby, they report that:

> Simon noted that because Jane was feeling fragile about her role and capacity as a mother, his attempts to care for their daughter Sally were more often rejected than welcomed by her . . . Simon expressed his sadness at the continual exclusion he felt from providing any care at all for Sally. He had wanted to help but felt actively prevented by his partner from doing so.
>
> (Lupton and Barclay 1997: 130)

Lupton and Barclay concede that mothers' desire to take on the mantle of principal childcarer, thereby excluding fathers, may be partly due to cultural stereotyping:

> the cultural imperative on women to be 'good mothers' may mean that women may wish to involve their partners more but find this difficult. To be shown to be overly willing to hand over more responsibility to one's partner . . . however much a woman may want to, may seem too cavalier an approach to one's responsibilities as a mother. Men's subject position as a 'good' father appears not to depend . . . upon demonstrating expertise in, and dedication to, the care of . . . children. As Walzer [(1996: 228)] contends, 'A father can be perceived as a "good" father without about his baby; in fact, his baby may pose a distraction to his doing what he is expected to do'.
>
> (Lupton & Barclay 1997: 132)

Nevertheless, the implication of their argument is that, if men do not spend enough time with their children, this must be the woman's fault. This analysis of fatherly involvement with childcare (or lack of it) is consistent with a recent study by Pasley *et al.* (2002), in which it is concluded that fathers are more likely to undertake childcare if wives are encouraging and positive in response to fathers' involvement. Once again, this implies the assumption that emotional labour within a heterosexual relationship where there are children lies with the mother, who is expected to be responsible for mediating involvement with children on the father's behalf (as in Ribbens 1994). However, it is arguable that this only applies when mothers are present. In her study at Amerco, Hochschild (1997) provided some evidence to show that when mothers were out at work and fathers were at home with their children, they were obliged to take on the principal carer role and deal directly with children, even if they were keen to 'hand over' when women returned to the house.

The position and role of fathers in the above studies (and also in Allen and Hawkins 1999; and Walters *et al.* 2001) is presented as complex and ambivalent, with fathers wishing to develop their role as involved nurturers of children but prevented from doing so by territorial wives/partners and by external forces. Particularly post-divorce, children are regarded as a source of power between couples. However, part of the reason why fathers are seen to be locked into economic roles lies in social expectations that they should construct their social identities as men through their occupational status. Several writers on fatherhood (e.g. Dienhart 1998; Lupton and Barclay 1997: 53; Lewis 1986: 125; Horna and Lupri 1987) link this explicitly to Parsons and Bales (1956). Some writers even imply that Parsons' work is responsible for causing this effect, Horna and Lupri (1987: 54) stating that:

> Parsons . . . has lent credence to role complementarity in the family in assuming that sex-role segregation is necessary for family stability . . . husbands and wives perform different tasks (functions) that combine to meet all family 'needs'. The roles of the father/husband are those of provider and protector. His contribution to child-rearing consists largely of providing a strong economic base for the family's survival . . . His actual involvement in nurturing and emotional tasks is limited.

Although it may seem surprising that this should be the case in the twenty-first century, the image of the father within a marriage is still one of a parent who may care deeply for his children but who nevertheless resides in the background of family practices and family life. The writings on fatherhood within marriage discussed above still give the impression that fathers' main activity is focused on the outside world, and imply that their social identity remains linked inextricably to occupational status (as suggested by Parsons as long ago as 1956), because they are constrained by social expectations.

Fatherhood post-divorce/separation

Although the body of literature concerning the role of fathers *within* marriage is growing, this is not as prolific as the rapidly expanding range of published work on fatherhood and divorce. This might seem surprising given that in 1992, the British Household Panel Survey (sample size around 7500) demonstrated that 73% of fathers were in their first family situation and were living with all of their children under age 18, with only 13% of fathers not living with any of their children under 18. It is possible, however, that recent interest in researching fatherhood post-divorce may have developed in response to changes in family law, as well as in response to social change.

It is argued here that, for fathers outside marriages/relationships, roles and responsibilities are less ambivalent than for fathers within marriage because the function of the post-divorce/post-separation father, whether or not he is married to the mother of his children, is formally outlined in legislation such as the Children Act 1989 and the Child Support Act 1991 (Burghes *et al.* 1997: 36–42). Collier (2001) outlines the role of the ' "new" [involved] father" ' and asserts that the 'desire to promote good fathering has become a central element of . . . the distinct paradigm shift which has taken place in recent years in Britain in how the state relates to the family'. Collier asserts that central to this is the idea that 'there can be no rights without responsibility', and notes that a new attempt to 'promote the new father as active parent . . . has proved an important feature of the . . . heightened conversation about fatherhood . . . which has taken place in recent years' (Collier 2001: 527–8). Critically, Collier argues that this new focus on the role and responsibilities of fatherhood centres on fathers following divorce and relationship breakdown. He further links this to the increase of academic publications in law journals on post-divorce fatherhood. There are certainly many examples of articles on the legalities of post-divorce fathering – for example, Rhoades (2002) writes on the enforcement of post-divorce contact between fathers and children.

Collier (2001: 528–9) explains that, from the mid-1980s onwards, a 'new consensus' among makers of family policy was marked by a desire to maintain contact between fathers and their children post-separation or divorce. He argues that part of the reason for this was the ideology that men should no longer be allowed, financially, to establish future partnerships without accepting a life-long responsibility for their first family (this leading to the establishment of the Child Support Act and related Child Support Agency in 1991) (Collier 1995: 227). Although the new emphasis placed on contact between fathers and children in both the Children Act (1989) and the Child Support Act (1991) was ostensibly due to a concern for the welfare of children, Collier sees this in harsher terms: that if policy makers seek to enforce fathers' financial obligations, these will be difficult to maintain unless they also seek to establish a father's right to have contact with, and/or parental responsibility for, children: 'Without legal rights, put crudely, why should men be financially responsible? . . . What we can see in law is an acceptance of the potential irresponsibility of all men and the . . . argument would appear to be that without *rights* there would be no *responsibility* on the part of men' (Collier 1995: 209; emphasis added). Collier's argument is consistent with the observation that:

> While the Children Act 1989 might be thought to reflect the new 'model' fatherhood – emphasising parental responsibility and active parenting – two years later in the Child Support Act 1991, an earlier model of fatherhood – that of economic provider – was dominant. Moreover, it enshrines the view that making financial provision for one's children is of an enduring nature irrespective of changes in the parental relationship or co-residence with children.
>
> (Burghes *et al.* 1997: 11)

Collier argues that the problematic nature of fatherhood in law has highlighted some uncomfortable issues about the economic basis of fatherhood, as well as 'the uncertain nature of masculine "responsibility" in the family' (Collier 1995: 209). He indicates that this provides an explanation for why research on fathers *within* a relationship, is 'a less traditional area of family law scholarship than the field of divorce, separation and contact' (Collier 2001: 528). Collier's hypothesis seems reasonable, and given that so many studies of fatherhood produced during the 1990s concentrate on the role of heterosexual fathers following relationship breakdown, it could be extended beyond the field of family law into other areas such as sociology and psychology (e.g. Smart and Neale 1999; Grief and De Maris 1995; Seltzer and Brandreth 1995).

As has already been observed, the social identity of 'father' post-divorce is firmly grounded in his role as provider/breadwinner for his children. This remains the case whether or not fathers are married to the mothers of their children, and whether or not they choose to apply for a parental responsibility order, which in effect 'places the unmarried father in the same position as his married counterpart' (Burghes *et al.* 1997: 37). It is a guiding principle of family law in the UK that 'Unmarried fathers are also under a duty to maintain their child financially whether or not they have parental responsibility' (Burghes *et al.* 1997: 37–8). This even applies to fathers whose partners chose to have a child without informing them, or if men provide sperm for artificial insemination as known donors, and it can be imposed retrospectively (Burghes *et al.* 1997: 41). It is observed by Burghes *et al.* (1997) and Dienhart (1998: 13) that post-divorce/separation fathers are judged, both in law and by society (especially in the media) *by their ability to provide financially for their children*. Fathers who fail in this duty (e.g. the very young, or the unemployed, even if their female partners undertake paid work) are seen as 'feckless' (or, in the USA, as 'deadbeat dads'), especially if this means a reliance on the benefits system – regardless, presumably, of whether they are involved with the day-to-day care of their children.

Fatherhood and occupation versus 'invisible' fatherhood

This suggests that, far from steering away from the institutionalized role of father, as might be expected at the turn of the millennium, the recent changes in law which define fathers principally as financial providers only serve to ensure that the social identity of 'father' becomes more deeply embedded in occupational status, the concept of involvement (or even contact) with children being equated mainly with the provision of money. This applies not only to the post-divorce father, but also to fathers living with their children, because the emphasis on money reinforces the stereotypical idea of father as economic provider. Thus, in a society where some men 'may want a more involved role with their children' (Burghes *et al.* 1997: 11), they might still find themselves constrained by the expectations of a wider population that they should go out to work and earn money, while mothers stay at home and care for children. Arguably, therefore, the strengthening of men's economic provider role has led to a phenomenon which has been described by Mike Durham (2002) as the 'invisible father'. Having reduced his career commitments, Durham is the principal carer for his two small children, while his wife is the main breadwinner. He notes (of his decision to be at home with his children) that 'the only real negative, and it is a big one, is not being able to acknowledge the path I've chosen . . . there is a layer of hostility (toward carer-fathers) that specifically denigrates men and threatens to make fatherhood a trial and a humiliation'. Durham observes that, when trying to combine parenting with his part-time work, he faces hostility and disbelief from colleagues and employers:

> This denial of fatherhood, creating invisible fathers, is a serious business. If motherhood is regarded as inconvenient [by employers] fatherhood is beyond the pale . . . When I left to take over from the childminder, [one colleague said:] 'You're a wimp, tell your wife to do it.' There was an undercurrent of incomprehension, hostility, small mindedness, and – who knows? – perhaps jealousy.

On another occasion, on being honest about missing an appointment due to a child's illness Durham realized:

> It was the wrong thing to have said. I should have made another excuse. Little boys don't count . . . Nowadays I am more discreet . . . Fathers have to lie, lie and lie again about being a Dad. It is what being an invisible father is all about.
>
> (Durham 2002: 6)

Durham's argument is consistent with the hypothesis presented by Dienhart (1998), who argues that some married/cohabiting fathers with children are attempting to make significant shifts to their role within their family unit, but that these changes are hidden within contemporary discourse on fatherhood. Dienhart interviewed 18 couples selected specifically for their self-reported agreement to share parenting responsibilities. Although she does not give it this precise title, Dienhart also observes the existence of the concept of 'invisible fatherhood' in her thesis and expresses concern about this:

> An embedded question may be, what do we really expect men to be as fathers? Only distant observers, perhaps! . . . I despair at the hidden judgement that [men are] not as good as the mother in caring for the children . . . Would men be noticed if more were participating in the public routines of children's lives? [Or] does it even matter how many men participate if we secretly harbour beliefs that family and children are really a woman's domain? . . . I despair that policies and the social environment at the workplace are changing very slowly, if at all, for working parents, especially for men who want to be involved in their children's lives.
>
> (Dienhart 1998: 11)

The concept of 'invisible fatherhood' is relevant in the context of this book, in that it is experienced very acutely by some of the research participants (and is described in Chapter 8). Also relevant is the observation, by Dienhart, that fathers who are primary caregivers and living with their wife/partner are usually happy with their situation if their wife's earnings are high and their role as principal childcarer was a choice they had made. However, as we shall see, is also notable that

> the negative aspects [of stay-at-home fatherhood] echo the issues widely reported in the literature on women's experiences – such as loss of freedom, problems of adjusting to being at home, lack of 'work status', general lack of social support, the desire for greater community support and the need for more flexibility in balancing work and family life.
>
> (Dienhart 1998: 28)

Summary

In this chapter I argued that, often, fathers only become responsible for mediating their own relationships with children post-divorce. Within relationships, this task has traditionally fallen to mothers, who are criticized for excluding fathers if they do it well! Additionally, I contended that the 'institutionalized' role of fathers as main breadwinners has been perpetuated by recent laws constructing post-divorce fathers as economic providers before all else, which adversely affects couples who do not conform to these expectations.

5 Working for love or money?
The commitment of mothers to paid work

Babies turn women into jelly-heads
A solicitor was offered a lesser job when she returned from maternity leave because, she was told, 'women who have babies go jelly-headed'.

Nicola Bilsborough had been shocked to see her job advertised while she was off work to have her son Jack.

An employment tribunal heard that personnel consultant Jenny Halpin told her that women who have babies go 'jelly-headed' and struggle to return to their previous standard of work.

(McIntyre 2002)

Focus on:
Working for money
Working for a sense of self
   Social identity theory
'Being a breadwinner': The power of earned income
The attributes of power
   A 'modern' definition
   . . . and a 'post-modern' definition

Introduction

The issue of money, in relation to the motivation and commitment of career mothers to their paid work, is important both because of contemporary questions about women's commitment to their career, and because of the questions raised (but not fully answered) in quantitative studies about why professional women may choose to return to work when their children are of pre-school age. Highly educated women are more likely to remain in their jobs for longer once they have returned to work, than are women with few qualifications, 60% of those educated to degree level having remained in the same job for at least 5 years (Macran *et al.* 1996: 287). Macran *et al.* also observe a polarity between those women who earn a high enough income to pay for childcare and those who do not. They speculate on what motivates highly qualified women – 'the privileged group at the upper echelons of the occupational scale' – to return to work and argue that 'some women may want to maintain their occupational status, pension rights or chances for promotions . . . others may need to have a job due to financial necessity . . . by remaining in a job . . . these women are less likely to suffer occupational downgrading and more likely to retain their employment benefits' (Macran *et al.* 1996: 290). However, they do not provide evidence for these arguments. Dex *et al.* (1998) assert that mothers may return to work due to 'financial pressure from mortgages', but this also appears to be speculative. Unfortunately, the issue as to whether mothers work through choice or necessity is not one to which there is a single, or a simple, answer. Issues of motherhood, money and marriage/partnership have been examined in detail by several writers, for example, Hakim (1995), Potuchek (1997), Pahl (1989), Vogler and Pahl (1993, 1994), and Brannen and Moss (1991), each of whose work is discussed below to show the breadth of explanation for mothers' commitment (or otherwise) to their paid work. The work of the latter four writers has various links in common and there are two key issues worth noting. Firstly, issues about commitment and paid work are inextricably bound up with family practices, roles (mother, father, spouse, breadwinner) and identities; therefore answers to any question about money, or breadwinning, are likely to be complex and multi-faceted. Secondly, there is evidence of rapid recent changes (Potuchek 1997), meaning that even research published in the early 1990s may not quite reflect the situation as it is today.

Working for money

One of the best-known writers on women's employment, Catherine Hakim, argues that women are less committed to work than men, and that part-time female workers are even less committed to their work than full-timers (1995: 434). It would be easy to dismiss Hakim's work on the basis that, even though her publications are recent, her views nevertheless appear rather outdated in the light of the increasing trends for mothers of small children to return to paid work. However, this would be a serious mistake, because it is Hakim's view that seems to be most frequently reflected by influential agencies such as the Institute of Directors, as well as in the press and other media. The media, which draw upon academic research for news stories, aim to produce stories which 'create an emotional response, or a lot of people can share in, because they relate to a common experience. Stories which prompt joy, fear, excitement, pity or outrage clearly make "strong" copy. So do stories which affect a large number of people' (Silver 1985: 68). In this regard, it is unsurprising that the UK media shows an awareness of the increasing trend for the professional mothers of young children to continue in paid employment. The press appears to have picked up on the debate stimulated by Hakim's work, and this is usually focused on the group under consideration here – professional women with small children. Every week a wide range of news stories is presented, often portraying professional mothers as uncommitted to (and unhappy in) their paid work but 'greedy' for the lifestyle extras that a career provides. Driscoll (2002: 19) argues that women do not wish to 'break through the glass ceiling' because 'most regret the impact working has on their family lives', but that they go out to work merely to pay for 'a lifestyle they'd rather not forgo'. In an article accompanied by a picture of Cherie Blair (lawyer and wife of the British Prime Minister) cuddling her baby son Leo, Hitchens (2002: 29) claims that 'modern [working] mothers do not enjoy motherhood which ought to be one of the happiest times in a woman's life because their lives, which should be full of joy, are bleary eyed and strained'. He argues that we should 'free our wage-slave mothers'.

Part of the reason why Hakim's work is so well known – apart from reviews of her work by other writers, such as Crompton (1997) – is her association with the British Institute of Directors, which produces policy documents on behalf of its members for use as reference points by the media (e.g. Malthouse 1997). Hakim (1995) questions the entire basis of the evidence for rising female employment – though as Ginn *et al.* (1996) argue, Hakim does not seem to account for the number of women in part-time work, basing her evidence on the total number of hours of female employment. Surprisingly, however, Hakim does not comment on the marked increase in women's commitment to their work over a five-year period shown in her own research, which is surely a significant finding (1995: 433). Using very old (1950s and 1960s!) data, Hakim claims to demonstrate that women – especially part-time women workers with children – are less reliable and less committed to their work than their male counterparts. According to Hakim (1995: 438), only those women who opt to remain childless are serious about their careers. Hakim argues that this is because:

> The unpalatable truth is that a substantial proportion of women still accept the sexual division of labour which sees homemaking as women's *principal* activity and income-earning as men's *principal* activity in life. This acceptance of *differentiated sex roles* underlines fundamental differences between the work orientations, labour market behaviour and life goals of men and women.
>
> (Hakim 1996b: 179; emphasis in original)

Hakim (1996b: 178) suggests that this is especially true of women who are employed part-time: 'On balance, the research evidence shows that part-time work does not change a woman's primary self-identity as housewife, does not change her bargaining power and weight in decision making and does not change her role in the household'. Speaking of women who 'choose' whether or not to undertake paid work (Hakim 1995: 434), Hakim appears to take no account of whether this choice might be socially constructed. Hakim does admit that her 'evidence is incomplete', but nevertheless she argues that it is 'consistent with the thesis of women's polarization into two groups: ... a group giving priority to marriage and child-rearing as their central life activity and another group giving priority to market work as their central life activity' (1995: 438). At no point does Hakim appear to consider that there might be a third group who are committed to both career and family and might hope to achieve a balance between the two. Even in her two most recent publications about women's work orientations (Hakim 2000, 2003) where she acknowledges that some women can combine mothering and paid work with success, she appears to dismiss the possibility that mothers may also have strong work orientation, describing them as undertaking a 'job' rather than a 'career'.

As noted above, Hakim's is the view quoted by some powerful agencies and in a wide range of popular literature. Quoting Hakim's work directly, the Institute of Directors (IoD) has argued that mothers are a bad investment in employment terms because they are uncommitted workers/colleagues. This is supposedly due to the fact that they would prefer to be undertaking motherly/ wifely duties at home, and would expect unreasonable flexibility from employers. It is noted by an IoD member that 'If a woman wishes to have a child, she ... should impose, by doing so, no penalties on anyone else other than those party to the decision' (Malthouse 1997). Ironically, if they are committed to paid work, mothers are constructed by the IoD as failing in their duties to society. The IoD quotes Hakim's suggestion that 'women who remain at home do so mainly by choice' and argue that this sacrifice should be recognized and these women supported as 'those who guard our future generations' (Hakim, quoted in Malthouse 1997: 2). The IoD asserts that 'It is for discussion whether Government should do anything to further increase the number of women in the work force or create a better climate for childcare (at home) and the future of the next generation' (Malthouse 1997: 2).

In my view, the writings of Hakim and the IoD continue to validate the 'either/or' choice between babies and career that Oakley (1981: 3) challenged over 20 years ago. Additionally, their work has opened the door to a spate of literature which presents women as unfulfilled by paid work, longing for the opportunity to have babies and to be dependent on a man for whom they can keep house. For example, Hewlett (2002) and Tooley (2002) have claimed that careers may cause women unhappiness, and support the hypothesis that women are more likely to be fulfilled by motherhood than by career. Hewlett

(2002: 37) explains how she was badly let down by the American university system which, following her miscarriage of twins, forced her to 'step down from a job I both loved and felt I had sacrificed a great deal for'. Hewlett, who supports women's work orientation, nevertheless argues that they should downplay career ambitions and focus on finding husbands while still young, so that they can conceive babies. Tooley, in particular, argues that women secretly yearn to remain in the home, playing the role of wife and mother. (He observes that a lack of ambition makes them better marriage material.) Tooley portrays mothers as singularly unenthusiastic about paid work. This is because, once she has given birth, a good mother will realize that *'There was something more important for her to do'* (Tooley 2002: 111).

The image of mothers as failing in their duties to both child and employer is frequently represented in popular literature (e.g. women's magazines). The suggestion is made that mothers return to work purely to collect a pay cheque, rather than for reasons of personal fulfilment. A recent survey by the private health insurer BUPA suggests that half of working women 'yearn to be women of leisure' (*Top Santé* 1999: 94). *Top Santé* argues that few women (less than 25%) would choose to pursue careers if money were no object. This is consistent with the recent view expressed by Knight (2002: 4) that:

> women would pack in work tomorrow if they could. An unbelievable amount of rubbish is written about women, work and, more often than not, gender politics, usually by female academics from the more ludicrous universities (think facial hair, galloping loneliness and a preoccupation with cats). Under this deluge of dross we've lost sight of the fact that in the vast majority of cases, work is a means to an end and this end is purely financial and, quite frankly, we'd much rather be at home with our children or, failing that, lying on the sofa with a good book and a bottle of wine.

In accordance with Hakim's assertions, some writers in the popular press draw the conclusion that working mothers are 'an absolute pain' because 'they think work is a waste of time; the new baby is everything' and they expect 'maternity leave and other benefits' (Boase 2001: 1). It is argued that child-less or child-free women are productive workers who are unfairly penalized by having to work long hours to compensate for mothers' inadequacies in the workplace: 'non-parents are being cheated; done out of perks they have earned by hard graft'. Meanwhile, working mothers 'read the papers over a cappuccino' (Boase 2001: 1). It is also argued that career mothers are disadvan-taging their children – who may therefore turn out to be 'moral degenerates' (Malthouse 1997) – because babies need their mothers to be at home: 'Chil-dren are our future and to my mind the person they really need when they are young is their mother' (Appleyard 2000: 48). It is notable that highly qualified, professional mothers in heterosexual relationships are particularly likely to be criticized for undertaking paid work, because they are seen to have a 'choice' about this, in a way that poorer, less qualified women may not. In letters to the *Sunday Times*, both Yates (2001) and Towers (2001) sum up this view neatly:

> I have every sympathy where both parents work on low wages to provide basics . . . for their children. However [middle-class mothers are] 'struggling' to provide designer lifestyles for their children and perhaps even more to the point for themselves.
>
> (Towers 2001: 4)

> Working mothers never pull their weight . . . They cheat the system and demand that others contribute to their selfish lifestyles.
>
> (Yates 2001: 4)

In the light of the views expressed above, it seems unsurprising that mothers are reported to feel a requirement to 'prove' themselves at work (Freely 1999: 6). Notably, in a survey of 3000 first-time mothers, more than one-third said that they 'felt under pressure to work harder during pregnancy to prove that they remained committed to their job' (Freely 1999: 6). It would be easy to assume that Hakim's views (even if they did not apply to 'professional' women), might be accurate in relation to those with fewer qualifications in low-paid jobs. A word of caution is sounded here, however, in the context of recent work by Backett-Milburn *et al.* (2001) which suggests that, for a variety of reasons, less qualified women may be very committed to their paid work. Because of its significance in both popular and academic literature, the question of women's commitment to their paid work is seen as highly important in relation to this research and is discussed at length, in relation to the empirical research, in Chapter 8.

Working for a sense of self

There are a number of writers who link mothers' commitment to paid work with their social identity. Potuchek's (1997) work on heterosexual couples and employment was conducted in America, and related to a piece of research in which it transpired that most young male university students felt that it should be their spouse's decision whether to work or not, whereas 80% of young women students expected their husbands to take the role of main breadwinner, regardless of the women's earning capacity. Potuchek maintains that a professional woman's desire to maintain her career following childbirth is closely bound up with social identity. She cites the case of a couple with two children (one aged 3 and the other of school age) who share a job in a law firm.

Their reasons for choosing to job-share were that neither was prepared to give up their professional identity, though at the same time neither was happy at the idea of their children in full-time childcare. Potuchek notes that 'In their interviews, Ellen and Bob minimize[d] gender boundaries and emphasize[d] the extent to which they share both work and parenting'. She also observes that 'Although Ellen and Bob fully share the responsibility for providing, it is not at the centre of either of their lives. . . both emphasize the importance of their roles as professionals' (as opposed to breadwinners). The woman in this case ranked her identity as a professional as equal in importance to her role as spouse and parent. Potuchek argues that once couples like Ellen and Bob have dispensed with traditional gender boundaries in relation to breadwinning, they are unlikely to re-create these at a later date, whoever the main bread-winner may be.

Brannen and Moss (1991) provided a detailed exploration of the experiences of working mothers in Britain (mostly in full-time employment) at the close of the 1980s. They noted that there were significant issues relating to the symbolic importance of women's earnings within households. Often, women's earnings were characterized as almost incidental to household income, and less important than the man's, even if salaries were at similar levels to those of the male partner. This was sometimes the case even when women earned more than their partners. Where there appeared to be financial flexibility within households, women's salaries were used for savings and payment of nursery fees, this giving both partners the feeling that the woman's income was 'dispensable' should she decide to give up work – even though she may not have had plans to do this. This relates to Potuchek's early findings that work may be seen as 'optional' for women, but not for men. Conversely, however, it is noted that discourses on twentieth-century motherhood and Bowlby's arguments that a child could 'suffer psychologic-ally if a mother did not provide her child with "constant attention, day and night, seven days a week, 365 days a year" ' (Brannen and Moss 1991: 91, citing Bowlby 1965: 77) are likely to produce feelings of tremendous guilt in the mother who chooses to work. In addition, a mother was also supposed to 'derive personal enrichment and joy from her devotion' (Brannen and Moss 1991: 91). It is arguable, therefore, that mothers who felt guilty about a wish to leave their children with others in order to be able to work may find that this burden is eased if their earnings were constructed as essential to family main-tenance. Significantly, in relation to the present book, Brannen and Moss argue that women, just like men, develop work orientations which are central to their social identity (whether in high- or low-status jobs). Brannen and Moss (1991: 78) note that 'while motherhood for some women overshadowed the previous importance of employment, for others it gave a new significance to employment . . . being at home [with a baby while on maternity leave] could make women realize their need for a sense of fulfilment and challenge which might not be met by motherhood'. Importantly, employment was also seen as salient to establishing a separate social identity from that of the domestic roles of mother, wife/partner and cleaner.

Social identity theory

This suggests that the commitment of mothers to their careers is complex, and relates to social identity and attitudes as well as to practical and financial needs. Rich and Oakley portray mothers as a distinctive social group which is undervalued by society, and it is clear from the literature discussed earlier that mothers' sense of identity and self-worth can be negatively affected if giving birth is associated with sacrificing career. Oakley (1981: 12–13), discussing the loss of self-esteem experienced by women who give up their jobs to become full-time mothers, states that: 'Becoming a mother is more than a change of job: it involves reorganising one's entire personality . . . motherhood seems . . . often to lead to a sense of lower ("depressed") self worth: children take the centre of the stage; the mother is merely a supporting player'. The question of positive (or negative) social identity and self-esteem was clearly an issue for the present book because one of the issues at the heart of the research was the question of the level of commitment of career mothers to their paid work. The women interviewed for the research project had all chosen to maintain their professional standing (sometimes with considerable effort) once they had children. This raised the query as to whether they may have been motivated to continue paid work due to a fear that being categorized as 'mothers' would relegate them to a lower social standing than if they continued to be associated with their profession of teacher, doctor, lawyer, and so on. In this respect, I considered that the work of Skevington and Baker (1989) in relation to motherhood and identity would be a useful framework through which to enhance the understanding of the work/home orientation of mothers. These authors have updated social identity theory (originally a psychological concept) and related it to women (in particular, to mothers and professionals). In my view, the authors succeed in their aim to make social identity theory 'more accessible' in the hopes that it can contribute to debates about 'the changing social identities of women in contemporary societies' (Skevington and Baker 1989: 1).

Skevington and Baker (1989: 1) state that 'The essence of Social Identity Theory is its concern with those aspects of identity that derive from group memberships'. They argue that 'Social Identity Theory has a potential as a way of understanding both the nature and content of women's group identifications in the course of women's lives, and also the intergroup relations between women and men and their consequences in social action' (1989: 4). Society is made up of various social groups that 'stand in power and status relations to one another'. Social identity theory is founded on the belief that individuals establish their identity, and evaluate their self-worth, not only through inter-personal comparisons and experience, but also via their membership of various social groups. The measuring of self-worth through group memberships (sex, race, occupation, etc.) is known as 'intergroup comparison' (Skevington and Baker 1989: 2). 'Members of dominant and higher status groups gain a positive social identity and high self-esteem from group membership; members of the lower-status or subordinate groups have a less positive social identity and lower self-esteem'. Members of social groups will estimate the relative status of their own groups and seek to optimize this in a number of ways. If individual upward mobility is achievable, then individuals will seek to attain this through their own effort. If this is not the case, then members of groups may consider options for collectively enhancing the status of their own group – for example, by trying to create a new and positive image for themselves (the National Childbirth Trust would be a good example of a collective attempt to improve the status of mothers in the UK). (Significantly, this issue is highlighted by Marshall and Wetherall 1989: 124, who describe their research with a group of trainee lawyers, in which participants equated a positive social identity with career, and ascribed a 'negatively defined base or standard identity concerned with child-rearing and a lack of career'.) In the light of this, social identity theory provides a useful perspective through which to try and understand the experiences and feelings of mothers and fathers – and it may provide a social explanation for the motivation underpinning the desire of career mothers to maintain their professional status.

'Being a breadwinner': The power of earned income

I have already observed that the social capital associated with motherhood and childcare is low, and that the status of breadwinner (especially if this is at a professional level) is higher by comparison. Since men's status has long been associated with economic provision for their families and since men have long been regarded by feminists as having more powerful status than women, this would imply that power and economic status are linked. As Pahl (1989: 125) has suggested: 'Being a breadwinner is often regarded as a burden, but it can also be a source of pride and power'.

Studying heterosexual partnerships and the distribution of household income, Vogler and Pahl (1994) and Pahl (1993: 630) have focused on how 'the social relations of employment intermesh with gender relations, with the workings of the household'. A key theme in their studies is the significant link between 'control over household finances and more general power within the household' (Vogler and Pahl 1994: 263). They noted that couples operate their household finances in a variety of ways, making the analysis of matters relating to marriage, money and women's motivation to work complex. In her study of *Money and Marriage*, Pahl (1989) had already underlined the status of the breadwinner role and noted that within heterosexual couples, both partners tended to portray the husband as the 'breadwinner' whose income should be devoted to the needs of the family, in contrast to the wife, whose earnings were seen as more peripheral. The frequent attribution of the breadwinner role to men was seen to reflect the desirability of this role, as well as the larger wages often earned by men due to freedom from childcare responsibilities. However, Pahl observed a reluctance on the part of female partners to regard their husband's income as 'shared', even when husbands were trying to convince wives that 'his' income was really 'hers' as well. Pahl (1989: 128) suggests that this may have been linked with an ideology in which the husbands' 'sharing' of money was seen as a reward for the wife's domestic work, which women rejected. Pahl (1989: 130) notes that: 'Earning was important to wives . . . because of the independence it brought them. Two-thirds of all the women said that it was important for them to "have some money you know is your own" '.

Vogler and Pahl (1994) focus on the association between control over money and power. They demonstrate that in households where money was 'pooled' (20% of their sample), relationships between the couple were relatively egalitarian. However, households in the higher income bracket where the male was in control of finances were among the least egalitarian, with women having little control over important decisions. This is particularly relevant to the research sample for the present book, where some of the employed men were highly paid. In an earlier article, Vogler and Pahl (1993: 93) note that 'The shift to greater equality [for women is extremely complex and] will depend not only on women's . . . participation in the labour market but also on effective changes to the husband's traditional status as main breadwinner in the family'. This suggests that the issue of earned income and power within intimate relationships is an important one. Predicting the way forward, Pahl (1993: 630) suggests: 'The smart money . . . is now on fragmentation and flexibility. It is not simply what goes on [at work] that provides the focus but how this activity meshes with all the other activities that [heterosexual couples] do'. Potuchek observed that, during the early 1980s, high-earning women in intimate heterosexual relationships tended to construct male partners as breadwinners, even if this was not the case. However, in Potuchek's (1997: 98) study, which researched couples from various backgrounds between 1987 and 1993, it was evident that there was a distinct trend away from 'using breadwinning as a gender boundary. This was particularly the case for wives; more than 75% of their reported changes in the normative and job centrality dimensions were in the direction of shared breadwinning'. Women were more likely to define their earnings as 'breadwinning' as opposed to 'pin money' if their earnings were high and they had children. Potuchek (1997: 100) asserted that women in the 1990s were more likely than women of previous decades to regard their own jobs as important because of their feminist attitudes, or because of fear of divorce. Potuchek (1997: 165) notes that 'the issue of whether the relationship between the breadwinning and mothering boundaries is complementary or compensatory [is complex because] just as husbands and wives do not always agree about breadwinning, they do not always agree about mothering'.

This is consistent with the views of many writers on family practices, patriarchy and the oppression of women, who recognize the importance of the power wielded by men in paid work, especially in situations where women are reliant on their husband's/partner's earnings for household and personal income. The literature on women's oppression and capitalism is immense, and I do not attempt an historic overview here. However, it is worth noting that the power wielded, historically, by employed men is not seen as accidental by writers such as Morris (1990), who suggest that much responsibility for this lies with the trade union movement of the late eighteenth and early nineteenth centuries. Morris notes that the unions fought for the rights of men not to have to compete with women for paid work by oppressing women, the goal of unions being 'to "bring about a condition where [women] would be in their proper sphere – at home" '. She notes that:

> The process by which these 'separate' spheres [of economic and domestic labour] came to have a gendered identity has yet to be fully understood, but there is a general agreement on a number of central points [including] . . . women's assumed responsibility for childcare . . . an associated constraint on women's activities, their growing exclusion from waged labour outside the home and a subsequent move on the part of male-dominated trade unions to secure male advantage in the labour market.
>
> (Morris 1990: 61)

Morris's linking of the connection between paid employment and power, and the impact this can have on the balance of power within heterosexual relationships, also concurs with Somerville's (2000) view. Somerville also notes the undesirability of being responsible for domestic labour by default and notes (as asserted by Dienhart and mentioned in Chapter 4) that men who find themselves responsible for children and household by circumstance, rather than by choice, are less likely to be satisfied than those who choose to be principal childcarers:

> Not only have men slowly lost the material comforts of the willing slave at home, but also the social status and self-esteem of a masculinity tied up with the capacity to be a breadwinner and afford a full-time housewife–mother. When the dual-earner mode was

chosen voluntarily by couples, it enabled an incremental modification of gender roles and a quiet renegotiation of masculinity and femininity. When it became an economic necessity in situations where it was often easier for women to get and keep jobs than it was for men, it presented a stark challenge to the self-esteem and sense of identity of both partners and the relationship between them.

(Somerville 2000: 241)

The attributes of power

I have already suggested that children, and the mediation of parent–child relationships, may be regarded as a source of power and conflict between mothers and fathers, particularly post-divorce. In Part 2, I will argue that within their marriage/relationship, parents are aware of the power of direct involvement with children's lives and may compete for their share of this. Given the issues of power and status related to the care of children and paid employment, both within relationships and in the context of the wider setting, it seemed important to consider the issue of 'power' as a concept, and I apply some of the theoretical ideas considered below to the findings discussed in Part 2. There are many writers on power in the areas of feminism, organizational theory and post-modernism. From the wide range of views and ideas available, therefore, I have chosen to consider two ways in which power can be understood which are particularly relevant to the present project.

A 'modern' definition

Modern writers on power in an organizational context (MacMillan and Jones 1986; Morgan 1986) define power as 'the medium through which conflicts of interest are ultimately resolved' (Morgan 1986: 159), and 'the ability to restructure situations' (MacMillan and Jones 1986: 18). These writers regard power as located in identifiable characteristics, the ownership of which can influence the status of individuals and other agencies, because these features may be used to initiate change. They list the key characteristics of power as: possession of resources; control of alternatives; leverage of existing influence; use of authority (formal and informal); and control of knowledge and information. Morgan, in particular, sees the power of resources as key, especially if this relates to money, which as Morgan (1986: 61) suggests, 'is the most liquid of all resources and can usually be converted into others'. In my view, these definitions are useful in understanding power relations within marriages/intimate relationships. For example, the concept of control of knowledge and information (such as how the child should be dressed, or what s/he might be given to eat) could be particularly relevant in a situation where either parent wishes to be territorial about relationships with children. The possession of resources as a source of power might be useful in terms of understanding why either partner in a marriage/relationship is motivated to continue working. Possession of resources could also be linked to the ability to control alternatives (such as the type of childcare used). Leverage of existing influence and informal authority might be less important sources of power within an existing relationship, but might be present in the background of a partnership/ marriage which is faltering. For example, in a contested residency case, courts may take into consideration existing responsibilities for childcare, in terms of which parent wields day-to-day influence and authority in the home, before awarding formal authority to one parent as principal carer.

. . . and a 'post-modern' definition

Post-modern writers and philosophers such as Michel Foucault, Bruno Latour and John Law write extensively on power. I do not intend here to cover the vast and complex literatures on power, philosophy and post-structuralism, but will make some key points and explain how these are relevant to this book. The first of these is that post-modern writers see power as less 'tangible' than organizational theorists such as Morgan, quoted above. Foucault, who was an important influence on later writers such as Latour (Law 1994: 105), came to the conclusion that although power might 'present its image' through political life (Foucault 1990: 118), nevertheless 'The relations of power are perhaps among the best hidden things in the social body' (Foucault 1990: 169). For Foucault, the challenge is less in the discovery of how people use power to influence the actions of others, than in the discovery of the origins of power – of where 'power' comes from in the first place: 'Who exercises power? How? Who makes decisions for me? Who is preventing me from doing this and telling me to do that? I don't believe that this question of "who exercises power?" can be resolved unless that other question "how does it happen?" is resolved at the same time' (Foucault 1990: 103).

Foucault theorized that, in a capitalist society, domination by the state is widespread but hidden because the state and related agencies regulate individual behaviours through setting the 'norms' by which people live. This has the combined effect of reducing freedom and increasing the state's power, with the eventual consequence that 'the role of the state is increased more and more' (Foucault 1990: 108), but in such a way that this may happen without people noticing, or realizing the consequences, until it is too late to alter things. Speaking of his own work, *The Birth of the Clinic*, Foucault even admitted that this had happened to him, as the regulatory power of the state could easily be overlooked in a study where the economic interests and the constituent subject were the priority. He notes: 'I scarcely ever used the word [power], yet when I think back now, I ask myself what else it was I was talking about?' (Foucault 1990: 116). As McNay (1992: 68) notes:

> In relation to the state, [the notion of] governmentality is used [by Foucault] to explain how the modern [*sic*] state is not a unified apparatus of domination, but is made up of a network of institutions and procedures which employ complex techniques of power to order social relations. . . . In this respect, governmentality is linked to disciplinary power in so far as it annexes disciplinary techniques in order to achieve its aim of the regulation of populations.

Although Foucault argued that the practices of the individual are regulated by insidious state power, or 'governmentality', he nevertheless believed that the nature of power was unstable and subject to change. This is because Foucault also deduced that, once people were *aware* of the rules of conduct set by the state, they were capable of resisting these. As McNay (1992: 68) notes: 'Like disciplinary power, governmentality also targets the individual as a means with which to maintain social control [but] individuals can resist this "government of individualisation" . . . and resist power through the very techniques by which [they are] governed'. In other words, individuals are responsible for ordering their own lives within a 'free' society, and while they may be constrained by the domination of the state, they may also choose not to conform to what is expected of them and may even, therefore (if they do this in large enough numbers), influence state policy. This philosophy has, as noted by McNay (1992: 69), some consistency with Giddens, who believes even more strongly that 'all social actors, no matter how oppressed, have some degree of penetration of the social forms which oppress them'. Foucault's view of a state which exercises power by regulating social behaviour (but which may face resistance from individuals) is highly relevant to the present book, which aims to set the experience of individual research participants in a wider context, with the objective of questioning current policy.

An explanation of the consequences of resistance to power is given by Latour (1986) and Law (1992) on the basis that those who exercise power may do so only through the consent of others. Once this consent is withdrawn, 'Order comes crashing down' (Law 1992: 379) and those who once 'made the rules' may find they are no longer 'Master of the universe' (Law 1992). As Latour (1986: 276) argues, 'No matter how much power one appears to accumulate, it is always necessary to obtain it from the others who are doing the action . . . to define who is acting, why it is necessary to act together, what are the boundaries of the collective, how responsibility should be allocated'. This view seems relevant to a book where, both within relationships and in the context of a wider setting, research participants are struggling to define their roles as both childcarers and economic providers, dealing with the conflict involved in giving up power on the one hand (by, for example, 'giving ground' on the issue of who is the principal carer for children) and seizing it on the other (by, for example, being 'territorial' in connection with relationships with children).

The issues of power, social identity and commitment to paid work are a constant theme which is threaded through the experiences of research participants in Part 2. As I draw Part 1 to a close, it seems that career women who combine mothering with paid work face some acute dilemmas. As they struggle to maintain their professional status (knowing as they do this that genuine 'equality' with men is almost impossible in terms of salary, promotion and status), they face the prospect of 'losing ground' in the home, in terms of their relationships with children. At the same time, they are no nearer to losing responsibility for domestic labour, which appears to lie with women no matter how many hours they work or how much they earn. Furthermore, whichever choice they make – whether to continue employment or to give up paid work – mothers 'can't win'. They face the conundrum discussed by Chira (1998) and Cusk (2001): that society disparages mothers who stay at home, while accusing working mothers of 'producing children who are emotionally damaged' (Chira 1998: 117). Fathers who want to change things – perhaps by explicitly combining childcare with paid work – may not find things much easier. The institutionalized role of the father as 'economic provider' is now so strongly embedded in tradition and in law that men in heterosexual relationships who wish to care for their own children at home may find themselves simultaneously challenged and ignored as they 'defy' expectations.

Summary

I argued in this chapter that mothers' commitment to work is questioned by key writers on women's labour who construct women (especially mothers) as a poor employment prospect and a drain on the economy (in Part 2 I shall challenge this idea very strongly). I acknowledged, however, that 'commitment' is difficult to define and involves complex concepts such as power and social identity, both of which I considered in some detail. I also recognized that power relations between men and women, within a heterosexual relationship, are difficult to dissociate from earned income and the history of women's oppression in the labour market. I ended on a note which sets the scene for the beginning of Part 2 – with a summary of the dilemmas faced by parents who wish to combine childcare with paid work, within a relationship.

PART 2
Doing it All (and having some of it)

He maketh . . . woman to keep house: and to be a joyful mother of children.
(Church of England, Book of Common Prayer, Psalm 113: 8)

Introduction

The purpose of Part 2 is to understand the experience of research participants in the context of the literature described in Part 1. In Part 2, I will highlight some of the key issues raised by the mothers and fathers who took part in the research for this book and will explore these in the context of wider debates (e.g. how far mothers are committed to their paid work). I seek to establish what the group of women and men concerned are *actually* doing with their lives, in contrast to what those who criticize career mothers argue they *ought* to be doing. Research participants held strong views on all of the topics under consideration, which had been thought out over a period of time. In order to bring their situations to life, therefore, and to allow them a 'voice', interviewees' opinions are, as far as possible, reported in their own words. The views of the 38 parents who took part in the project cannot be said to 'represent' the wider population, because the sample size is small in comparison with the total number of parents in the UK who are combining parenting with paid work. However, Part 2 will generalize and theorize about parents' experiences, building on Part 1 and providing explanations for parental choices and behaviour: what has motivated participants to make certain decisions and to remain in (or, in the case of some fathers, to give up) paid work. These explanations are set in the wider context of social structures and practices.

Summary of similarities to, and departures from, the literature

Before going into detail about the research project, I will give a brief overview of what follows, which might help readers decide how and in which order they wish to approach this part of the book. In the following chapter, I shall argue that there are some areas where the experiences of participants are very similar to the situation outlined in the literature, which were therefore in line with expectations. These include the transition to motherhood, which is portrayed by participants in a way that recalls the descriptions given by writers such as Oakley (1981) and Rich (1977) – as a huge emotional and physical shock. The experience of pregnancy and giving birth is also reported in terms comparable with key writers on the subject, such as Kitzinger (1992a), who focuses on the battle between mothers and health professionals for control of the maternal body. The same can be said for the description of poor health suffered by new mothers in the sample, which follows the patterns indicated by the work of Graham (1993) and Popay (1992). Mothers' experiences relating to the domestic division of labour also follow the pattern outlined in the work of Delphy and Leonard (1992), Dryden (1999) and Maushart (2002): that is, in most cases, mothers are responsible for household and domestic chores, no matter how well they are paid or how many hours paid work they do. In addition, it will be seen that women experienced discrimination in the workplace and found employers unsupportive of their maternal status, which tallies with descriptions provided by Cockburn (2002) and Halford *et al.* (1997). Significantly, this finding also applied to some men who wanted workplaces to be flexible to accommodate childcare.

However, there were some areas in which the findings from the research for this book broke new ground. The feelings expressed by mothers towards their paid work were in marked contrast to the assumptions made by Hakim (1995), Dex *et al.* (1998) and others that mothers are uncommitted to their jobs, and may be trapped in paid employment because they want the money to purchase lifestyles associated with success, involving expensive cars and houses. A discussion of fathers' commitment to work raised the question whether this might change once they became involved with the raising of small children. In this respect, perhaps the most outstanding departure from the existing literature on families and parenting was demonstrated in the practical involvement by almost all fathers in caring for their children *within* their marriage or partnership. Fathers not only undertook practical duties, but also took some responsibility for managing their own emotional relationships with children, rather than leaving this task to their wives (as described in the work of Ribbens 1994). This marks a change from previous studies (e.g. Smart and Neale 1999), in which it is shown that cohabiting or married fathers usually leave the emotional labour of care to mothers, only establishing their own relationships with children post-divorce (if at all). My research also showed that, although some fathers in the sample 'tolerated' their partner's wish to work, and dreamed of freedom from domestic chores (for themselves), many associated full-time motherhood with a drop in social capital. In contrast to what is suggested by Hewlett (2003) and Tooley (2002), they esteemed their wives/partners more highly when they were in paid work than when they were at home full-time. A further group of fathers were financially dependent on their spouse/partner, meaning that the women in the relationship were not the 'second income earner' as assumed by those writing in the 1980s and early 1990s (Lewis 1986; Pahl 1989; Brannen and Moss 1991). Given the social changes outlined in Chapter 1, it might be supposed that these discoveries are unsurprising. However, it appears that while the demographics and the social behaviour of mothers and fathers may be changing, the social attitudes of some agencies and individuals remain almost the same as they were in the 1950s. In my view, it is the forging of new and diverse ways of living, in the face of disapproval, that is mainly responsible for the difficulties faced by those who are at the vanguard of new social trends – in this instance, the women (and their partners) who are combining career with child-rearing.

The research project

The research for this book took place between 1999 and 2001 and consisted of in-depth, qualitative interviews with 20 women and 18 men. In order to protect the identity of those who took part, participants were drawn from all over the UK. This was important because some mothers had reached a level within their profession where numbers of women were small, and an indication of their address might have made them identifiable. Locations included Durham, Cheshire, Cumbria, Essex, London, Lancashire, Manchester, Merseyside and Yorkshire. For the same reason, pseudonyms have been given to all participants, the numbers and ages of children are not identified (other than in Table 3) and the ethnic backgrounds of individual participants are not described. Most of the participants were white and originated from England, Scotland, Wales or Northern Ireland. However, two interviewees (one male, one female) had emigrated to England from Australia and New Zealand respectively, and two women, although British, had rich cultural backgrounds, one with one Chinese and the other with one Asian parent. The sampling strategy was designed to generate a range of participants who would reflect (but not necessarily represent) the demographic trends outlined in Chapter 1. Parents who took part in the project were recruited through snowballing, so some were self-selecting, and some went to a good deal of trouble (taking time off work and paying for childcare) in order to take part. This inevitably means that some participants were predisposed to believe that the subject was important at the start, and some had a political agenda. They felt that improvements in policies for working families were necessary and hoped that, by taking part in the research, they may have made a direct contribution to this change, however small. In the carefully considered selection of participants, however, the above concerns were offset by a strict adherence to the sampling criteria. Mothers were the 'gatekeepers' of the research, and all women interviewed were qualified to degree level and had at least one baby or pre-school child. At the time of the interviews they were all in paid employment at a professional or managerial level and they were living with the father of the pre-school child(ren) in question. The ages of children ranged from 2 months to 8 years, and the numbers of children per couple ranged from one to five (Table 3).

Mothers were drawn from a broad range of professions, spanning both private and public sectors. Mothers and fathers were interviewed separately, unless they requested otherwise (as in the case of three couples). All of the women carried a high level of responsibility, and nine could be described as 'employers' in the sense that they were responsible for recruiting and managing staff. Sixteen of these women described themselves as working

Table 3   Ages and numbers of children (at date of interview with mother)

Couple	No. of children	Ages
1	1	3 years
2	2	3 and 5 years
3	3	1, 3 and 5 years
4	1	4 years
5	2	3 and 6 years
6	2	10 months and 4 years
7	1, 1 expected	2 years
8	2	3 and 8 years
9	2	2 and 4 years
10	2	2 and 4 years
11	5	1 (twins), 3, 4 and 6 years
12	2	1 and 3 years
13	2	6 months and 3 years
14	2	3 months and 3 years
15	1, 1 expected	3 years
16	2	2 months and 2 years
17	1	10 months
18	2	2 and 4 years
19	2	2 and 4 years
20	3	2, 4 and 6 years

'part-time' and four as 'full-time', though a word of caution is sounded here in that, for some interviewees, working 'part-time' might mean working a minimum of 40 hours per week. For others, it might mean flexible working in terms of how and when tasks were achieved but might still involve a full-time commitment in terms of hours. Two women, who described themselves as working '80%', earned more than their husbands did. Table 4 lists the pseudonyms and professions of the interviewees.

Table 4   List of those interviewed

Women	Men
Amanda, *architect*	Alan, *academic*
Angela, *academic*	Andy, *hospital pharmacist*
Diane, *television news producer*	Charles, *scientist*
Eleanor, *senior education manager*	Chris, *chemist*
Elisabeth, *hospital doctor*	David, *psychiatrist*
Estelle, *psychotherapist*	Edward, *GP*
Jane, *A-level teacher (head of department)*	Henry, *lawyer*
Jayne, *electronic engineer*	Jack, *GP*
Joanne, *tax consultant*	James, *electronic engineer*
Lianne, *A-level teacher*	Jeremy, *academic*
Louise, *public sector manager*	Joseph, *at home, principal childcarer*
Lucy, *hospital pharmacist*	Mark, *secondary school teacher*
Pandora, *lawyer*	Nick, *lawyer*
Penelope, *social worker*	Peter, *social worker*
Rachael, *NHS chief executive*	Sam, *lawyer*
Sarah-Jane, *hospital doctor*	Stephen, *GP*
Sophie, *lawyer*	Tony, *computer programmer*
Sonia, *nurse manager*	William, *architect*
Suzanne, *lawyer*	
Victoria, *academic*	

The descriptions of the posts held by those concerned are of necessity general, in order to assist in protecting the anonymity of research participants. For example, the description 'lawyer' covers roles such as solicitor, barrister and Crown prosecutor. Fathers, although living with their wives/partners, were interviewed separately, and after the mother had been interviewed, unless couples requested otherwise, as it was felt that some couples might find joint interviews constraining.

As can be seen in Table 5, in five of the couples interviewed, the woman was the principal earner within the household (and therefore by implication did not have the choice to 'opt out' of paid work). In a further three instances the woman was equally responsible for household income. This is interesting

Table 5   Summary of financial, childcare and household responsibilities of mothers in the sample

---

Principal or equal earners (8 mothers):
2 mothers principal earners, in full-time paid work, with fathers at home as full-time childcarers (one father is the main houseworker, the other not so – this job is left to the mother).
3 mothers principal earners, in full-time paid work with fathers in part-time paid work, and acting as principal childcarer. Mothers still carry the main responsibility for household work.
1 mother equal earner, in full-time paid work; the responsibility for children and household is shared equally.
2 mothers equal earners, working approximately 80% of a full-time equivalent, with childcare shared equally (but mothers still carrying the main burden of household responsibility).

Second or incidental income earners (12 mothers):
9 mothers 'second income' earners, in part-time paid work, principal childcarers and houseworkers (husbands/partners in full-time paid work). Two of these couples are working towards the situation where responsibility for earning and childcare work can be shared equally.
3 mothers' income incidental to household finances, as the cost of childcare leaves a deficit. All three are in part-time paid work and have the principal responsibility for childcare and household work. However, one couple is actively and explicitly co-parenting on days when both are working.

---

as it limits the possibility of couples choosing to characterize the woman's salary as 'incidental' to household finances, which is what some couples with financial flexibility chose to do in the late 1980s (as noted by Morris 1990; Brannen and Moss 1991). This finding is in contrast to much of the literature on dual-earner couples, where it is generally assumed that the woman's income (especially where she has children) will be of secondary importance to that of her husband/partner (e.g. Pahl 1989). This may be because some of the key texts were written over 10 years ago and circumstances are changing rapidly (although this remains the assumption of Maushart 2002). While the sample of 20 couples is small, the results from my research raise questions about whether changes in the way couples operate their household responsibilities may be taking place in the wider population.

6 'Baby, you changed my life'
The transition to motherhood

A lot of my friends have conformed to the perfect mother role model of staying at home and not working. And I don't feel as if I ever do anything right, I mean I don't feel I get the balance right, so I feel guilty because if I'm at work, and because I'm fairly dedicated and enjoy doing my job, then there's the guilt bit about 'Well, I should be at home'. And it's fine if everything is working but if the youngest throws a tantrum, then I get the guilt bit about: 'It's happened because I'm a bad mum'. And I do struggle with that and I don't think I'll ever come to terms with it, the guilt, I really don't. If I was going to, I think I might have done it by now.

(Rachael, NHS chief executive)

Focus on:

Losing control: The experience of pregnancy and giving birth
    Depression and lack of maternal control
    Physical health problems
The shock of the new
'Domestic goddesses'? Childcare, wifework and emotional labour
    The value of experience
Guilt and the 'bad mother'
'Built-in' behaviour? The emotional bonds of motherhood versus the 'institution of motherhood'
'Pink jobs and blue jobs': Women's responsibility for domestic labour
    'Help' with the housework
    Working to pay for help with the domestic chores
'I should iron his shirts': Laundry, and the symbolism of tending men's shirts

---

Introduction

This chapter considers the empirical study in relation to key themes which emerged in Part 1. It begins by focusing on transition to motherhood, which can cause physical and emotional upheaval for months. The birth of children (particularly a first child) had a major impact on both mothers and fathers, which is consistent with the observations of Oakley (1981), Rich (1977) and Cusk (2001). Unfortunately it would appear that, despite government initiatives to make childbirth more mother-centred (Department of Health 1993; Audit Commission 1997), birth is still very much the domain of hospitals, technology and male obstetricians who may be unsympathetic to the concept of maternal choice. The birth process and the associated issue of maternal control (or otherwise) has already been shown to be key to mothers' mental health in the years following childbirth (Kitzinger 1992a, 1992b). Perhaps predictably, therefore, there appeared to be a link with post-natal depression where mothers felt out of control during the birth. Many women in the research sample also suffered physical health problems following childbirth and few had sought help in these matters. This is significant because all the women who took part in this project were returning to work less than 12 months after the birth of their children (in one case after only 6 weeks). The determination of mothers to continue their careers, often despite poor health and a lack of support from employers and other agencies, indicated a deep personal commitment to their profession – in contrast to the arguments put forward in the media (e.g. Boase 2001; Knight 2002) and by some academic writers (e.g. Hakim 1995, 1996b). Pressures on mothers (and fathers) were at their height following the birth of first babies. Research participants loved their children but were shocked by the stress that the arrival of a new baby placed upon them as individuals and as a couple. The combining of paid work with mothering meant that women devoted less time to husbands/partners, which caused concern to both partners in some relationships, although women (to their frustration) found themselves spending even more time on domestic labour than before their children arrived.

Losing control: The experience of pregnancy and giving birth

No matter what they had read, or how many ante-natal classes they had attended, all the parents who took part in the research for this book were shocked by the transition to motherhood, which had a deep and irrevocable impact on the mother and her relationship with her male partner, as well as with the workplace on her return. This accords with the arguments of Cosslett

(1994), Davidson (2001) and Cusk (2001) that motherhood changes a woman profoundly, as her body literally creates another life and a new social role is thrust upon her. For this reason, the transition to motherhood, and how this was managed by health professionals and the mothers themselves, was pivotal in terms of how well women coped with paid work, relationships and life in general over the following period. The argument put forward by writers such as Kitzinger (1992a, 1992b), Oakley (1981, 1984), Graham and McKee (1980), and Rothman (1982), that 'the *beginning* of motherhood could be immensely important and the way in which a birth is managed could influence a woman's whole experience of becoming a mother' (Oakley 1981: 2; emphasis in original), has been established in Chapter 3. In other words, a badly managed hospital birth, in which a mother felt herself to be deprived of choice and information, could affect her mental and physical well-being for months or years afterwards. This point was made by many mothers. While they did not object in principle to the idea of medical intervention, all women found it difficult if this robbed them of a sense of control during the process of pregnancy and birth. Additionally, the transition to motherhood was compounded by the fact that mothers experienced difficulties with physical and mental health for a lengthy period (in some cases, for years) following the births of their children. This is consistent with the arguments of Graham (1993) and Popay (1992), who note that new mothers often struggle with ill health because they are offered little support from health services and can see no option other than 'keeping going'. Given that all the women in the research sample returned to demanding jobs within 6 weeks to 12 months after the birth of their babies, their state of health was important because the strain on women who are trying to combine child-rearing with paid work is already substantial, without the added pressure of poor health.

Depression and lack of maternal control

Although the number of women who took part in the research was small, it is worth noting that seven women who experienced traumatic births reported being depressed for up to 3 years afterwards. Their unhappiness seems to have been exacerbated by the feeling that they had lost any sense of control or choice during the pregnancy and birth. This is not to suggest that some mothers did not enjoy the experience of being pregnant, or that they rejected the concept of regular medical checks for themselves and their babies:

> I fell pregnant and I was ecstatic, the whole period I was happy, it was just the thing I wanted most and she was, the minute I became pregnant, she was loved. I felt a real wanting to do the right thing for her, and the mother in me was probably at its most extreme.
>
> (Louise, public sector manager)

However, many mothers resented the feeling that, from the moment they became pregnant and throughout the birth process, their bodies had become public (or at least health service) property and they were allowed little or no say in the nature of the treatment they experienced, but were expected to submit to this without question – especially if all was not well. Their feelings in this regard accord absolutely with the arguments put forward by Davidson (2001) and Miles (1992). For example, Estelle, who was warned that her baby might have Down syndrome, wanted to refuse a third trimester scan on the grounds that the result would make no difference to her decision whether to have the baby. She described her experience thus:

> There had been some anxiety about him on the first scan. And then we had another scan in the routine way of things. And then they wanted us to go back for a follow-up scan and I remember getting very cross actually, because this scan was just for their records and I thought, well there is no medical or management decision we're going to make that will change in the slightest in the light of what is seen on the scan, so we'll just have to wait until he's born and then we'll find out. And we did try and take some control but I faced real hostility on this and the [hospital staff] were just appalling. And in the end what I said was 'I can't have this baby in this hospital.' Anyway we decided to have the baby at home, we were trying to take some control and that was great, that bit was *very* good. But then we got sort of dampened by having to go into hospital. And when he was born he was perfect. What a huge sense of relief.
>
> (Estelle, psychotherapist)

Women who had experienced a loss of control indicated that this had robbed them of self-confidence and self-esteem in all aspects of their lives for a long time to come. The writer Rachel Cusk (who was unhappy and depressed for months after her baby was born) attributes this to the trauma of the birth process and records her frustration at being required by the hospital system, against her wishes, to 'submit' to various medical procedures. She recalls her experiences thus:

> I am told I must remain in hospital ... A militant junior doctor keen to practise inserting things into veins ... offers blood tests [which] ... I refuse. Quietly enraged, she disappears and returns with back-up. It is explained to me that I must undergo these procedures. I argue and eventually submit ... Chastened, I am put to bed in a ward.
>
> (Cusk 2001: 139)

Cusk's description is similar to that given by one of the interviewees for this research. Louise, who was seriously ill following the birth of her only child, remembers the feeling of vulnerability and the need to 'fight' the system which 'bullied her into submission' when she realized that something had gone wrong, and she was seriously ill, following complications. Four years later, having survived after a long period of illness, she still felt as if her body had been violated; her experiences are consistent with those described by Kitzinger (1992a), Rothman (1982) and Cusk (2001) and noted in Chapter 3. Another research participant described a similar experience and made a direct link between the lack of control during the birth process and her subsequent depression:

> [although I did not want this] they induced me because by their dates I'd gone a week or 10 days over, which I was annoyed about. It didn't work the first time and I think it made for a very, very difficult birth. He was slow to come out and I was slow to dilate. The room was like Piccadilly Circus, there must have been seven or eight people in it at various times. I was very badly sort of beaten about at the end, because he had to be ventoused [suctioned] out . . . And then later my [GP], because I did get very run down and depressed, kept saying 'Stop breast feeding and let me give you some anti-depressants or whatever' . . . And I said 'No, no, it's OK I'll keep doing it' 'cause it took me so long to perfect it and at long last *I* was in control of what I was doing and I just wanted to go with it as long as I could, so I did. And I felt better for that.
>
> (Joanne, tax consultant)

It is significant that of the seven women who reported depression following difficulties in childbirth, only one had sought formal treatment. This may be partly due to the fact that close family and GPs are unlikely to take women's depression seriously unless it 'interferes' with their ability to manage their domestic or paid work effectively (Kitzinger 1992a). It may also be that new mothers lack the energy to tackle this problem, or that they quickly reach the point where they take their poor health for granted and just accept it as part of post-natal life, as suggested by Graham (1993) and Popay (1992). However, women could also be reluctant to seek help because they were embarrassed about admitting to mental health problems, even if these problems were long-term (as suggested by the description of depression given by Sophie, quoted below). Perhaps this desire to avoid the label 'depression' is because highly qualified career women who feel used to being 'in control' are shocked to find themselves with mental health problems, and are unaware that many other women in the same situation are experiencing similar feelings (Kitzinger 1992a). Sarah-Jane recalls:

> By the time [my baby] was 6 months I was actually quite depressed. Although I think I never acknowledged that at the time, and I got very angry if anyone tried to suggest it to me and especially if [my husband] tried to suggest that perhaps I was depressed, I'd end up getting very angry and then it would end in tears and then [my husband] would be rather afraid to broach in case it sort of upset me again. And by the time I went back to work I was really wanting to be back at work.
>
> (Sarah-Jane, doctor)

In some cases, like Sarah-Jane's, mothers found that returning to work helped them cope with depression because it provided them with a sense of being in control of their lives once again. This is in accordance with Hochschild's (1997) argument that work can provide a solace for parents who are struggling to cope with the demands of household work and small children. One mother, who felt that control of the birth process had been denied her during a difficult hospital delivery, linked this with depression and found that returning to work was helpful:

> I was never actually diagnosed as having post-natal depression but I found life very difficult after I had [my son] and was keen to go back to work quite quickly, and once I got back to work I felt much better, but I found it very hard to be at home with this small baby.
>
> (Sonia, nurse)

Some women (and their partners) made a positive link between maintaining their paid work and good mental health:

> I consider work and motherhood as going hand in hand. I feel it's really for my sanity, for my life, it is my life and I don't [want to] give it up.
>
> (Amanda, architect)

> It enables [my wife] to keep sane really, to carry on with what she was doing beforehand and I think, you know, self-esteem and independence and it's something she has worked very hard for.
>
> (Sam, lawyer)

In other instances, however, the women concerned hoped that work would help but found that, in the long term, it simply compounded the pressures they were under. Sophie, who underwent a particularly lengthy labour (36 hours) and was so distressed by the process of childbirth that she rejected the idea of further children, reported:

I wouldn't say I had a mental illness but I did hit a depressive time, there is no doubt about that at all. And that was during that six-month period when I was at home. It wasn't post-natal depression, it was . . . though I suppose it could have been described as that . . . It was born in that time but it didn't actually manifest itself till [my baby] was 2 and I'd sort of been keeping it all here and all tensed up about it . . . I was this lunatic woman who just didn't know what she was doing and tearing her hair out. And I think I was assisted [initially] by going to work because there I knew this security, this certainty . . . but having said that, work did not help [in the long term] because I was tired from doing that, so it was all a big combination of everything.

(Sophie, lawyer)

Several women who had 'planned' a natural birth were (like Cosslett 1994) shocked to discover that the description of natural childbirth offered by Kitzinger (1984) and Natural Childbirth Trust classes was somewhat 'rose-tinted'. They did not find it sexy, easy or joyful, but far more painful and frightening than they had anticipated. Many mothers entered hospital armed with lavender oil and relaxation tapes, only to find themselves confronted with a terrifying world of pain, drugs and fear as things spun out of their control. However, some women saw the medical profession as being partly responsible for this situation because they found themselves under pressure to 'hand over' control of their bodies to hospital staff, on the basis that refusal would make them 'irresponsible'. This is in keeping with Kitzinger's argument that modern medicine renders intelligent women powerless 'in the production of babies' by threatening risk to unborn children if mothers fail to conform to medical conventions (Kitzinger 1992a). Despite the evidence provided by writers on childbirth that 'choice' and 'control' in childbirth are important to the well-being of mothers (e.g. Department of Health 1993), the experiences of the women in my research sample indicate that, at least in the case of first births, maternal choice is almost as difficult to achieve now as it was in the 1970s and 1980s when Oakley and Rich were writing. Significantly, women with more than one child were assertive on subsequent occasions, and managed to exercise some control over the birth process. Some chose a 'natural' route and had their babies delivered by a midwife at home. Sarah-Jane describes her experiences thus:

[the midwife] came and she said, 'yes you are 5 centimeters dilated'. And then we pottered round and at about 6 o'clock in the evening [my other child] said he wanted to go to bed. And he'd been lovely really, he'd rubbed my back and he'd been in and out playing and then he went to bed. And at 8 o'clock [my baby] was born. And the next morning my partner went and got [my eldest] out of his cot and he came in and sang Happy Birthday to the new baby. And it was lovely, there was no disruption to family life.

(Sarah-Jane, doctor)

Most chose to go to hospital (one woman even electing to have a Caesarean birth), but they made it clear that they were not prepared to simply 'hand over' all the decisions about their pregnancy and the birth to someone else. In a broad sense there is an implication that the ideals espoused in *Changing Childbirth* (Department of Health 1993) may not be working, especially in the case of first babies. Although the 'silly rule that husbands could not see their children being born' (Oakley 1981: 3) has fortunately been laid to rest, Oakley's description of her 'first birth [when I was] a passive patient, bewildered, afraid . . . controlled rather then controlling, his birth more the [health professionals'] achievement than mine' (Oakley 1981: 3), still has much in common with the first births experienced by many of the women in this sample. In my view this is highly significant because it implies that there could be a link between births where mothers feel out of control and post-natal depression. This suggests the need for further research, post *Changing Childbirth*.

Physical health problems

As well as depression, many women struggled with physical health problems following the birth of their first and subsequent children. For example, two had to return to hospital for further operations following badly executed stitching and pelvic floor problems. Two reported back pain and another suffered from persistent cystitis. One mother reported suffering from stress incontinence, which was inconvenient: 'a continuous thing there that I just have to be a bit careful with'. Lucy reported that she may need an abdominal operation to repair damaged stomach muscles and also mentioned that she suffered pins and needles and numbness in her legs for months following an epidural. Talking about her tummy muscles, and grimacing at the thought of her forthcoming operation, Lucy explained:

I've very damaged stomach muscles at the front because my babies were very big, they were 10 pounds, which is why I had C-sections because I couldn't get them out. And this time particularly, it's four months since I had [my baby] and I still look five months pregnant, you know, which if I was to wear a bikini or something . . . So that's a problem [because] if these muscles don't meet together I'll have to have them surgically repaired which is you know, a bit . . .

(Lucy, hospital pharmacist)

Many women reported permanent tiredness, caused partly by the combined workload of child, husband and housework, as well as their paid work, but also by consistently broken nights. This is in keeping with the contention of Popay (1992) and Graham (1993) that many mothers simply accept exhaustion as a fact of life. One mother summed this up neatly:

> It seemed like for the first two years of his life I was just constantly ill really and that's why I couldn't even think about having another child because I was just so run down. And I think as well with breast-feeding . . . it took so much energy really. The general run-down, ground-down sort of feeling really has been the main thing.
>
> (Penelope, social worker)

All of the women in the 'Hard Labour' project had returned to work between six weeks and one year after the birth of each child. Thus, many were returning to work while still under par, often not having come to terms with the arrival of a new baby. Unless they took the trouble to pursue this themselves, there was no post-natal 'aftercare' provided for mothers, apart from the initial home visits from the midwife (up to 10 days after the birth) and the standard six-week check by their GP practice. Neither health services nor occupational health services nor personnel services offered any support to any of these mothers, who were returning to work a relatively short time after giving birth. (This situation must be even more difficult for women in the USA, where maternity leave is often limited to six weeks). Given the pressures on the health and relationships of mothers at the time they returned to work, this was a serious omission. In my view it could only be beneficial – to mothers and to employers – if confidential support was provided by health agencies for women returning to employment after maternity leave.

The shock of the new

On arriving home with a new baby, especially if this was their first, most mothers (all of whom had read parenting texts and attended classes) were completely unprepared for the physical and emotional rollercoaster of new motherhood. Sarah-Jane, whose first baby cried a great deal, and Joanne each described their situation as follows:

> Of course [my husband] and I had this very rosy picture of what it was going to be like and all the things we'd do, we thought we'd be off up mountains with him on our back and be doing X, Y and Z. And of course the reality was we had no sleep, we completely disintegrated . . . and the moment [our baby] woke up he cried and it was awful and

[when my husband] went off to work I'd be on the telephone every hour saying 'somebody has got to come and help, he is just crying and crying', it was absolutely awful and it was such a shock. It wasn't what I had expected motherhood to be. I got very tired and then once you're tired everything seems so bleak . . . and so when I was off with [the baby] I felt I was very isolated with a very difficult baby and . . . [I felt] no good at being a mother and I *had* thought I would *love* it, you know: this is really what I've been wanting to do and it is going to be wonderful.

(Sarah-Jane, doctor)

It hit us like a brick wall. All the books we read, we just weren't prepared. We'd gone into it feeling we had done our reading but we weren't prepared at all.

(Joanne, tax consultant)

Like Marshall (1991), Joanne and others criticized parenting texts and ante-natal classes for providing an unrealistic picture of what 'motherhood' really meant. Despite the deep love they felt for their children, they admitted feeling ambivalent at times, and worried about the impact of motherhood on their own social and personal identity. Victoria's description seemed to sum this up very precisely, and echoed the poignant descriptions provided by Rich (1977) – see p. 50 above:

Physically it's messy, and emotionally it's messy too. When my daughter was born I fell in love with her. You are torn between this wonderful little creature you have brought into the world . . . I was so in love with my daughter . . . but in recognizing that I could be in love with her but also not necessarily want to look after her . . . there is this *guilt* thing. I feel it's emotionally messy. You *don't* want to lose your own sense of identity which you've spent many years building up.

(Victoria, academic)

It must be emphasized that the shock of the transition to motherhood did not mean that the mothers interviewed did not want or love their children. All but one of the mothers was explicit that babies had been planned, and all babies were much wanted, one mother having undergone surgery in order to become pregnant. Nevertheless, all but three mothers recalled the experience of being at home alone with a tiny baby (especially if this followed a difficult birth) as traumatic. They were taken aback by how exhausting and unpredictable the responsibility for a baby can be, as well as by how 'tied down' they felt, having temporarily given up their jobs to be at home full-time. The sense of shock and frustration is described by research participants in remarkably similar terms to Oakley (1981: 12–14) and Cusk (2001):

> When I had [my son], I had enormous problems . . . I didn't really know what I'd done; I'd given up this calm, collected, controlled position to become this sort of completely demented mother . . . I was very isolated with a crying baby, I'd given up this position where I was *always* in control, to being completely *out* of control, I mean this child governed everything we did and it was very, very difficult.
>
> (Sarah-Jane, doctor)

> It was terrible, I remember *screaming* at my husband, 'I am *trapped*' (I was so trapped, like in a cage, because I can't get out of this), 'I am *trapped* with this child, I'm not working, there's nothing I can do', . . . all your choices are taken away. But now I am back at work and we've come through all that now.
>
> (Lianne, A-level teacher)

As noted above, only three women in the sample acknowledged few problems adjusting to the responsibility of mothering a small baby. They considered themselves relatively unusual in this. One woman described her experience thus:

> I think I've been really lucky to bond with my children quite early on. You know, whereas friends have had six months of hell and wondered what this thing was that was screaming at them. I just got joy out of them and feeling as one with them really. And you know being besotted and all these things, it's true, they say you fall in love with your baby and you do and you feel that's just part of you.
>
> (Amanda, architect)

'Domestic goddesses'? Childcare, wifework and emotional labour

As argued by Kitzinger (1984: see Chapter 3 above), there was recognition among couples that the arrival of babies had changed their relationship with one another. Some of these observations related to a change in the level of investment (particularly on the part of mothers) in the intimate relationship, others to the relentless pressure of the domestic details which must be considered when both parents are combining childcare with paid work. Victoria described her situation thus:

> I don't mean this in a nasty way, but sometimes you can forget why you married this person ... sometimes you get so caught up in the operations management that you lose the excitement of being with the other person ... the niceness of being a couple gets lost somewhere.
>
> (Victoria, academic)

Some mothers related pressures on their intimate relationships to the change in parental social identity which is brought about by the birth of (especially first) children:

> Our relationship changed so instantly, from the moment the child is born you suddenly stop calling each other by your [own] name. Literally, one minute we're going to the hospital as '[husband's name] and Sophie', and we came out 'Mummy and Daddy' and you lose a certain identity I think ... And your own parents are no longer 'Mum and Dad', they are 'Granny and Grandpa'. And suddenly everyone is speaking this completely different language and so the relationship does change hugely between husband and wife and this can have a big impact.
>
> (Sophie, lawyer)

It was also observed, by nine of the mothers, that the amount of 'quality time' spent with their partner/husband was substantially less than before and that the number of social activities undertaken as a couple had reduced dramatically. When not at work, mothers were concerned to spend time and emotional labour on children, feeling that this was important, given that children were cared for by others for at least part of the time. All mothers went into detail about the intricacies of children's days, and those who reduced their hours of employment did so specifically in order to spend time with children, leaving little time for their own needs. Eleanor, a senior education manager, explained how she ensured that any free pockets of time were channelled into the children:

> I get tremendous pleasure out of spending time with the children. My idea about an ideal mother is one that spends time with the children. I don't mean never-ending time, I don't necessarily think you have to be with them all the time, but I like to listen to them, to talk to them, to do things that are about building memories for them ... and (despite my work) we do have lots of fun together and I really try hard to keep in touch with what's going on at my little boy's school and my daughter's nursery and that's not easy because I'm not there a lot of the time ... and I'm not able to take my little boy to school and that's a big, big regret. I do feel quite bad about that and on the odd

occasion when I go to a meeting [in city] I can leave a little bit later and I just love taking him to school and dropping him off.

(Eleanor, senior education manager).

Many mothers admitted that they became very tired, and were concerned that they should protect their children from the effects of this, taking trouble to try and remain calm at bedtimes even if their own patience was wearing thin, so that the children went to bed happy and settled. Mothers' working days (no matter how senior their jobs) were organized around children's needs, and women went to great lengths to accommodate both paid work and the detailed requirements of children's lives (see also Chapter 9). However, mothers were less able (or less willing) to play the role of 'domestic goddess' when it came to their partners' emotional needs, even if this had been a priority before children arrived. Some fathers were deeply resentful of this, a situation which both concerned mothers (because they did not wish to compromise their intimate relationship) and irritated them (because they felt it to be childish and self-centred). One mother said:

> You feel torn between your child and your husband and he is jealous sometimes, I think, of the attention I give to the children. I've had him shouting 'What about *me*?' and I've said 'Well, what about you? You're 38!'

(Lianne, A-level teacher)

As a result of this, women were aware that they were doing less wifework in the sense described by Delphy and Leonard (1992), Maushart (2002) or Lawson (2000). This was partly because they resisted the expectation that they should undertake more than half the domestic labour in the household, a responsibility which they considered had fallen to them at the moment they became mothers. However, it was also because they felt under pressure to fulfil their roles as mother and paid worker to the best of their ability, meaning that the husband/partner had slipped in the list of priorities. This is in keeping with the observations of Duncombe and Marsden (2002), who report that 'passion' within intimate relationships declines due to the 'distractions' and hard work associated with child-rearing. This caused concern among some mothers, who were anxious to retain their marriages/partnerships at the same time as caring for children and keeping up at work. It seemed to be the case that all mothers felt responsible for the emotional stability of their marriages even if they worked full-time, with husbands mainly responsible for childcare (as in Louise's case):

> It's difficult, your whole emotional thinking is difficult, your feelings for your husband are not the same after you've had children and that

is really back to lack of time again. I just have less patience with my husband, less sympathy. When we go away sometimes and there are just the two of us it's quite good for us. I suppose we're not as close, you see, we don't hug and kiss as much because when you're with the children, you're touching *them* all the time, kissing *them*.

(Lianne, A-level teacher)

I find learning to develop this new relationship [with the child] and with your partner as a 'unit' is difficult and I find that a challenge because inevitably [my husband] suffers. Obviously my daughter wants my attention when I'm at home and then when she goes down at night then there might be some work to do. And then maybe you drift into a position where you're not talking as much as you should together, I mean life isn't as it was. And I wonder whether this is an area, you know in terms of marital breakdown, it's about just how *do* you work as a unit? I am aware that [the role of wife] needs working at and I'm aware that possibly it's the third-place or fourth-place role . . . Because first it's the child, then business, then the third place is me, but then really I'm in fourth place because I don't seem to give myself any priority at all. So third place would be my husband, so he is actually in third place and that's the area where I think people like me need [to work at] if they want to avoid marital breakdown.

(Louise, public sector manager)

This indicated a tension for working mothers who were trying to maintain a balance between children, partner/husband and paid work. Some mothers felt guilty that they were no longer lavishing attention on male partners. At the same time, however, they felt resentful that they were expected to manage this when they were caring for a new baby, particularly once they had returned to work. In my view, the assumption by those in heterosexual relationships that mothers should undertake wifework – no matter what their other commitments may be – is problematic, since the combining of wifework with child-rearing and paid work would seem to be an impossible task, especially if mothers are also responsible for domestic labour. This expectation may be particularly intimidating for mothers, in the light of Giddens's (1992) argument that men are now aiming for perfection in their 'pure relationships'. This presumably means an ever-present threat that men might flee relationships if wives/partners prove unsatisfactory once the initial excitement has worn off and women have less time (or inclination!) to construct themselves as 'a cross between Sophia Loren and Debbie Reynolds . . . a weekend alter-ego winning adoring glances and endless approbation' (Lawson 2000: vii). It is notable – and disappointing – that this is exactly the fate which befalls Kate Reddy, the heroine in Allison Pearson's (2002) novel, who is forced to abandon her career because the combining of her job with mothering does not allow her to offer the required amount of 'attention' to her husband.

The value of experience

Although the transition to motherhood was difficult for most women, it is notable that, where there was more than one child, the birth of the first child proved the most difficult to adjust to. Second and subsequent children were easier. This was because, initially, mothers had been unprepared for what was involved in giving birth to and caring for a tiny baby. The births of second and subsequent children, while they created additional work, were less of a shock. Mothers felt more in control, and more confident about what they were doing. This was the case even if second and subsequent children were difficult to settle, or unwell. One mother explained:

> I enjoyed my time off so much more with [my second baby] than I did with [my first baby]. Despite the fact that she didn't sleep, I still enjoyed those first few months so much more with her than with my first. She was actually a very difficult baby, with horrendous colic and really didn't sleep at all, but it was still a better experience.
>
> (Sonia, nurse manager)

This would explain Macran and colleagues' (1996) observation that women who return to work after the birth of one child will probably continue employment after subsequent births.

Guilt and the 'bad mother'

It was noted in Chapter 3 that arguments about whether mothers should be the exclusive carers of pre-school children are often centred on 'maternal instinct' (Appleyard 2000: 48) and the image of women as 'natural' carers (Malthouse 1997). Given the years that have passed between 1956 and 2002, it might be assumed that legal forces for change such as equal opportunities legislation would have transformed attitudes towards working mothers – even though policy statements suggest that we should not be too hopeful on this score (Lea 2001). It would appear, however, that although the law has moved forward, the attitudes of some agencies towards working women remain firmly in the 1950s. Although the pieces quoted below by Malthouse, (1997) and Appleyard (2000) were written over 40 years after Parsons' seminal texts on family life (Parsons and Bales 1956), the sense of what is said about institutionalized motherhood is not far removed from what Parsons wrote. Malthouse (writing for the Institute of Directors in the UK) and Appleyard (writing in the *Daily Mail*) contend that mothers are responsible for ensuring children are 'disciplined' in accordance with society's 'norms'. This is consistent with Marshall's (1991) argument that (especially working) mothers are often blamed for society's problems. Malthouse (1997) states that '[women staying at home] is simply the most suitable arrangement for the emotional and physical development of a child, particularly between the ages of 0–3 . . . Day care actually threatens youngsters' development'. Appleyard (2000: 48) underlines what she believes the consequences of working motherhood to be: 'We read more and more about the dangers of not being there for your children . . . our children are our future and . . . the person they really need when they are young is their mother . . . having children is a full-time occupation in itself'. As noted in Chapter 3, views such as these put pressure on women who are trying to combine work with motherhood, as it may imply that their mothering is deficient. Brannen and Moss (1991) and Scott (1999) suggested that this might make working mothers feel very guilty, which was certainly the case among my respondents. Mothers explained that they were conscious of the powerful effects that 'institutionalized' roles had upon them and that these social expectations induced deep feelings of guilt. It was felt by research participants that popular literature and the media only dealt with what mothers 'ought' to be doing, and had failed to recognize social change:

> The books just failed me . . . maybe I wasn't reading the right literature, so once the babies were born I relied instead on the experiences of other mothers like me.
>
> (Victoria, academic)

Unsurprisingly, given the kind of pressures described above, all of the women expressed guilt and anxiety about leaving their children in the care of others. This is in keeping with the concerns of the many popular authors on working mothers, who write sympathetically about the difficulties of leaving very young children in order to re-enter the workplace (Franks 1999; Figes 1998a; Buxton 1998). One mother said:

> I am sure there are some negative effects . . . I think my children feel rushed, my oldest particularly is always being told 'hurry up, eat your breakfast' and I don't think they feel relaxed. Childhood is only so short and they spend a considerable amount of it either missing their mother or missing their father or being rushed off to some place where they are being looked after.
>
> (Elisabeth, doctor)

Some mothers found that female relatives and friends who had sacrificed career for full-time motherhood were very disapproving of their career status.

This accords with Buxton's (1998) argument that full-time mothers and career women are set against one another by the media, and experience conflict because of this. Penelope explained:

> My sister's just totally opposed to [mothers working] because she decided she wasn't going to and its almost like sinful to actually work and she's just totally, I think, unfair . . . She's made it quite clear [in her] attitude, just when I talk about people going back to work . . . she's just been totally on and on, 'its not right' and that sort of thing.
> (Penelope, social worker)

It was further reported by mothers that they felt as though they were failing to fulfil the role of 'mother' because they were unable to be involved in all aspects of children's daily lives due to work commitments. This seemed to exacerbate the feelings of friction and competition between stay-at-home and employed mothers. As noted by Brannen and Moss (1991), mothers felt guilty, and were criticized on occasions where the demands of paid work prevented them from being part of children's activities. One mother explained:

> [Full-time motherhood] makes you conscious of what you don't do, I do try to go to everything there is to go to. But things like school trips, you can't just do everything, you can't be the mum that accompanies on the school trip. I don't know whether I've a chip on my shoulder about it, but there are certain mums that are professional mums who make a point of being at the school all the time and volunteering for everything and being classroom helpers and wearing the [mantle] of the perfect mother . . . And I do feel some of these sanctimonious mothers really get up my nose, and [my relative], you know, she was working [before she became pregnant] and I asked whether she's returning to work and she said something like 'no, I can't see the point in having children if you palm them off on other people to look after' and . . . how insulting that was to me.
> (Suzanne, lawyer)

Remembering her own mother, Suzanne added:

> I am conscious that you can't do, in two days [during the week] and two days at weekends, the same as a mum does in seven days a week.

Another observed:

> Things like nursery, or breakfast clubs at school, don't convey a sense of, you know, 'great, this is so both parents can work.' They convey a

sense that 'somebody's got to mind the children whilst the "bad mother" isn't there.' And I sometimes feel more despairing about that than I do about anything else.

(Estelle, psychotherapist)

Two mothers cited the response of their own mothers when they explained that they would be combining motherhood with career:

My mother was an institutionalized mother and my parents were absolutely horror-struck when I suggested I was going to go back to work. And I think a lot of the guilt I found myself struggling with came from other people's perceptions about what you ought to do. And by implication you're a 'bad mum' if you go back to work, so partly I think the family perceptions were the most difficult to deal with.

(Rachael, NHS chief executive)

Another recalled a similar experience and recounted how she dealt with this:

I [got] the comment from my mother: 'Why bother having children at all if you are just going to farm them out?' And I said, well, let's sit down and look at this . . . 'Do you really want me to have the kind of life that you had? Because all you do now is complain when I ask you how it was, when you were trapped in the house with two young children, do you want me to do that?' And yet she still keeps saying that, it's almost like a mantra, it's very weird.

(Joanne, tax consultant)

As Maushart (2002) points out, this is a pressure not suffered by men, who are not presumed to be bad fathers if they undertake paid work, but instead are defined as 'good' fathers because they are providing for the family, as advocated by Parsons 50 years ago.

'Built-in' behaviour? The emotional bonds of motherhood versus the 'institution of motherhood'

Although they may have felt guilty about not being 'stay-at-home' mothers, there was a strong reaction, among women, against being identified with the 'institution of motherhood'. Significantly, however, although they may have rejected motherhood as an institutionalized role, all mothers believed that there was a special bond between mothers and their babies/pre-school children. When discussing their feelings about the birth of their children, all expressed strong emotions in specific terms which reflect Rich's (1977: 36) description of the 'invisible strand' which binds mother to child. Words used were those such as: 'bonding', 'falling in love', 'biological ties'. This was the case no matter how difficult women had found the adjustment to motherhood to be. Typical descriptions were as follows:

> suddenly you have this little person and you're breastfeeding and it's a wonderful sort of bonding, I think, it's very intimate.
>
> (Eleanor, senior education manager)

> Motherhood has amazed me with my capacity to love. When [my son] came along, I couldn't believe I could love anything so much and it was quite scary.
>
> (Joanne, tax consultant)

> the minute I was pregnant [my daughter] was loved . . . biologically, I think there's something there.
>
> (Louise, public sector manager)

Fathers also acknowledged a strong tie between mothers and newborn babies, referring to this either directly or by inference:

> Becoming a mother is actually a very private, very biological event.
>
> (David, consultant psychiatrist)

> a lot of motherhood is sort of built-in really, I think mothers have this sort of built-in relationship with their new babies.
>
> (William, architect)

However, although it might be argued that it could be expected from this group, all of the women were clear about the distinction between the strong emotional bonds they felt for their children, which they felt to be biological, and the institution of motherhood, which they considered to be socially constructed. Diana summed up her feelings explicitly:

> I never considered having a child meaning the typical thing of motherhood, I *never* thought it meant giving up my job. I certainly loved [my daughter] but it was a very biological love. I mean I worried about her constantly, I worried that she was breathing, worried that she'd eaten something . . . but I didn't have a problem about the concept of mothers coming back to work and that is why I am here now – work is a part of who I am.
>
> (Diana, television producer)

This implies an affinity with the views of some radical feminist writers on motherhood such as Oakley, Rich and O'Brien, who argue that women should be able to enjoy mothering without having to relinquish ambition and career. It also distances the mothers in this research from writers such as Firestone and Valeska who, as noted in Chapter 3, have argued that career should take the place of motherhood and mothering. Significantly, however, when asked to define the qualities that make a 'good' mother, both women and men were clear that 'good' motherhood did not necessarily mean being at home with children full-time:

> It can be a combination of work and home, to be a good mother you don't have to be at home . . . mothers in the 1950s weren't necessarily 'good'. I think the pressures of women in the home can be very great which can create tensions in the house, which then don't necessarily mean they are being a good mother.
>
> (Sam, lawyer)

'Pink jobs and blue jobs': Women's responsibility for domestic labour

> There is a general myth that you can 'have it all', but my sense is that you do it all. You just end up doing more; women are under tremendous pressure and that is not recognized at all – you've got it made because you've got washing machines and disposable nappies.
>
> (Victoria, academic)

As far as the domestic division of labour was concerned, the situation for mothers was depressingly familiar, and echoed the findings of key writers on domestic labour during the previous two decades in that women bore the brunt of domestic work, no matter how many hours of paid work they undertook. The discovery that mothers were burdened with the domestic chores is consistent with the work of many writers: Scott (1999), Dryden (1999), Delphy and Leonard (1992), Oakley (1981) and, discouragingly, Gilman (1998), who was writing at the end of the nineteenth century!

'Help' with the housework

In accordance with the literature on heterosexual women and domestic labour, the mothers in all but one partnership took responsibility for managing the household work (laundering, ironing, cleaning, shopping, cooking), no matter how many paid hours they worked. However, the extent of this varied among couples, as did the mothers' attitudes towards it. At one end of the scale, women reported taking almost total responsibility for household work, a claim which was verified by their husbands. One father said:

> Domestic? Oh well, um, I'm no good at washing, ironing and I'm not very good at washing up, I'm hopeless at washing up. I hate the pans, the fat, the grease.
>
> (Henry, lawyer)

Some fathers admitted that they had to be pushed by their partners into doing anything and that they saw their role as household 'helper' rather than 'manager':

> [My wife] will prompt me by saying 'the bath hasn't been cleaned for ages', which usually means, 'Charles, go and clean the bath,' and I'll do it. But I *won't* do it *then*. I'll do it when I've got a free slot.
>
> (Charles, scientist)

At the other end of the scale (especially if paid help could be afforded), the remaining chores were shared out more equally. However, the women still carried the main burden of responsibility for ensuring things got done, which involved mental, if not physical, labour:

> In general terms, I'm the chief executive of the household in organizational terms, in that I'm the one who thinks it out and organizes it and says this is what is happening, this person is doing this, that person is doing the other. But [my husband] does a huge amount of practical stuff. On his own initiative he is quite domesticated, but the decision and organization is me.
>
> (Suzanne, lawyer)

Maushart (2002) suggests that the burden of unpaid labour within the household begins the moment the relationship is formalized into marriage, but accepts that this is exacerbated once children are born. Although all but two couples in the research sample were married (and the remaining two were in committed relationships), the inference from interviews was that the domestic division of labour became a serious issue following the birth of the first baby, in keeping with Oakley's (1981) hypothesis. Five women explicitly dated the point at which they became 'responsible' for domestic management from the moment their children were born and they stayed at home full-time (even though, for these women, this was for a relatively short period). It was felt that, once they had taken on the management of the household, it was very difficult to hand this back:

> It quickly became an expectation that I would do all this [domestic]
> work.
>
> (Victoria, academic)

As discussed by Dryden (1999), the expectation that women should be responsible for domestic matters was regarded as an issue of power and equality (or lack of it) within the couples' relationships. In respect of this, there are several interesting points of note. Firstly, it appeared that the women did not regard this division of labour as 'equal' or 'fair' (as suggested by Dryden 1999), and some strongly resisted the mantle of 'housekeeper'. Secondly, in all cases, fathers' reports of the level of domestic labour were comparable to the women's descriptions, contrasting with Maushart's (2002) suggestion that men tend to overemphasize their contribution. Furthermore, at variance with Dryden's (1999) findings, it appeared that research participants were aware of the inequality of the domestic division of labour and were open about this during their interviews (which may be due to the fact that most couples were interviewed separately and not together). This is consistent with Giddens's (1979: 71) argument that people are often aware of the social constraints which oppress them, even if they choose to comply with these. One couple, who were interviewed together, referred explicitly to the gendered domestic division of labour within their marriage as 'pink jobs' and 'blue jobs'. In this instance, like so many others, the humdrum burden of domestic routine (pink!) was left to the wife, who expressed her resentment of this, while the husband undertook occasional and traditionally male (blue) jobs, such as putting up shelves. Although Crompton (1997) suggests that male partners who undertake traditionally gendered tasks such as DIY deserve some credit, this was not the view taken by the women in this research. One mother (who works full-time while her husband works part-time) noted:

> I think what's really important are not the things you have to do once every three to six months, but what has to be done every single day, what has to be done to keep the family and house ticking over. And it's my experience that women still bear the brunt of that, even women in professional jobs . . . they are not just thinking they have to have this paper written or seminar [organized], they're thinking: they haven't got any bread for the sandwiches in the morning, we've run out of bread, loo roll and that sort of stuff which is the humdrum detail of everyday life.
>
> (Eleanor, senior education manager)

During the interviews, nine of the women who took the lead responsibility for domestic labour inferred that they were not happy with this, but felt more or less resigned to it. This is in keeping with Maushart's suggestion that women will accept an unfair domestic division of labour because they fear that resisting it will threaten their relationship. Joanne said:

> I used to come home and think, 'I'm not going to start trouble' [about domestic chores] because they're horrible jobs, nobody wants to do them, so if [my husband's] attitude is 'if I leave it long enough, she'll do it', I can kind of understand.
>
> (Joanne, tax consultant)

In six cases, however, the mothers (all of whom worked at least four days per week) expressed serious frustration about the assumption that domestic chores should be their responsibility. They questioned the acceptability of husbands/partners 'helping with the housework' (Delphy and Leonard 1992: 240), and four of them challenged this situation:

> I feel I'm dragging (my husband) like a donkey, and he has said on occasion, 'I'll help you out, I'll help you out by cleaning the bath' and I always make a big fuss about it because there's no '*helping* me out' to it . . . *we* live here, it's two *adults*, you and me.
>
> (Lianne, A-level teacher)

> At one point we were both equally responsible for the house. And then something happened when I went on maternity leave where suddenly all these boring domestic chores became my responsibility and I don't remember having discussed this but somehow it happened . . . whereby suddenly [my partner says]: 'well I'm really good because I help'. And I think . . . well, why are we not equally responsible?
>
> (Angela, academic)

Some women indicated that the pressure of doing the majority of domestic chores, if partners did very little housework, made them think seriously about their relationships. For example, Sophie explained:

> I couldn't cope with the change in our relationship [following birth of baby] because I felt I was doing *everything* and he was doing *nothing* . . . so I had to take a long hard look at me, and a long hard look at [my husband] . . . and how we interacted.
>
> (Sophie, lawyer)

Among the group of research participants it was, in all cases but two, usual for the mother to manage responsibility for the repetitive tasks of cleaning and laundry. Three women expressed real loathing for the latter chore:

> The washing, the amount of washing is absolutely . . . horrendous. I've got to do a load every day otherwise it builds up and then I say 'Oh my God how am I going to get it all dry' . . . I don't enjoy washing, in fact I hate it.
>
> (Jayne, electrical engineer)

> domestic management, the really boring repetitive stuff, the ironing, the washing, etc. is a bone of contention. I hate the chores, I hate laundry and the endless repetitive trips upstairs, empty the airing cupboard, put stuff away, fill it with new things, put another wash on . . . and then you look round and the linen basket's full and you've got to start again.
>
> (Angela, academic)

In five cases, men took 'lead' responsibility for supermarket shopping (including making a list of what to buy) and others were prepared to do this with advice from partners about what was needed. In some cases, fathers were obliged to deal with cooking children's tea because wives/partners were at work. The specific involvement and investment by fathers in childcare is important, and is discussed in detail in the next chapter. There was only one mother who took less responsibility for domestic labour than her husband. All other fathers interviewed were unenthusiastic about the tasks they did have to perform, though five men accepted the principle that this should not automatically mean that their wife should undertake the tasks (even if she was doing so at the moment). In keeping with Maushart's (2000) argument, like 'Quiche man' (BBC Radio 4, 11 January 2002), these men knew the language of equality but did not always put it into practice where boring and routine domestic work was concerned. Two of these five worked part-time and two were, with their partner, working towards a situation where both mother and father could undertake part-time paid work. One father described the situation thus:

> Society is 'men' and I think we are conditioned and socialized into believing that as a man you take on the dominant role and, traditionally, that power is something that as men we are given by other men. And you have a choice whether to use or abuse that. And having experienced injustices in my own life . . . I don't want to put other people in that position.
>
> (Peter, social worker)

However, these sentiments did not necessarily extend to the practicality of actually doing household chores:

> We both see that we've got a house, we've both got jobs ... but occasionally there is conflict [about domestic chores] and I think that's really the social conditioning coming out ... [I resent doing household work] when I've had a stressful day at work.
>
> (Peter, social worker)

Working to pay for help with the domestic chores

As Gregson and Lowe (1994) and Maushart (2002) point out, paying for household help is not uncommon in 'professional' households where both parents work, but it is usually the woman who takes responsibility for organizing this – an observation that was clearly reflected in my research. Half of the couples had some paid help with domestic chores and in all cases the responsibility for managing this lay with the mother. Delphy and Leonard (1992) argue that the mental and creative energy involved in managing paid helpers in the home is not shared because fathers just assume that this does not concern them. The culpability for the market in low-paid domestic work is also laid at the door of employed mothers, and not fathers (e.g. by Ehrenreich and Hochschild 2003), since by implication these jobs only exist because women are going out to paid work rather than staying at home (in which case cleaners and nannies would not be required). For women in my research, help with housework involved cleaning (especially of kitchens and bathrooms) and, in all but one case, ironing. In one case, some meals were prepared and frozen by the person assisting. Even if paid help was on hand to assist with chores (e.g. the ironing) it was usually the mother's responsibility to ensure that items were ready to be pressed on the correct day of the week. Furthermore, in all but one case where there was paid help with household chores, it was the mother's responsibility to finance this, as well as arrange it. Two mothers described the situation thus:

> I manage it and I organize all the stuff that needs to be done and that amazes me how much time that takes. So I organize that the washing is done, to leave out in the basket so that [the cleaner] can take it out and iron it, and I tidy up so that it isn't too bad when she is trying to clean.
>
> (Eleanor, senior education manager)

> The responsibility for [cleaning washing and ironing] is mine, the responsibility for managing it. I can choose how I do that, I can pay somebody and do without something or I can have a bit of extra money in my pocket and not pay them but the responsibility is mine.
>
> (Angela, academic)

'I should iron his shirts': Laundry, and the symbolism of tending men's shirts

It is interesting that the management of laundry and ironing – especially shirts – was a bone of contention among both men and women, all but two interviewees having discussed it at length, without prompting, during interviews. Of the two who did not mention ironing, one had a husband who was at home full-time (and therefore may not have worn shirts that needed pressing), and the other had a husband who bore the brunt of the domestic chores. The prominence of washing and ironing of clothes as an issue among couples supports Kaufmann's thesis that laundry is a symbolic of

> the folds of the conjugal fabric. Laundry . . . is ubiquitous, always on the agenda, clinging to the couple just as clothes cling to the skin, constantly charged with significance. It is a reminder of a feminine role which has been modified by the notion of equality.
>
> (Kaufmann 1998: 8)

The particular focus on ironing men's shirts could also be because this is seen to be symbolic of wifework (Maushart 2002) and the social expectation that a mother's priority is to support her husband's business lifestyle at the expense of her own (even if she also has a career). Notably, in the sample for this research, two husbands who felt 'a bit hard done by' due to the lack of wifework performed by their partners, centred on the lack of clean pressed shirts as a key reason for their dissatisfaction. Peter explained:

> Occasionally, obviously, there is conflict and . . . I might get a bit annoyed that a shirt of mine hasn't been ironed, it's more a case that *I've* got to iron my bloody shirt, and I'm a bit unhappy about that because I've had a stressful day at work or something like that. But the fact is that [my wife] hasn't *got* to do that, I might just have *liked* her to do that.
>
> (Peter, social worker)

Conversely, however, one father appeared to accept his wife's assertion that it was 'demeaning' for her to iron his shirts. He therefore accepted the responsibility for ironing his own and made a point of mentioning this when interviewed. Another father (who incidentally did not iron his own shirts but left this to his wife!) described the requirement to iron shirts as 'corporate invasion of family time' and said:

> I resent big corporations feeling that they can invade my family life and that goes as far as having to iron shirts. As far as I'm concerned if

I've got to come to work in an ironed shirt I should be able to iron it in their time, not mine, but of course they wouldn't like that!

(Tony, computer programmer)

Given that shirt-ironing may be seen as metaphorical of wifework, and hence, as Van Every (1995) suggests, of the power relations between couples, it is significant that only one woman was prepared to iron her husband's shirts herself. Nine women who could afford it dealt with shirt ironing by paying someone else to do it. Where mothers did not have paid help in the house, they carried the lion's share of domestic labour, undertaking the drudgery of cleaning and washing of clothes and appliances themselves. However, their partner's ironing was the one issue on which they 'made a stand'. All but one woman simply refused to do it. This may be because, given the responsibility they already carried for childcare and paid work, they were symbolically rejecting the role of unpaid housekeeper that is associated with the role of 'wife' (Van Every 1995: 262 and 267). The women in this research all made it clear that they wished to feel on equal terms with their husband/partner and, therefore, even if they were resigned to undertaking other aspects of domestic labour, denied their responsibility for shirt ironing:

I can't stand ironing, can't be doing with it. If he needs a shirt ironing he can do it himself because it's only *his* stuff for work that needs ironing.

(Penelope, social worker)

I do all the washing and ironing except for [my husband's] – he can do *that* himself!

(Victoria, academic)

You can get him to iron if he's watching a football match or something, you can just dump the clothes in front of him and he'll iron.

(Jane, A-level teacher)

I do a load of washing in the evenings and put it out after they've gone to bed ... but [my husband] irons his own shirts, *he* irons his *own* shirts in the morning and if *I* iron anything, well, it's just for myself or the children.

(Jayne, engineer)

Three women mentioned that they had a household policy of buying non-iron items for themselves and the children. They implied that they did not iron anything else (such as sheets), which meant that only the shirts were left.

> I don't buy things that need ironing, we made a vow not to do ironing. [My husband] does have work shirts but he's got 20 so we wait until there are 20 to iron and then he will take the kids out the park and I'll just stand there and iron 20 shirts . . . the one thing he can't do is iron, but that's the only ironing I do.
>
> (Joanne, tax consultant)

Significantly, in Joanne's situation, her husband had at one point taken over a month's unpaid leave to be with his baby daughter while his wife worked full-time. Following this, Joanne noted a change. Although she still ironed the shirts, her husband undertook a reasonable share of domestic tasks without being asked:

> The month he had off with [our daughter] really brought it home to him, what exactly what was involved in running a house. Because [before that], I used to get in from work and he wouldn't even have switched the dishwasher on or even loaded it and there would be piles of dirty clothes and he wouldn't have thought . . . and I used to walk round the house thinking, 'Right, well the dirty clothes fairy isn't going to move these for you' . . . but [once he spent time at home] that attitude improved and within a week the washing was done, it was pegged out, you know.
>
> (Joanne, tax consultant)

In one further case where the mother worked full-time and the father remained at home with the baby, the roles were completely reversed. Significantly, the father in this case is responsible for all the shopping, cooking, cleaning, washing and ironing, most of which he undertook on his 'day off', while the mother was responsible for driving and maintaining the car.

Crompton (1997) has argued that women's professional status can have a positive effect on the amount of domestic work done by male partners. Crompton's hypothesis was not borne out in my research. Even though, as noted earlier, some men accepted the intellectual argument that responsibility for domestic chores should be shared, this did not provide enough motivation for them to actually do anything about it. Unless their wives/partners took an assertive stance, most men were quite prepared to abrogate responsibility for household matters. With the one notable exception referred to above, few men were prepared to take on what Joanne described as the 'horrible jobs' that 'nobody wants to do'. This appeared to be the case whether or not women were principal providers in the household. Perhaps this is because, as Delphy and Leonard (1992) argue, men have for many years been protected from the boredom and drudgery of domestic chores. Arguably, this gives them two sources of power – that of status, and that of time – neither of which they are prepared to relinquish even if (as Peter noted earlier on) they feel a bit guilty about it. Paradoxically, some fathers felt badly done by because of the reduction in the level of wifework undertaken by employed wives/partners once children arrived. This was ironic, because some mothers indicated a regret that their intimate relationship had 'slipped' down the list of priorities due to the pressures of paid work, childcare and housework. It is possible that if the 'hard done by' men had spent more time undertaking domestic labour and had accepted the principle that they were equally responsible for the housework (not 'helping' with it), their time-starved partners would have had more energy available to invest in the management of the intimate relationship.

Summary

This chapter considered the impact of motherhood on the health of mothers in the research sample, as well as on their marriage, on the relationship between mother and father and on the amount of wifework mothers are able (or willing) to do following (especially first) births. It was noted that women receive little support from health or other services beyond the first few days after giving birth, and I argued that this is a serious omission. Additionally, working mothers are made to feel guilty due to criticism by the media and family members. I contended that in the light of these factors, and given the pressures they face trying to combine paid work with mothering, it is remarkable that women were managing to continue with their careers. Consequently, I asserted that mothers must be very committed to their work, in contrast to arguments put forward by Hakim and others. Finally, no matter how many hours of paid work they undertake, women in heterosexual relationships are still expected to be 'domestic goddesses' where household and emotional labour is concerned, and this is a source of resentment and conflict between couples. I suggested that fathers hoping for a little more 'wifework' might find this more likely to be forthcoming if they ceased to 'help' with the housework and became equal partners with respect to responsibility for domestic labour.

7 A labour of love (and a sound investment)

The division of childcare work and the centrality of children to fathers' lives

I find a lot of the traditional ideals just totally unpalatable, to be honest. I think the important thing for children is that they have the love, and care and attention of *both* their parents equally, rather than just what would have been traditionally mostly the mother and much less the father. And there might be women walking around feeling guilty about not being good mothers who may have partners who are much better at being a parent than they are, it's not true in our case, I think my partner is actually more patient with the kids than I am but we do split it fairly evenly between the two of us. And if I had the sort of job where I worked inordinately long hours I would miss a huge chunk of their lives and that would sadden me enormously. So I won't let that happen. I want to be a part of their lives.

(Chris, industrial chemist)

Focus on:
'What about me?' The transition to fatherhood
Fathers' involvement in childcare
    Fathers who choose to prioritize children over career
    Fathers who learn to embrace the responsibility for childcare
    Emotional labour
'Good fathers'

Introduction

In contrast to their participation in domestic labour, the fathers I interviewed demonstrated a far greater involvement in the physical and emotional aspects of childcare work than I had anticipated. This marks a departure from the research of previous decades (e.g. Ribbens 1994; Dryden 1999; Smart and Neale 1999; Lewis 1986; Warin *et al.* 1999), which suggests that, although some fathers become involved with childcare post-separation/divorce, this is relatively unusual within an existing relationship. In my view, this change is due to the acknowledgement, by fathers, of the value of close relationships with their children once they became 'involved' with their day-to-day lives. I contend that fathers in my research saw children as central to their lives, and took practical steps to develop strong bonds with them. This may be because children were seen by fathers as a longer-term investment, with better 'returns', than marriage or a career. It is well known that Western countries have high rates of relationship breakdown. Additionally, the rapidity of workplace change and increasing levels of workplace stress mean that even those in traditional jobs such as banking or insurance may no longer be able to rely on the idea of a 'job for life'. Children, however, might be expected to outlive their parents and an increasing number of fathers are beginning to realize what many mothers have always known: that good relationships with children can provide rewards over a lifetime.

'What about me?' The transition to fatherhood

Although most fathers became involved in the care of their children as time progressed, many found the initial transition to fatherhood, and from 'couple' to 'family', very challenging. For some fathers, the difficulty in dealing with the arrival of a new baby related to their sense of being 'downgraded' in the household hierarchy (which was acknowledged by mothers in the previous chapter). Before the arrival of their first child – in keeping with the arguments put forward by Maushart (2002), Delphy and Leonard (1992) and Duncombe and Marsden (2002) – nine men in the sample had regarded themselves as the first priority in their partner's life. These men resented the expectation that they should be more self-sufficient than previously, because their wives/partners had less time or inclination to undertake what Oakley (1981) terms 'husbandwork' and Maushart (2002) calls 'wifework' once children came along. Some men clearly disliked this and tried to 'win back' their partner's attention:

> He's the first child I've ever had so it was difficult for me in the sense that I wasn't quite used to her attentions being more in favour of someone else . . . and in particular coming second! So that was a big transition and it took me some time to come to terms with that. . . . And I suppose even now [this feeling] rears its ugly head, but [I] have to be sort of tolerant in that regard, or try to be.
>
> (Henry, lawyer)

Others were, like their partners, just shocked by the impact that new babies had on their lives, and several observed that books and parenting classes had left them ill prepared to cope with a new baby. Nick and Charles's experiences are described below:

> Initially your other half is in hospital with the baby, and then they come home, and suddenly you are in the position where you are both left on your own at home with the baby for the first time, so obviously whatever preparation you have had in any classes or literature turns out to be completely . . . well, shall we say it doesn't help much! Shall we say it's still a 'novel' experience being at home with this baby despite all your preparation [laughs] because you've no idea, just *no idea* what to do when the baby makes a noise or cries.
>
> (Nick, lawyer)

> How many men just have no idea how it is going to change their lives? Just have not a clue what they're letting themselves in for, it's a dramatic change in your lifestyle . . . you adapt to it but at first there's a lot of 'well, I was just not expecting this' . . . it hits you like a ton of bricks and men either get stuck in or turn their backs on it, I know a lot of men who do that.
>
> (Charles, scientist)

Those fathers with more than one child agreed with mothers' views, however, that once they had survived the shock of the first baby, subsequent children were easier to manage:

> Adjusting to having a child, certainly from being able to live your life as you want to . . . to have some other body who takes precedence, is quite a hard transition, I found; well, we both did. And certainly the first six months with [our son] were very stressful because he was not a settled baby at all, he cried a lot . . . I think the transition from one to two [children], compared to the transition from nought to one, was much easier.
>
> (Stephen, doctor)

Significantly, nine fathers were involved in dealing with children who were up in the night, and reported feeling tired during the day due to disturbed sleep. Two of these said that they had become accustomed to this and considered themselves to be managing it reasonably well. However, four who shared with their partners the responsibility for children who did not sleep, reported feeling weary to the point of exhaustion, which is in keeping with Popay's (1992) suggestion, noted in Chapter 3, that 20% of new fathers are permanently fatigued. This challenges the assumption reported by Cockburn (2002) that only mothers' efficiency in the workplace is likely to be disturbed by the arrival of children, since presumably exhausted men are just as likely to be 'under par' as exhausted women. The four men under consideration noted that they felt obliged, at work, to cope with the effects of sleep deprivation without complaint since it was automatically assumed by others that their wives would deal with broken nights. This is consistent with the concept of the 'invisible father' recorded by Durham (2002) and inferred by Dienhart (1998). One father described his feelings thus:

> What I didn't expect of course was the level of tiredness, and I mean at work they just assume that [my wife] does it all . . . you are OK to admit [that you are tired] for the first few weeks but after that you are just supposed to get on with it as though nothing had happened.
>
> (Charles, scientist)

Mothers' reports that pregnancies had been planned, and babies eagerly anticipated, accorded with the fathers' accounts, 17 men having also referred to 'planning' the arrival of their children. Some fathers who talked of positive outcomes to planned pregnancies attributed this to 'luck', others referred to it with a sense of pride. Lewis (1986) notes that heterosexual fathers feel under pressure to 'provide' their partners with a child. It could be inferred from this that the fathering of children is associated with social expectations of masculinity because 'expectations . . . in terms of bodily performance . . . have been met' (Morgan 2002: 413), this suggesting to the outside world that husbands are virile. This accords with Parsons' definition of manhood, discussed in Chapter 2, in which the identity of adult men is seen to be closely bound up with the requirement to father children, and to make economic provision for them. One father described his reaction to his partner's pregnancy thus:

> Well initially, I mean obviously you're pleased, you are surprised because obviously you are never quite sure, um, that your wife will become pregnant, I mean we have friends who have difficulties having babies, so obviously if you're a bloke you feel quite pleased and you know that in nine months' time that obviously things will be rather different.
>
> (Nick, lawyer)

It has been indicated in the literature that the transition to parenthood is easier for fathers than it is for mothers (Maushart 2002), though fathers in my research, like those in Lupton and Barclay's (1997) study, also experienced difficulties adjusting to parenthood. However, fathers' choices may be also be circumscribed in a different way. It is notable that in Appleyard's (2000: 48) profile of an 'ideal' family, the father concerned is portrayed as 'thrilled' that his highly educated wife has relinquished her career, because this enables him to leave the child-rearing and domestic work to her, while he remains 'anchored in the occupational world' (Parsons and Bales 1956: 15). In my view, however, by excluding men from the responsibility for children's development, writers such as Appleyard and Malthouse are denying a role for fathers in the emotional upbringing of their own children (and also circumscribing women's choices). This indicates a discrepancy between demographic change and the social roles defined for parents by post-war governments and writers. The behaviour of heterosexual parents may therefore not accord with popular views of what it 'ought' to be.

Fathers' involvement in childcare

As recently as 2002, Susan Maushart has argued that 'Where there is a mother in the household, the day-to-day responsibilities for childcare are, as they say, "her baby" . . .. Mum remains the default parent and Dad the back-up' (2002: 121). 'After the birth of her first child . . . a wife will . . . assume major, and in the majority of cases, overwhelming, responsibility for childcare' (2002: 123). The experiences of mothers and fathers who participated in my research indicate a significant departure from arguments outlined in the literature on motherhood and wifework (e.g. Oakley 1981; Rich 1977; Delphy and Leonard 1992; Maushart 2002). This is in the area of day-to-day management of childcare, including emotional labour and emotional mediation on behalf of the children which has traditionally been the mother's role (Ribbens 1994; Oakley 1981). In contrast to this expectation, once their wives returned to work, all but two fathers who took part in this research did *share* a significant proportion of the practical and emotional responsibility for child-rearing, even if the couple still regarded the woman as the principal carer.

Five fathers whose wives/partners were in full-time paid work took lead responsibility for childcare. Three couples, where both partners worked full-time, shared the childcare equally between them. A further three couples, where the wife worked part-time, divided up the childcare equally on the days when she was working or were both at home, but she took the main responsibility when at home with the children on her own. A further two couples who both worked irregular hours and weekends were keen to describe their situation as 'co-parenting' – that is, whoever was at home was in charge and if both were at home together things were shared equally. In all but two of the remaining couples, although the mother was the primary carer, fathers nevertheless took a substantial proportion of childcare work. This is at variance with the findings of Dryden (1999), where couples claimed to share out childcare equally, when in fact most tasks fell to women. In my view, the sharing of childcare labour between mothers and fathers is directly linked to mothers' paid work, and this is consistent with Lewis's (1986) observation that fathers within dual-earner marriages (although they were few in number in his research sample), tended to be more involved with childcare than others. In contrast to arguments put forward by Maushart (2002), fathers who took part in my research undertook practical tasks such as cooking children's tea, as well as the 'fun' aspects of childcare such as playing. All but one father also took responsibilities connected with emotional labour, such as taking time off work to care for sick children, which, as already noted in Chapter 2, involves the giving of 'emotion as much as any kind of physical labour . . . physical care and monitoring, handling the fears and frustrations experienced by the sick child . . . and drawing on one's own emotional resources and exercising emotional control while doing all of this' (Morgan, 1996: 105).

In most cases, the fact that fathers' input was higher than anticipated was not due to a social conscience about equality for women (although five men did mention this). The relatively high levels of childwork undertaken by fathers were linked to their own desire to establish and maintain a bond between themselves and their children without an intermediary, because (in accordance with the views of Beck and Beck-Gernsheim 1995) they realized that this was an important and worthwhile investment. In some respects this is not as surprising as it may sound, given that this desire was expressed by fathers in the work of Lewis (1986) and more recently Lupton and Barclay (1997). In these texts, as discussed in Chapter 2, many fathers felt they had less of an opportunity than mothers to establish intimate relationships with their small children because they had less access to them on a day-to-day basis, their own lives being closely bound up with occupational responsibilities and long hours. Thus, they rarely found themselves in the position of having to care for their own children for long periods because (in most cases) their partners were at home full-time. For most of the men interviewed by Lewis (1986) and Lupton and Barclay (1997), the idea of reducing hours or even staying at home full-time was not a realistic one, because they were principal breadwinners. This was different for many men taking part in my research because they were married to highly educated women in relatively well-paid work, meaning that downshifting their career was a viable option for those fathers who wanted it.

Fathers who choose to prioritize children over career

There appeared to be two reasons why fathers became more involved with childcare than might have been anticipated. The first of these was because they chose to. In this respect, it is significant that in all but one of the five cases where the father was the principal carer for children, they had made a positive decision to reduce career commitments in order to increase involvement with children. Joseph explained:

> I suppose it was me who thought: 'I'm missing something here, it
> doesn't feel right, my daughter's only a few months old and I'm
> not seeing her' ... I felt pretty dreadful about it. So I discussed
> with [my wife] about myself giving up work and she was happy to
> go with it if it was what I wanted, and it wasn't a hard decision for
> me to make really ... I missed [my daughter], I never saw much
> of her and I wanted to see more of her. I was quite upset about it
> actually.
>
> (Joseph, full-time childcarer and houseworker)

Tony described his situation thus:

> I was determined (when my second child was born) that this time I
> would not miss out, because I felt angry for a couple of years, really
> angry that I had missed out on [my son's] time as a baby due to my
> job. So I changed my job and took a pay drop but the employers are
> much more flexible and I am able to cope with the job and enjoy the
> children.
>
> (Tony, computer programmer)

In two further cases, where the mother worked part-time and the father full-
time, couples were proactively aiming for a situation where the father would
be able to drop his working commitments by 40% so that they could share the
childcare between them. This is in marked contrast to the findings of Smart
and Neale (1999) and Collier (1995), who argue that many employed fathers
do not co-parent within a marriage/partnership, and choose to adopt a co-
parenting role only when the relationship with the mother is over. It is also
in contrast to the writings of Lewis (1986) and Lupton and Barclay (1997),
who suggest that for many fathers still living with their wives/partners, social
identity is still associated with the traditional provider role as described by
Parsons and Bales (1956). However, this change was perhaps less surprising
than it might seem, given the expressed wish of some fathers for greater
involvement with their children, should the opportunity arise *within* a
relationship (Lupton and Barclay 1997) – rather than having to establish their
rights *post*-divorce (as described by Collier 1995).

Whether or not the findings from my research reflect a change among
the wider population of fathers, social constructions of fatherhood appear
to remain entrenched. Although it is around 50 years since Parsons'
work on family life and social roles was published, the attitudes described
by him in relation to fathers remain in existence today, because men are
still '*expected* to be a good provider, to be able to secure for the couple a "good
position" in the community' (Parsons and Bales 1956: 163; emphasis in
original). The literature on fatherhood suggests that, within a marriage/

relationship, fathers are still expected to construct their social identity through their occupational role (Lupton and Barclay 1997; Warin *et al.* 1999). This is certainly true of contemporary fathers who are also public figures, such as the British football player David Beckham, who was openly disciplined for missing a training session at Manchester United when his son was ill. In accordance with Beckham's story, the experiences of fathers in this research suggested that, from their perspective, social attitudes had changed little from the Parsonian image of father as 'economic provider'. It has already been noted that mothers felt criticized for maintaining their career instead of being full-time mothers. Conversely, although fathers escaped criticism if they went out to work, they were regarded as 'odd' if they chose to reduce their commitment to paid employment in order to be principal carers for their children. In accordance with Dienhart's (1998) observations, the five fathers who chose to be principal childcarers suffered inflexibility, opprobrium or disbelief when others realized that they were 'in charge' of their own children. Interestingly, fathers were not aware of media or academic criticism of their decision to be stay-at-home parents, in the same way that mothers felt censured for going out to work. This is possibly because articles on stay-at-home fathers are fewer in number than those about working mothers – in keeping with the concept of 'invisible fathering' identified by Durham (2002) and discussed later in this chapter. However, fathers nevertheless believed that gender roles were assigned to them by their social circle and external bodies, and this was resented by some research participants – especially if they had given up their 'status-giving and income-earning function' (Parsons and Bales 1956: 15), in favour of caring for their children. Male principal childcarers faced criticism from parents and colleagues, who disapproved of what they were doing, and failed to understand why they were doing it. Joseph, a social worker who had given up his job to be a full-time childcarer and houseworker, was heavily criticized by a close colleague, who accused him of being 'weak', and by his parents, who described his wife as 'heartless'. He said:

> When I said I was going to finish work, in a lot of cases it was viewed as rather strange, the fact that I was giving up *my* job to go and look after my daughter and why wasn't [my wife] giving up *her* job? It was viewed as very odd that I was going to be at home, which I found very difficult to deal with. I thought people were more understanding and had a wider view of female and different roles in the house. But no, it was viewed as odd, the fact that I was spending not just two hours a day with [my daughter], but all day. It's time people were a bit more in touch with what is going on. More and more men are deciding to stay at home.
>
> (Joseph, full-time childcarer)

Joseph's experience reveals a conflict between the social construction of fathers as breadwinners (partly encouraged by the laws discussed in Chapter 4, which cast post-divorce fathers in the role of economic providers) and Joseph's desire to attain a 'more involved' relationship with his children (Burghes *et al.* 1997: 11). In her study on the centrality of mothers to their children's lives, Ribbens (1994: 199) notes that 'acting on behalf of the child' is usually the mother's role. This can lead to discrimination against men who wish to look after their own small children at home because society fails to acknowledge their existence, this rendering them metaphorically 'invisible', as noted in Chapter 4 and argued by Durham (2002) and Dienhart (1998). This is unfortunate because, for as long as society continues to regard men who care for their own children with opprobrium (or as 'invisible'), employed women will find themselves similarly constrained. It also causes some very practical problems. For example, in the five cases where mothers worked full-time and fathers were the principal carer, 'official' external agencies were not prepared to accept that fathers were undertaking the role of mediator/ negotiator on behalf of children – even if this role was taken by the father. Rachael recalled:

> My daughter is at the school nursery part-time at the moment, she starts school full-time in September. And when they came to do the pre-school home visit, we wrote on all the forms that the main carer was the father, but they *insisted* on meeting me. So I took some time off work for the home visit, because the teacher didn't want to come home and meet my husband. So that kind of thing reinforces some of the stereotypes, I think people just make assumptions about who should be doing what, really.
>
> (Rachael, NHS chief executive)

Rachael went on to explain how difficult it was for her husband to undertake normal tasks associated with childcare because of his gender:

> He was asked to leave Mothercare, . . . because they don't like men in Mothercare so they asked him to leave the store and I don't under-stand it but they said they don't have male [baby] changing rooms, only rooms for mother and baby, so they won't let men go into changing areas. If you put some of this in print, in the *Guardian* or whatever, you'd think, 'Oh, some silly person's made this all up'. It isn't until it actually *happened* to you that you think, 'this is *barmy* in this day and age'.
>
> (Rachael, NHS chief executive)

Fathers who were sharing the care of their children and trying to reduce their hours of paid work, experienced similar difficulties. In one instance, a male doctor (who has changed his job because of this) experienced discrimination in his job when he took time off to care for a very sick child:

> My partners were very traditional, they felt that the woman should have to give up *her* job to look after the child . . . they would say, 'well, shouldn't your *wife* look after your children?'
>
> (Jack, GP)

In another instance, where the father worked full-time and the mother four days per week, the father was responsible for journeys to and from the paid childcarer. Although she saw the father four days per week, the carer was reluctant to discuss with him details about the child's day, such as whether she had eaten well or soiled her nappy, so the mother had had to make alternative arrangements:

> [That was difficult because] I don't have any day-to-day contact with this carer, but now I have telephone contact and it's been sorted.
>
> (Sonia, nurse manager)

The five fathers who spent part or all of their time at home, found themselves excluded from social groups set up for mothers and children, in accordance with Dienhart's (1998) observations. Joseph had persisted with his attempts to be included until he was accepted:

> I was extremely nervous at first but I got friendly with a lady up the road and she eased me into it. Once I got mixing with them it was great, we had a lot in common [as regards caring for small children] even though we were male and female.
>
> (Joseph, full-time childcarer)

The others had felt too awkward to go at all, or had given up.

It is significant that two fathers began caring for their babies at a very early age due to the illness of their wives following complications post-partum. One of these fathers eventually gave up work to look after his daughter full-time, and his descriptions are similar to those of Oakley (1981). This indicates that looking after a baby full-time can be stressful whoever is doing it – mother or father – and reflects the experiences of some fathers who took part in Dienhart's (1998) and Lupton and Barclay's (1997) research.

> I found it difficult, initially, being full-time at home, I found it extremely difficult . . . I thought everything would be rosy but at first it was extremely difficult, 'cause I'd given up something. I was at

home full-time with [our baby], I was getting no stimulation and I was exhausted.

(Joseph, full-time childcarer)

It is notable that Joseph and the other fathers discussed in this section felt that the birth of their children had significantly reduced their commitment to paid work. The fact of their partners' employment had offered them an unexpected alternative to the 'economic provider' role and as a result they elected to take on the childcarer role more traditionally associated with women. This is interesting because the academic and media spotlight rests on mothers who 'choose' to work, and mothers' commitment is questioned in this context (Hakim 1995; Knight 2002). However, it is rare to read an article arguing that men's commitment to employment is reduced once they become fathers. This is not only hugely unfair to employed mothers, but it may also fail to reflect the attitudes of some fathers. This is discussed in greater detail in Chapter 8.

Fathers who learn to embrace the responsibility for childcare

I suggested in the previous subsection that there were two principal reasons for fathers' increased involvement with childcare. The second, and most common reason for this, related simply to the practicalities of having a wife/partner in employment while children were very tiny and unable to do things for themselves. If mothers were out at work, fathers were obliged to take on some responsibility for childcare because there was no one else to do this. This is in contrast to the findings of Lewis (1986) and Lupton and Barclay (1997), where most fathers could rely upon wives/partners to look after the children because they were living with stay-at-home mothers. In this context it is important to note that 13 of the 20 couples whom I interviewed could not rely on grandparents to help when mothers were at work, because they were deceased, too elderly, or located in 'home towns' where the participants no longer lived (though in a further three cases, grandparents were able to come and stay when a crisis occurred). Thus, once mothers returned to their professional jobs, men became involved in the day-to-day care of their children out of necessity. In 15 cases, men were involved either in taking children to and from nursery, or providing day-care themselves, having organized their working hours to facilitate this. This is in contrast to Dryden's (1999: 42) observation that fathers were reluctant to take pre-schoolers to nursery because this was seen as 'in some ways a demeaning thing to do' – though it is in accordance with the work of Dienhart (1998), who focused specifically on fathers who wished to share childcare responsibilities. It would appear that the involvement of fathers with their children had the effect of a 'virtuous circle'. Lewis (1986) noted that fathers who worked long hours outside the home reported doing less childcare as a consequence. Conversely, fathers in this research, who were obliged to put boundaries on the amount of hours spent at work because of childcare responsibilities, spent more time caring for their children when mothers were absent. As a consequence, they began to build up direct relationships with their small children in their own right, without these being mediated by the mother. Descriptions of the responsibilities of four fathers are given below, demonstrating the practical involvement of this group of men in activities more traditionally associated with a mothering role (as noted by Dryden 1999 and discussed in Chapter 4):

> In the morning I get up and I'll be in work for about half-past seven, so . . . I go to work and [my wife] takes [our baby] to nursery and the elder two go to a neighbour who takes them to school and we pay her for this. Then in the evening I leave earlier than my peers and I go home, I pick up [the baby] from nursery and I pick up the other two from after-school club. I take all three of them back home and give them some food. They'll have a bath, teeth, whatever and they are generally in bed by 8 o'clock. And as I say, I'm lucky that they go to sleep. At some point I'll have something to eat and then [my wife] will come home, having worked late.
>
> (Nick, lawyer)

> I usually bath [the baby] at night and prepare the bottles. Most mornings I get up about half past six, get myself dressed and then deal with [the baby], take her downstairs, feed her and so on . . . then I wake up [our little boy], then my wife goes to work and I take the children both to nursery, and I collect them both at five.
>
> (Tony, computer programmer)

> . . . on the Tuesday [my husband] takes [the children] to nursery and school, a nanny comes in for the day for the baby (and also after school) and I pick up [our son] in the evening. And we share bedtime arrangements so we both bath the children, I tend to feed them, [my husband] puts them to bed. On Wednesday and Thursday it's more or less the same and on Friday I look after the children. But [I am undertaking a course of study] which involves being away, so every other weekend [my husband] will look after all the children all weekend.
>
> (Pandora, lawyer)

One father, whose wife regularly stays overnight at the hospital where she works,

> does it all . . . makes up their lunches the night before and gets up even earlier, at quarter past six to get them organized . . . and gets them to the nursery on time.
>
> (Elisabeth, doctor)

Emotional labour

In cases where grandparents could not be called upon to help, all fathers but one were just as likely as the mothers to take time off work if children were ill, and had done so when this occurred. Most couples worked out between them whose commitments were the most pressing, and fathers took sole responsibility for the 'emotional labour' involved in caring for sick children (Morgan 1996: 105) when it was their 'turn'. The accounts of mothers and fathers on this point were consistent:

> I have almost never had time off work because of the children because if there is something critical [the father] will not go to work, he would do it or it would definitely be split, there would be no assumption that it would be me.
>
> (Lianne, A-level teacher)

> What we have done is talk to each other and whoever can leave most easily, or first, does. When it happened last time, in fact my husband was the one who could go. And he was worried, I think he would put [our daughter] before more or less anything anyway, so he's very quick to say he'll do it. He left, got her from nursery and ran to the doctor with her . . . And I hadn't actually left work, I was still here because it seemed stupid us both leaving.
>
> (Diana, television news producer)

> I've changed since I had children and I would not have wanted to admit, before I had children, that I was staying at home looking after them, but now I don't mind, I'm quite . . . not exactly happy to do it, but I just do it, I don't mind because it's easier for me than for [my wife] and it's what is best for the children, they need their parents really when they're ill.
>
> (Sam, lawyer)

All fathers were regularly involved in feeding and bathing the children and putting them to bed. One father dresses his 2-year-old every morning:

> He decides what she wears. He's got better at it and I've got less fussy.
>
> (Victoria, academic)

Another working father looks after the children by himself when his wife is away, and also deals with disturbances in the night when both parents are at home:

> I will get up at nights, yes, generally me, [our son] is very good but [our daughter] will get up and go to the loo, I think I am repaying [my wife] for all the nights when she was feeding, so yes, I tend to do it now.
>
> (Sam, lawyer)

At first, the men concerned may have been reluctant to take on this level of responsibility, because of the amount of work it involved, which initially came as something of a shock. This is in keeping with the observations of Lupton and Barclay (1997) that well-intentioned fathers may be prone to retreat into their occupational roles once they have experienced the reality of managing childcare. Nick, who was a senior partner in a big law practice, explained:

> During that initial period [my wife] was away from work [and] . . . clearly she was the major carer for the baby because I returned to work full-time after my week off. So whilst I had involvement with the baby at nights or at weekends, the major role was with the mother. Then of course she returned to work, so obviously that had a change in the routines and affected me more . . . and that involves arranging your life or working commitments around making sure that one of you is there either in the morning or in the evening to either drop off the children or pick them up at the end of the day and that can be pretty tiring . . . but the actual transition to parenthood came as something of a shock. Obviously you have to plan things a lot more . . . and obviously a lot more of your time is directed [towards them].
>
> (Nick, lawyer)

It appeared, however, that the majority of men, once they had become accustomed to managing the additional burden of childcare work, began to see advantages in this, regarding the practical and emotional aspects of childcare as a long-term 'investment' (a sentiment that could not be applied to domestic labour!). Once they had begun to undertake a substantial share of childcare, most fathers were prepared to continue doing so because they had begun to realize the long-term benefits of this – 'genuine intimacy with . . . their children' (Maushart 2002: 132). Interestingly, part of Beck and Beck-Gernsheim's (1995) discussion centres upon the argument that both parents set great store by relationships with children because these may be more durable than relationships either with spouses or with work. However, these writers do not appear to base their assumptions on empirical work and the inference is that this issue comes into sharp focus only following separation or divorce. Arguably, for many men within relationships, the ideal of investing in the day-to-day lives of children has previously been unattainable because until recently the major burden of childcare work usually fell upon mothers, who stayed at home with children while fathers were out at work. However, the group of fathers considered in my research were establishing relationships with their children within the marriage/partnership without an intermediary as a result of, and in direct proportion to, the amount of childcare work they carried out. This included emotional, as well as physical, labour.

In her text on child-rearing, Ribbens (1994) indicated that mothers bore the responsibility for 'emotional labour' within households. Mothers managed parent–child relationships on behalf of fathers, and also dealt with external contacts (relations, carers and school) on children's behalf, as a matter of course. This argument is consistent with the image of the mother as an 'angel in the house' (Oakley 1993: 15, 2002), or the more contemporary 'domestic goddess' (Lawson 2000). Significantly, fathers in my research remained keen for wives/partners to manage relationships with family and friends on their behalf. Alan, who was employed part-time, noted:

> With things like birthdays, I mean, I remember [my wife's] birthday and the children's birthdays but with everything else, as with the rest of society [my wife] remembers but I don't. [Laughs.] I don't know whether its genetic or what, I don't know. But it's true, that's the way it is.
>
> (Alan, academic)

Men also continued to assume that women would take responsibility for the emotional management of the marriage/partnership even after the arrival of children (as observed by Duncombe and Marsden 1993, 2002) and, as discussed earlier, some men felt resentful if this did not happen. Conversely, fathers were keen to manage their own relationships with children and, in contrast to what is suggested in previous research (e.g. Ribbens 1994), were reluctant to let mothers do this on their behalf. Alan, who had exchanged his academic job for a less prestigious part-time post, described his own situation thus:

> I decided, well, we both decided that I was going to move over to part-time teaching . . . and that will give me flexibility to fit in with the children. I mean the nursery is open long hours but we don't want [our daughter] to be there eight hours a day if we can help it. And I think having that extra flexibility and the extra time . . .

I think there's a big difference between just being there with the children and spending quality time with them and giving them attention. It's not just getting up in the night and, you know, doing all the toilet bit and the rest of it, what's important to maintain – and that's the difficult bit – is the constant attention. I know some people think well, that's just spoiling them, but that's for every individual to decide.

(Alan, academic)

This suggests a change in attitude and behaviour on the part of fathers in this research, who, once they began to glimpse the benefits of this, desired a direct relationship with their own children. Although some men had initially been reluctant to take on the role of 'involved father' (Smart and Neale 1999: 55), all but one man valued this highly at the time of the interview, whether they had chosen to embrace it or whether it had been forced upon them. This mirrors Smart and Neale's (1999: 55) finding that some post-divorce fathers 'develop a new identity as fathers as a consequence of . . . spending more time with their children'. However, in the case of fathers in this study there has been an obligation to 'become more responsible for their children' (Smart and Neale 1999: 55) *within* the marriage/partnership, because the mothers are employed. This reflects Beck and Beck-Gernsheim's (1995: 105) hypothesis that 'having children . . . is increasingly connected with hopes of being rooted, of life becoming meaningful and with a claim to happiness based on the close relationship with the child'. It is also consistent with Dienhart's (1998) hypothesis that some heterosexual fathers are making significant changes to their social identity, which is shifting in favour of involvement with children, even if this flies in the face of social expectations relating to the 'economic provider' role. As noted in Chapter 4, Dienhart observes that 'policies and the social environment' can challenge fathers who wish to adopt the social roles more conventionally associated with women, because governments and other agencies still expect married/cohabiting men to adopt the 'Parsonian' role of economic provider. The issue of relationships with children and who should mediate these is linked with a sense of power within the parental relationship, and this might provide part of the explanation for why, once they had gained this, fathers were keen to maintain their involved status, even if this made life difficult for them at times. The concept of power and children is considered by many writers on family practices and parenting (e.g. Maushart 2002; Smart and Neale 1999) and is discussed further in Chapter 8.

'Good' fathers

Not surprisingly, given that five of them were principal carers, some fathers were keen to point out that, in relation to the institution of motherhood, the qualities necessary to be a 'good' mother should also be included in the definition of a 'good' father:

> A good mother? Caring, being gentle, having time to spend with your children, listening, being fun, doing the sort of things that children want to do, in their way and at their pace – the same as being a father, really. You know, I can't think of anything in particular that would go for a mother that doesn't go for a father.
>
> (Alan, teacher)

Significantly, although they had discussed the close ties between mothers and babies, all fathers were very frank about their own bond with, and love for their children. One father noted:

> I didn't realize how much of an effect he would have on me in so far as how I would feel about him. I never realized how you'd feel about a child. People go on about how you feel about children, but I never realized how much I'd love him.
>
> (Andy, hospital pharmacist)

Some men saw themselves as becoming more involved with their babies as they grew older (from 6 months or so). In cases where men were working full-time, this was directly connected with the return to work by the mothers which precipitated more physical involvement in childcare on the part of the men, partly because the mothers stopped breastfeeding:

> when they are very tiny there isn't a lot you can do really, particularly as [my wife] is breastfeeding, that is the catch, I often find I'm holding the baby when he's crying. But when they get older, I'm fairly good at that, I give them a bottle sort of in the middle of the night and I found that I could do that much more easily than [my wife], you know, get up, give him a bottle and go back to sleep, and there's that sense of being close to them once you can take part in the feeding.
>
> (William, architect)

The involvement in childcare of fathers raises two important issues which will be dealt with in Chapter 8. The first is in relation to the concept of power, and fathers' desire to increase their involvement with their children *within the intimate relationship with their partner/wife.* While some women saw the practical involvement of fathers as a purely positive change (often meaning that both partners could work, minimizing the amount of time spent by children with paid carers), others were territorial about their role as mother and principal carer, and did not wish to see this threatened by the father. As Maushart (2002: 138) suggests, 'women have more to gain by the establishment of co-equal parenting but more to lose . . . Most research continues to indicate that women's support for "father involvement" cannot be assumed either within the marriage or without'. In accordance with this view, some mothers held ambivalent views about increased father involvement, fearing that it may change the balance of power in the parental relationship unfavourably as far as they were concerned. The issue of power and equality within parents' intimate relationships was a theme which ran consistently through research interviews and is discussed in detail in the next chapter.

The second issue centres on the relative commitment of mothers and fathers to their paid work. Given the level of involvement described by fathers in this research sample, the question is put as to how this has impacted on the time and energy that they are able (or prepared to) devote to the workplace. This is important because, as noted by Cockburn (2002), employers and other agencies such as the Institute of Directors routinely single out career mothers for criticism on the basis that mothers are less committed to their work than childless women, or men. The implication of the findings reported in this chapter is that married/cohabiting fathers also experienced changes in their attitude towards and behaviour within the workplace. This issue is explored specifically in the next chapter and the hypothesis is put forward that the findings from this research may extend to the wider population of dual-earner couples (or couples where mothers are the main economic providers). This signifies a need for further research to discover how far this may be the case.

Summary

This chapter focused on the involvement of fathers in caring for their children and revealed that, while they may be unenthusiastic about domestic labour, fathers felt very differently about physical and emotional labour which involved direct contact with children. I argued that this may be because involvement with children provides a better return on investment than marriage or paid work. I noted that five fathers reduced their hours of paid work in order to become principal carers, and all but two others undertook a high proportion of childcare work. This applied both in the practical sense (e.g. ferrying to and from day-care) and in the emotional sense. Fathers established their own relationships with children within the marriage/partnership (rather than expecting this to be done on their behalf by mothers) and mediated on behalf of their children with external bodies such as nurseries. This caused difficulties with some agencies who struggled to accept that principal childcarers were male, and it raises two important questions. If fathers place children at the centre of their existence, how does this affect their attitudes to work? Does increased father involvement with childcare change the balance of power in the marital/intimate relationship?

8 'Everything I do, I do for you'
The commitment to work and child

It never occurred to me that because I was a woman I would give up work, it just didn't cross my mind . . . and then I had my first baby and I knew it might change, I might not want to come back to work, but I did. I was absolutely happy to come back full-time – I wanted to come back full-time. Working is about needing to be me. I like working and I want to keep working . . . I mean, my profession is actually part of who I am.

(Diana, television news producer)

Focus on:

Working for love of the job
Working to retain a hard-won position – for 'me' and for 'the population I serve'
Working to 'earn decent money'?
The high social capital of 'career' (and the low value placed on full-time motherhood by society)
The low value placed on full-time motherhood by husbands/partners
Fear of 'institutionalized' motherhood
Working to remain equal: Power, earned income and the 'balance' of the intimate relationship
Freedom from domestic duties – and male oppression
110%: The commitment of mothers to paid work . . .
. . . and the pain of parting: The commitment of mothers to their children
'I want to spend more time with my kids than my Dad did': The commitment of fathers to paid work and children
Precious time
Whose children? Power, the children and the intimate relationship

Introduction

> I adore my [children], just adore them, but my own career (and especially my research) is still very important to me, so often I am burning the midnight oil long after everyone else is in bed so I can get things done because I am ambitious and I want to succeed at work as well as trying to be a good mother.
>
> (Angela, academic)

It has already been observed (in Chapter 5) that the definition of 'commitment' is complex and involves a good deal more than simply totting up the amount of time spent at home or in the workplace. However, it was apparent that the main reason why mothers chose to undertake paid work was not so much the financial imperative, as a deep commitment to their paid work. This was linked to a desire to retain the social identity of 'career woman' and a fear of being trapped by the 'institution of motherhood', which was associated with low social capital and negative equity within the marriage/partnership. Although some fathers were ambivalent about their wives'/partners' paid employment (because it meant a reduction in the amount of wifework undertaken) they nevertheless linked employment with their partner's self-esteem. Fathers also expressed a preference for being married/committed to someone with a professional identity, because they associated 'full-time motherhood' with negative social value. In my view, women's commitment to paid work must be high given the heavy emotional costs involved in leaving their children in someone else's care. In this respect it is notable that, although some women spent fewer paid hours at work, their productivity increased once they had children. Significantly (as I noted in the previous chapter), the attitudes of fathers towards paid work changed once they became directly involved with their own children. This is interesting because, as we have seen, although few relate this criticism to fathers many writers argue that women cease to be committed to their paid work once they become mothers, (e.g. Hakim 1995, 2003; Gaillie *et al.* 1998; Malthouse 1997; Boase 2001; Lea 2001; Knight 2002; Tooley 2002). Driscoll (2003) suggests that this is because women are 'reaching their late twenties or early thirties and finding that a career is not all it was cracked up to be'. She argues that they would prefer to give up their 'high-flying' careers altogether because they cherish the idea of being full-time mothers, 'getting in touch with their inner housewife, immersing themselves in the joys of flower arranging and cooking'. It has been suggested by Dex *et al.* (1998) – who make no judgements about whether or not mothers are 'good' employees – that mothers return to work for financial and lifestyle reasons, perhaps because of immediate concerns about mortgages or long-term plans about pensions. Significantly, the values of the women who took part in my research were in direct contrast to the hypotheses of Hakim (1995), Dex *et al.* (1998) and Knight (2002), and all the women interviewed, whether their earnings provided the main family income or whether their contribution to household finances was small, regarded their profession as a career to which they were deeply committed rather than as a means to a financial end. This is important because it suggests that assumptions about lack of commitment to paid work, on the part of mothers, may be seriously flawed.

Working for love of the job

Although, as in any job, including parenthood, they occasionally experienced 'bad days', mothers all spoke of their paid work in positive terms, in contrast to the arguments cited by Knight (2002) and Hakim (1995). Examples of research participants' descriptions of their feelings towards their paid work are as follows:

> You get a sense of achievement at work, it's not about the money, it's job satisfaction.
>
> (Lianne, A-level teacher)

> I really like my job, and other people have commented about how they're envious that I am so enthusiastic about my work, so I think I am lucky [to be doing] something that I really, *really* like doing and get a real buzz from.
>
> (Suzanne, lawyer)

> I do love my job intensely.
>
> (Joanne, tax consultant)

> I work because I enjoy work and get a huge amount of satisfaction out of it and I think I am good at what I do and have a contribution to make, that's why I work.
>
> (Sonia, nurse)

> I didn't feel that I was working for the money, I knew I was working because I wanted to be working and I enjoyed it.
>
> (Lucy, hospital pharmacist)

Seventeen mothers were explicit that they had missed their paid work while on maternity leave, and some explained that they would find it difficult to sustain the commitment of being home full-time:

> How do you entertain a 2-year-old all day long? How would you cope without the boundaries that work imposes? It is giving up *work* that would be a big adjustment.
>
> (Victoria, academic)

Two women in particular were honest about the fact that they did not find babies very interesting and were 'bored staying at home' (Jayne, electronic engineer). This accords with the findings of Brannen and Moss (1991), who observe that being on maternity leave with a baby might, for some women, reaffirm the need to maintain a career. It is also in keeping with Hochschild's (1997) argument that some parents regard paid work as an 'escape' from the drudgery of home and need the balance provided by remaining in work as well as caring for small children.

Working to retain a hard-won position – for 'me' and for 'the population I serve'

Part of the reason why mothers wanted to continue their career was because they had worked hard to establish themselves before having children. They did not want to give up a 'hard-won' position, because it had taken several years of studying and an average of 10 years in the workplace to get where they were. This is in keeping with the observations by Macran *et al.* (1996) and Dex *et al.* (1998) that highly qualified women are likely to delay the birth of their first child while they build up their career. It also accords with the suggestion of Macran *et al.* (1996) that professional women continue paid work after childbirth because of a desire to maintain occupational status:

> I had spent such a lot of time being educated in order to be a lawyer, achieving, you know, the sort of degree of seniority, that it seemed almost like a criminal act to give it up.
>
> (Pandora, lawyer)

> I thought, well I've got a good job, I won't be giving up a good job to stay at home, I have not got a job like this and I have not done a degree to give it all up.
>
> (Jane, A-level teacher)

Fathers also recognized the logic of their wives'/partners' reluctance to give up careers that they had worked for, and spent long years building up:

> It was what my partner wanted and that's why I supported it. . . . I think if you've trained and studied and spent [many] years in a

job and been very happy, very satisfied with it, I think it's a lot to give up.

(Sam, lawyer)

Four women stated they would have liked the option of a longer career break (of between 2 and 4 years). However, they felt unable to take this either because their employment did not offer it or because they were afraid of their skills becoming out of date:

You can't just take a career break as a woman and expect to go back to the same thing. You know it's going to be a struggle in the future. And I don't want that struggle.

(Diana, television news producer)

There is a need in me to work but I would have taken longer about [going back to] it.

(Victoria, academic)

Six mothers expressed a feeling of moral responsibility: having been trained by society to do something they were good at, they felt a duty (and in some cases a vocation) to continue their paid work. One doctor said, on treating a dying patient (a woman of her own age, with children):

I realized this woman needs me to be here, she needs the expertise I possess . . . it really reaffirmed my sense of vocation . . . a big part of me really doesn't feel I have the right to make that decision to stop work. It's not a moveable feast, it's just there and I have to do it. Part of who I am is a doctor and I can't . . . shrug that off and say it doesn't matter, it actually *does* and it isn't just to me that it matters but the population I serve.

(Sarah-Jane, doctor)

I enjoy the feeling that you're doing something for society, using the skills you've qualified for.

(Lucy, hospital pharmacist)

All of the female research participants were overtly ambitious. Those who had scaled down their hours to suit their mothering responsibilities found it frustrating if this threatened to slow down or limit their career progress because employers failed to take them seriously:

I'm an ambitious person . . . I always think of my career in the long term, I always have done, my long-term ambitions haven't gone

> away. Just because [you work fewer paid hours than before] doesn't mean you are less committed to your job. It frustrates me that mothers have to prove their commitment and are constantly being tested out.
>
> (Victoria, academic)

Fathers who had scaled down their careers in order to become the main carer for the children felt similar concerns to mothers who were in the same position. Alan, whose wife worked full-time, had chosen to change his job and work part-time in order to spend more time with his children. This had limited his career prospects and he expressed ambivalent feelings regarding his wife's career progress, indicating that he was supportive of what she was doing but stating:

> My parents think I get a raw deal, you know because of what *I'm* doing . . . looking after the children.
>
> (Alan, academic)

Working to 'earn decent money'?

It has already been observed that none of women who were principal earners cited the intrinsic value of money as a reason for continuing their employment. All doing well in their field, they seemed more focused on the intellectual aspect of what they were doing than the financial side. However, there were some pragmatic reasons why the ability to earn money was seen as important. Two women mentioned working for money because they considered it unreasonable for their partner to take sole responsibility for family earnings:

> I didn't want [my husband] to feel that he would always have to be the sole provider because that could put a tremendous strain on him. So by working part-time I could [retain the opportunity of] working full-time and that would just, you know, ease the burden.
>
> (Pandora, lawyer)

> The implication [of my not working] would be the huge pressure on [my partner] being the only earner . . . and the financial pressure of feeling that he was always in the corner, . . . always trapped, he could never ever give up work because there was no one else to cushion that.
>
> (Angela, academic)

In addition, although they hoped this would not happen, some women expressed concern about the possibility that they might one day be single mothers, and would wish to be capable of self-support should this happen. This reflects the argument put forward by Potuchek (1997) that women undertake paid work because they fear being disadvantaged in the event of separation or divorce:

> I like to think we have a strong marriage, but divorce is a fact of life.
>
> (Victoria, academic)

> I don't like to think it will happen, I think we are happy . . . but then I know from bitter experience myself that people do die and marriages do fail and it's not necessarily your fault, or anyone's fault really, it might just happen to you . . . so I need the option of being able to earn decent money full-time and although what I am doing now is part-time, it keeps the door open and if, at some stage and for some unexpected reason, I am left alone with my children I've got the wherewithal to support them myself.
>
> (Angela, academic)

It appeared that couples were open with one another about what they earned and how this was spent, in contrast to the findings of Brannen and Moss (1991: 148) that a proportion of mothers had no idea about their partner's take-home pay. Several women earned the same as or more than their partners and took either an equal share of, or lead responsibility for, day-to-day finances. This differed from the findings of Potuchek (1997: 185) and Brannen and Moss (1991) who observed that, even where women made a substantial contribution to family finances, they often constructed the father as the financial provider for the family, and played down their own contribution. This divergence from research published in the 1990s may indicate a more general change in the way that twenty-first-century couples operate family finances. However, at variance with the knowledgeable and responsible attitude taken by women towards day-to-day finances was the general lack of concern and interest expressed by mothers about their pensions, which I found disturbing. Only one woman in the sample cited her pension as a key reason for continuing paid work. Significantly, she suggested that this was not for her own benefit but because she did not wish to be a burden on her children in her old age! The other mothers interviewed – even those earning large sums in highly responsible jobs – were far more concerned about the immediate needs of maintaining a fulfilling career and being good mothers than they were about the longer term. They demonstrated little interest in their own pension arrangements and, when asked, were vague about what these were. Even those mothers who were actively involved in (or principally accountable for) managing household finances appeared to have given little thought to their own long-term future. To my surprise, some mothers indicated that they had left this aspect of their finances entirely to their partner/husband to deal with:

> The motivation to work in the long term, in terms of pensions never really crossed my mind . . . I suppose I vaguely think of pensions only in the sense that I should pay in more than I do.
>
> (Suzanne, lawyer)

> I suppose I should worry about money for when I'm old but I don't, the motivation for me is personal not financial . . . I leave all that to my husband and I think he does pay in some extra pension contributions.
>
> (Lianne, A-level teacher)

> [My husband] pays for, you know, these PePs and ISAs and things, which I've never bothered about.
>
> (Jane, A-level teacher)

This is in contrast to the argument by Macran *et al.* (1996) that saving towards a pension was a motivational reason for women to work. It confirms the arguments put forward by Smart and Neale (1999) that women are often financially disadvantaged by divorce (e.g. because they do not take responsibility for pensions) and flags up the need for long-term financial awareness among working mothers. Although this may be because they are too busy to do anything other than focus on the immediate future, I regarded it as surprising that among this group of women, who are fighting the traditional Parsonian role of stay-at-home mother, most had not thought seriously about their own financial independence later in life, but were either vaguely assuming that there would be enough to live on, or were relying on someone else to provide this.

The high social capital of 'career' (and the low value placed on full-time motherhood by society)

One of the main reasons for mothers' continued commitment to work after childbirth was the association of paid work with self-esteem and social identity. Brannen and Moss (1991) argued that paid work was just as central to women's identity as it was to men's. This came through strongly in my research, and is discussed below in relation to social identity theory. It was apparent that my research participants considered there to be a link between motherhood and negative social identity. As discussed in Chapter 5, feminist writers Skevington and Baker (1989) have adapted social identity theory with the intention of enhancing understanding of women's changing role in contemporary society. As a reminder of the relevance of social identity theory, it is worth repeating Marshall and Wetherall's (1989: 106–7) neat explanation of the meaning of social identity:

> when a group or social identity is salient, individuals begin to think about themselves and others in terms of attributes which are collectively shared and which define that group and, as a result, individual traits that mark out one's personal, unique and individual identity become less prominent in the individual's self-conception. Thus . . . when a woman categorizes herself as a feminist, what becomes dominant in her self-concept are the attitudes, traits, norms and values shared with other feminists rather than the idiosyncrasies of her individual temperament and personality.

Mothers who took part in this research clearly identified themselves with two social groups: 'mothers' and 'professional career women'. In accordance with the argument put forward by Marshall and Wetherall (1989), these identifications were so strong that, in the analysis of the interviews with mothers, it would have been difficult to separate out the characteristics of the individual from their group identity, as most women described their paid work as being an integral part of 'who I am'. In some cases, the woman's identification with her particular professional group was seen as important (as in the case of Sarah-Jane, who expressed her sense of vocation). Other mothers were also proud of their level of seniority (e.g. Jane and Pandora). However, the most significant finding in relation to social identity was a powerful sense that research participants equated high social worth with the social group 'career woman' and negative social worth with the group 'full-time mother'. All of the women interviewed expressed a fear that their social capital would decline if they were to become 'full-time' mothers. This related to their own sense of self and how they perceived they would be regarded by both family and friends and the wider society, if they became full-time mothers. All mothers were explicit about their feelings on this matter and some provided examples to illustrate the point. For example, on recounting her friends' response to the suggestion that she might give up paid work and be with her children 'full-time', Sarah-Jane reported that people were:

> aghast, I mean really aghast . . . they all said 'It will be boring and completely dull, so you wouldn't have anything to talk about any more'. We are *defined* by work and given *value* by work . . . and nowadays people don't think that being a mother is in any way a job or an occupation. They don't actually see it as having value – oh,

they might pay lip service to it having value, but in practical terms they don't see it as anything valuable. So if I gave up work, what would I be worth then?

(Sarah-Jane, doctor)

This is not to suggest that women denied the importance of motherhood in relation to their own children. On the contrary, mothers were keen to point out that they loved their children dearly and did not see personal ambition and motherhood as being mutually exclusive. As discussed in Chapter 6, it was apparent that, like Rich (1977) and Oakley (1981), participants celebrated their maternity, emphasizing their closeness to their babies:

I just adore my daughter and I'm delighted about having another baby, I love that feeling of closeness you have with small children and a new baby.

(Angela, academic)

Nevertheless, when interacting with others (even those close to them), mothers often preferred to be identified primarily with their professional grouping, and distanced themselves from the social group 'mother'. For example, in social situations, Diana made an intergroup comparison between the social group 'career woman' and the social group 'mother', choosing to identify herself with the former social group because of the higher value she believed was attached to it:

I was worried about not having anything of interest in my life other than [my baby] and [did not] think of having a child as being interesting to other people. And I was worried about not being interesting to my friends and my husband, and to myself, I suppose, in the end. [I worried that] what would concern me, if I did not go back to work, would not concern other people. The idea of 'the ideal motherhood' bores me. I could see myself . . . boring the people I liked. It's like valuing . . . you *are* what you *do*. And when you meet someone and you say that you stay at home and look after children (and I've seen other women have to do it) you sort of hold your breath and you see their eyes glaze over and I didn't want that to be me, which is horrid of me, because I'm not judging them, but I am aware that a lot of what I am is from work, it's fun and interesting here all day . . . it's a good job. And if I didn't have it, I wouldn't be who I am.

(Diana, television news producer)

Jane expressed a similar sentiment:

> If I had chosen to stay at home full-time I would never say to people 'Oh, I am just a housewife and mother.' I would say, 'Well I used to be a teacher, and a good one at that!'
>
> (Jane, A-level teacher)

All mothers were clear that being part of a group with high social capital (i.e. career woman) had an affirmative impact on their own confidence and self-value:

> I think work gives you some self-confidence, some self-esteem that I wouldn't have if I were at home all the time. It makes me feel, you know, I am actually a unique person in my own right . . . I have got a value other than just somebody who only matters in terms of how they relate to others . . . and who does all the boring jobs in the house.
>
> (Angela, academic)

Given their identification with the raised social capital of career, it is unsurprising that mothers linked their profession to a strong sense of their own personal identity:

> The motivation to work is to do with me and my identity, with finding me and getting 'me' back again. It's important for me to have a different part of my life and different part of myself fulfilled in a different way.
>
> (Penelope, social worker)

Many expressed their desire to maintain their professional identity in positive terms, for example because they thought it provided a good role model for their children:

> I think, particularly if you have daughters, I think if you have daughters *and* sons, you know, I think there is a responsibility to provide a kind of role model in which women actually do work and are ambitious and seen as achievers and so on.
>
> (Estelle, psychotherapist)

> I think if you give up your life entirely or your sense of identity it doesn't do [the children] any good in the end. I wouldn't like the boys to see me being a total floor mat, housewife, then going on to expect to marry someone like that you know because I'll be really appalled. Hopefully I'll bring them up to do their fair share of chores.
>
> (Lucy, hospital pharmacist)

However, 14 women displayed a 'darker side' to their need to work, in relation to the kind of person they feared they might become if they relinquished their careers and lost the status accorded to 'career woman'. For example, Suzanne had decided to retain her career partly because she saw negative consequences for her social status if she gave it up. Suzanne expanded this argument, suggesting that if mothers were valued negatively by others, this could adversely affect the way they valued themselves and could therefore lead to poor self-esteem. In keeping with the findings of Marshall and Wetherall (1989), she explained that keeping her job enabled her to align herself with the higher-status group 'career woman' and preserved her self-confidence as a consequence:

> I look at friends of mine who had very equal jobs and one of them hasn't gone back. And now, I don't think of her as an equal, and I don't think that's just me belittling her. I still think intellectually she is bright but her role is defined differently and she is the master [sic] of the home which is 'the wife' and she has let go the worldly reins and I think that is probably bound up with self-confidence. I think if you stay at home you lose confidence in your ability to do things which are measurable by your peers . . .. I can quite understand that people who have been out of the workplace lose confidence in a really dramatic way . . . but literally within days of being back I realized I am good at what I do and I like the respect you get from that. I think if I stayed at home I would just lose confidence and not be really the same person.
>
> (Suzanne, lawyer)

Other women expressed views which accorded with Suzanne's concerns, worrying that they might overeat, or become depressed if they relinquished their career.

> What people don't seem to understand is that my job is a part of me. It's a vocation, and it's who I am. And I feel a kind of black despair when people just can't seem to grasp that. Just because I am a mother – and that is part of me, too – doesn't mean I am prepared to give everything up. I worked so hard to get where I am. And maybe it shouldn't be the case, but the truth is, it is: mothers are not valued as highly as doctors.
>
> (Sarah-Jane, doctor)

> I am frightened of not working, frightened of what you become really. I am frightened that I would cease to be an interesting person. There are all sorts of fears and the other big problem, it sounds really

pathetic, but I'd put weight on, that's how important my weight is to me, I stay thin because I work and if I'm at home I'd eat and I'd go to eleven stone. I wouldn't be me, I'd be a different person.

(Lianne, A-level teacher)

These views are in keeping with Skevington and Baker's (1989) assertion that members of groups which are of high standing 'gain a positive social identity and high self-esteem from group memberships; members of lower status or subordinate groups have a less positive social identity and lower self-esteem' (Skevington and Baker 1989: 2), and with Chira's (1998) argument that a negative value is placed on motherhood as a full-time occupation. Marshall and Wetherall's (1989) arguments are also in keeping with observations that 'Looking after children is a low-status occupation. It is isolating, frequently boring, relentlessly demanding and exhausting. It erodes your self-esteem and your membership of the adult world' (Cusk 2001: 7). Cusk's account of the social status of motherhood reflected the views of all mothers who participated in this research and, significantly, those of some fathers – which were a further source of anxiety for mothers.

The low value placed on full-time motherhood by husbands/partners

As well as being explicit about the low value placed on motherhood by society, 17 mothers felt that if they lost their professional identity, this would be viewed negatively by their partners, and would adversely affect their intimate relationship. The remaining three mothers hoped that relinquishing their career would not change the balance of the relationship, but were not prepared to try this out in case it might. One mother, who was very concerned, explained:

When I went back to work [my husband] said that for him there was a huge change, I became 'me' again. He feels I sort of got back a lot of self-confidence by going back to work and a sense of my worth again which I lost in this horrible muddle in the first six months [at home with baby] . . . And so even [my husband] will sort of pay lip-service to me being at home and being a mother as being valuable. But he will probably negate it by saying something that really expresses his truer feeling about it all . . . he has only ever known me as a working person, which has always had a significance in our relationship . . . . Part of his initial attraction to me was that I am a very clear-minded person at work and for him that was very appealing. And when I wasn't at work he suddenly didn't know quite who I was anymore. He likes the fact that I'm working.

(Sarah-Jane, doctor)

This concern was entirely borne out by the views of fathers on equality and the status of the social group 'mother' versus that of 'career woman'. Some fathers expressed an explicit concern that their wife's social capital would diminish if she became a full-time mother and houseworker. This is in contrast to Tooley's (2002) assertion that men find career women unattractive because they prefer women to be meek and dependent. However, it is in keeping with the views of Marshall and Weatherall (1989), Chira (1998) and Cusk (2001), all of whom believe that society holds full-time motherhood in low regard. Fathers indicated that mothers needed to maintain their career in order to retain status and respect within the intimate relationship. Jack, Stephen and William described their feelings clearly:

> I feel if [my wife] hadn't gone back she would have felt diminished as a person really . . . I could never have envisaged marrying somebody who would have just stayed at home, I couldn't, I wanted to marry my equal and that is what I have done.
>
> (Jack, GP)

> I think part of the basis of the relationship is that we are both doing similar things . . . I think people probably get on better if they . . . both run professional lives, really. I think, otherwise, if you've got the mother at home all day looking after the children, complications can develop in the relationship, so I think equality must be quite a good thing really; also you don't get that sort of 'living two separate lives' thing.
>
> (William, architect)

> In terms of what was in it for me [that my wife works] I . . . find it difficult to deal with her being at home full-time when there is this difference in *weighting*. As in: how do you weigh up the *value* of different things because society very much values work, very much seems to value *work* and *careers* above the concept of looking after the children, motherhood. And so I felt a little uncomfortable when my wife was at home but I felt more relaxed knowing that she was back at work, so I suppose that is what was in it for me. Also, my wife at various times, with just looking after the children, has been quite stressful, she has been quite low and has been much happier when she's been back doing some work, so obviously that has a benefit for her and for me as well.
>
> (Stephen, GP)

Fathers also saw a direct link between the capacity to earn money, high self-esteem and high social identity. Those men (and one of the women) who were main breadwinners in their households admitted that they held their partner in greater esteem if she/he was earning money in her/his own right. One father noted:

> Having been married before, to a wife who never wished to work, I really admire [my present wife's] wish to develop her own career and earn her *own* money – I respect her for that.
>
> (Jeremy, academic)

Fear of 'institutionalized' motherhood

It has already been noted (in Chapter 6) that the institution of motherhood induced negative feelings in the women interviewed for this research – they did not wish to be associated with the role of full-time mother or 'domestic goddess', but at the same time they felt guilty about this. On a positive level, however, the institution of motherhood acted as a spur in motivating women to combine mothering with career. This fear of becoming 'institutionalized' mothers helps to explain why the women (all of whom were tired, guilty and pressured) nevertheless continued to retain commitment to their paid work. In particular, there were seven women whose own mothers had felt trapped and frustrated by the social roles defined for them at the time. These research participants saw a cause-and-effect connection between the dissatisfaction experienced by their own mothers and the lack of a career. Thus, the means of avoiding the unhappiness exhibited by their own, non-working mothers was linked to professional fulfilment. This provided a strong motivation for those concerned to maintain a career following childbirth:

> My own mother was so unhappy at home, she had a breakdown and that partly explains my fear, she had a breakdown when I did my A levels because just being at home made her really depressed, it's the futility, she had nothing . . . it did have an effect on me, you don't want to be the same, you don't want the nothing . . . and she's been adamant that 'you must have a career, you don't want to be giving up work' . . . I permanently felt responsible for my mother, she said 'I wanted to go into nursing but I got pregnant so they wouldn't let me go', because she's had me, she permanently feels she was robbed of a career.
>
> (Lianne, A-level teacher)

> my mother was tremendously bad tempered, she was always angry, aggressive, so I have a view of a mother who stayed at home being someone who was completely angry.
>
> (Pandora, lawyer)

the thought of not doing something was frightening ... and the thought of becoming my mother was probably too much. She was incredibly frustrated, a very bright lady who left work when her children were born and didn't go back for 25 years, and then to a role which did not reflect her abilities or qualifications.

(Rachael, NHS chief executive)

Although some of the arguments about social identity might seem convincing in relation to career women, it would also be easy to presume that, for lower-paid women, with 'jobs' rather than professions, the link between enhanced social identity and employment would not apply. However, as noted on p. 85, recent work by Backett-Milburn *et al.* (2001), which examines the experiences of a small group of less affluent, less well-qualified women in Scotland (described as 'working class'), implies that this could be a mistaken assumption. It is argued by these writers that paid work and self-esteem are also closely linked for 'working-class' women. Given the relatively small size of the two research samples (mine and that of Backett-Milburn *et al.*) it is difficult to be sure how far this argument would apply to a wider population. However, in my view the link between social identity and mothers' commitment to paid work is an important one, and suggests that policy makers, such as Lea (2001), should think much more carefully before dismissing the contribution to the workplace of women with small children.

Working to remain equal: Power, earned income and the 'balance' of the intimate relationship

As well as providing social capital, paid work obviously provided mothers with earned income, and this was seen as central to the balance of power between husband and wife. The idea that earning money enabled mothers to remain on equal terms with their partner was an important motivating factor for women to continue working (even if their income was not needed to run the household). The majority of mothers felt a loss of equality and a shift in the balance of power in their relationship (in their husband's/partner's favour) during the short period while they were at home on maternity leave. This provided an important spur for them to return to the workplace. This is consistent with the views of writers on family practices noted on p. 90, who recognize the power that has historically been wielded by men in paid work while wives have remained the 'willing slave at home' (Somerville 2000: 241). In contrast to this, women wanted to be respected by their male partners and treated as equals, which they felt would be difficult if they were at home with small children every day. Fourteen women were explicit that remaining at home, while their partner went out to work, had

had a serious impact on their marriage/relationship. Estelle and Lianne explained:

> When you have a child it changes hugely. One minute you are both equal, both working, next minute [my husband] sees me snapping into the sort of person his mother was; in his eyes I suddenly became like his mother, it was frightening, I was shocked by it, really shocked . . . this is what I couldn't believe, that he would not be equal with me, we had ceased to be equals because I became a mother and he carried on, I cried when he went to work, because he put a suit on and went to work and I sat at home and cried because *I* wanted to go to work, I wanted to put *my* suit on and not to have the responsibility of this child, I wanted to be a real person again, to be the same like I had been.
>
> (Lianne, A-level teacher)

> I could *not* be at home full-time . . . [because] there are points where I have felt my autonomy is being pushed, my space is being elbowed, you know like when my husband takes over the study, his physical manifestation of that. I can't bear it and I fight back. I am absolutely determined to get that inch back, you know.
>
> (Estelle, psychotherapist)

In relation to this, mothers were plainly reluctant to take on the role of 'wife' as defined by Van Every (1995) or to be completely dependent on, or beholden to, the fathers of their children, because they did not wish to concede the control of alternatives or the use of authority which might be associated with earned income (Morgan 1986). This is in complete contrast to the argument, put forward by Tooley (2002), that women secretly yearn for a dependent, wifely role. It is also at variance with the work of Delphy and Leonard (1992) and Maushart (2002) who imply that women accept the role of 'wife' in the sense that they are resigned to it, and undertake it without protest. In a wider context, this indicates a more general challenge to the idea that women should be subordinate to men, just because they are mothers. This is consistent with the views of some radical feminists, such as Rich (1977) and Oakley (1981), who have privileged women's reproductive status while also arguing that women are entitled to both motherhood and intellectual fulfilment. It also accords with Walby's (1990) assertion that motherhood is not in itself responsible for the male domination of women, but that patriarchy and a social structure which privileges men continue to perpetrate women's oppression. Personal access to money (which Morgan 1986: 161 described as 'the most liquid of all resources') in the form of a regular salary was seen as important, because of the power differential it would create if mothers were financially dependent on fathers. All research participants considered that earning power was linked to control of alternatives and authority regarding family decision making (MacMillan and Jones 1986). Should this responsibility be vested solely in fathers, it was feared (by the men as well as the women) that this could be abused, which is consistent with the findings of Vogler and Pahl (1994). Lucy and Pandora expressed their views on the power which income invests in the person earning it:

> You may feel that if you didn't contribute any financial input to the family . . . you would feel different about spending . . . I think that I would feel that . . . I'd have to either ask [my husband] or check with him and I'd *hate* to have to do that you know . . . I like that fact that I earn money as well . . . I know I contribute quite a substantial amount so I don't have to worry about what I may, or may not, buy.
>
> (Lucy, hospital pharmacist)

> I had a traditional mother who stayed at home and was very frustrated . . . she was *always* angry, always aggressive, and also financially and emotionally dependent upon her husband. My father used to say: 'I don't know what's wrong with your mother, I give her housekeeping on time every week, why is she so upset?' Which *I* didn't *ever* want to be in the same position as my mother.
>
> (Pandora, lawyer)

Fifteen fathers admitted that their wife's partner's ability to go to work and earn her 'own' money was a factor in maintaining a balance of power within the relationship (indicating that Pandora and Lucy had a point!):

> In that year being off the first six months was *very* hard and I think [my wife] was quite low in that period. And certainly I felt it started to equalize things much more again and there wasn't this . . . she was less . . . well, obviously it was just much more 'equal' when she was back working. But then when she was off with [the next baby] it was quite hard again at that point, because again the inequality thing came in a bit, which was an adjustment thing.
>
> (Stephen, GP)

> The one of us who was at home would almost certainly end up certifiable one way or the other . . . because I think the equality *would* shift in my favour. . . . that's what's so difficult about this equality idea.
>
> (David, psychiatrist)

> It would change things . . . in so far as, you know, she would have no money and she'd be completely reliant on me and I think . . . there is

always a risk that the partner who earns the money can wield that as a threat and . . . unintentionally, I think that might be there, so the balance of the relationship would change.

(Sam, lawyer)

Freedom from domestic duties – and male oppression

Several men also expressed concerns that if their partners/wives gave up paid work, not only would they cease to regard them as a partner of equal status, but they also would expect them to play the role of 'domestic goddess': the selfless being whose principal job was to provide 'material comforts' for her husband (Somerville 2000: 241). Although some considered the idea of having an unpaid houseworker, or 'wife' – in the sense defined by Van Every (1995) – to be a tempting prospect from the point of view of the domestic comforts it would provide, fathers feared that they would cease to have much in common with their wives/partners, should this occur:

> I think it's nice to have a partnership . . . from our point of view I think you are looking at a partnership. . . . I respect [my wife] and I think one has to feel that has to be an equal partnership . . . is it a housekeeper you want or a soul mate?
>
> (Edward, doctor)

> [I think] it would sort of creep in if she was more at home . . . one would sort of say 'Well, you're at home, aren't you? You can do that sort of thing.' There's a danger that could happen . . . Um, and then that's just laziness again, isn't it, on my part, but sort of absolving myself of the responsibilities that could be done at leisure by someone who's at home all day . . . There is a danger that I might say: 'Well, you're at home, can't you do that?' and you do it once then: 'Well – do it next time, you know!' So . . . that could lead on to greater things and a greater callousness or indifference.
>
> (Henry, lawyer)

However, while they may have wished for a 'soul mate', some fathers were nevertheless ambivalent about the benefits of having a partner in paid work. In five cases where there was no immediate financial imperative for the mother to work, fathers indicated a secret wish for her to stay at home and undertake wifework (Maushart 2002). It has been noted in Chapters 2 and 3 that heterosexual women have traditionally taken responsibility for the emotional management of intimate relationships, as well as undertaking routine chores, allowing men more freedom to pursue their careers. However, as noted earlier, although all mothers but one found themselves responsible for domestic labour, all 20 women recognized that wifework became less of a priority once they began to combine child-rearing with paid work. Five fathers resented this and were explicit about their feelings. Edward stated:

> I was talking to one of the guys at work the other day who is married to a lawyer. And he hit a chord, he said: 'You can intellectually agree with everything that is happening to you but there are periods where you just want that shirt to be ironed and you feel, "goodness why is that shirt not ironed or why isn't there any food in the fridge?" ' And at those points . . . I think, you think: 'Oh, it would be nice . . .'.
>
> (Edward, doctor)

This accords with Giddens's (1992: 11) suggestion that, although men may speak the language of equality, some are extremely 'nervous about what this means for them' (perhaps especially when it comes to household work!)

In my view, there is a vital link between earned income and the rejection of accountability for domestic labour. This point was not overlooked by mothers. Female research participants felt that paid work validated their right to decline personal responsibility for household work, or wifework (Maushart 2002). The capacity to earn money offered them the chance to side-step patriarchal traditions by buying their way out of the role of 'wife':

> I don't know if the money thing would end up being an issue, like [my husband] would feel like he was the breadwinner and it was his money . . . and certainly if I didn't work I would end up doing . . . a lot more of the [household, husband and childcare work] than I do now. Which, I think I would start to feel that he wasn't doing his share and I think we would probably fall into the habit where he came home and did nothing. If I didn't work he'd end up doing nothing, I'd end up doing the lot and I'd resent that.
>
> (Jayne, electronic engineer)

> I'm afraid if I stopped work then it would go back to me being taken totally for granted and I am not going to be just the doormat who just does all the dirty jobs because I'm at home . . . I'm not the dirty washing fairy, thank you very much.
>
> (Joanne, tax consultant)

> That is another reason I wanted to go back to work, because I knew otherwise I would be kicking against this, you know, 'I do everything and he does nothing syndrome'. And also I would have felt beholden to him, I would have felt he was bringing in the money, I was just pootling about dusting. And that he would have had no conception

THE COMMITMENT TO WORK AND CHILD   **169**

as to what that amounted to. And at least I now have the excuse of my job. I mean if there is a problem which arises as to 'Why haven't we done such and such?' he can't say to me 'Well, I've been at work all day' because then I can say 'Well, so have I'.

(Sophie, lawyer)

Despite these statements (and as noted in Chapter 6), in all but one case, even where men were principal childcarers and women main breadwinners, there was still no assumption by couples that fathers would take on the 'horrid' domestic jobs that 'nobody' wanted to do. This may be because male status remains distant from housework, which is historically seen as lowly female work (Morris 1990). As noted in Chapter 7, many women therefore chose to pay others to undertake those domestic chores which fell to mothers as 'pink jobs' but which they preferred not to do themselves. This was the case even where mothers felt guilty about paying other women to do the housework (a concern which worried three mothers in particular).

Significantly, especially in relation to women's resistance to patriarchy, it must be noted that both of the women who worked full-time, while their husbands remained at home full-time and were not in paid work, seemed concerned about their own tendency to seize the power in a situation where their partners were at home full-time and did not earn money. One of these women, Louise, made the point that:

This is not necessarily about gender. It's about roles in the social context and the position of being the one who doesn't earn any money.

Louise described her own situation thus:

We have a joint account . . . and all I ask him to do when he buys something is to give me chits . . . now I haven't set parameters there, but still, he sort of says 'Is it OK?' and I say 'Yeah', because he doesn't spend a lot of money . . . however, when we had problems I said I'll give you x amount a month just for, it's like pocket money but it's actually so that he feels more comfortable because it's been very much, *I've* been in control, so although he has complete access to [the money in the bank] he probably doesn't feel empowered.

(Louise, public sector manager)

This view was reflected by two of the men who were not principal earners in their households. One stated that in arguments his wife used her earning power in her favour as the 'medium through which conflicts of interest [were] usually resolved' (Morgan 1986: 159):

> It always comes down to who earns the money, I think. My wife does say, when she has a fit of anger, though this is very rare you know, but like: '*I'm* the one who's the main breadwinner'.
>
> (Joseph, full-time father)

110%: The commitment of mothers to paid work . . .

As noted at the start of this chapter, and in Chapter 1, many who write about women's employment (e.g. Knight 2002; Hakim 1996a), assume that women's commitment to work diminishes once they become mothers. Tooley (2002) argues – and Hewlett (2002) implies – that well-educated women are unhappy with their careers because they would rather be playing the role of 'domestic goddess' or 'angel in the house'. This was not borne out by my research, which demonstrated mothers' high commitment to paid work and raised productivity levels, despite their love for, and devotion to, their children. In contrast to the arguments put forward by Hakim (1995) and Boase (2001), those who had chosen to work part-time showed dedication to their employment and appeared to manage boundaries competently and honestly. Where women had to leave work 'on time' because of childcare commitments, they felt guilty about this and worried about how it might be viewed by their colleagues. Significantly, however, all pointed out that this did not mean leaving tasks undone, as they worked more efficiently during the day, and were prepared to take work home at night, or even return to the office when children were in bed:

> before I had the children I would have been prepared to stay after time if there were things to do and now I have to go so I just do. But that doesn't make any difference to how effective I am because the work still gets done – I just rush round more during the day to ensure that happens.
>
> (Elisabeth, doctor)

> I have to leave at 5.15 but if a job needs to be finished I go home [deal with baby] and then drive back to the office and do three hours, sort of 8 to 11 . . . or even leave both [children] with [my husband] on a Saturday morning . . . that's the job really, we are deadline related.
>
> (Joanne, tax consultant)

Some women had to be highly organized and go to imaginative lengths to deliver children to nursery and present themselves at work appropriately dressed and on time, which, in my view, revealed an exceptionally high level of commitment. Joanne, for example, cycled to work so that her husband could use their only car to take children to nursery and everyone could arrive on time:

> We are out of the house by 7.45. I then just cycle straight into work, my suits and tights and breast pads are here at the office (where I have a wardrobe) so I get dressed and, if there is time, get some make up on. I keep porridge oats and bananas here for breakfast because the office has a microwave.
>
> (Joanne, tax consultant)

Well over half the mothers reported that their productivity levels had risen sharply after they had had children, as their time at work was limited and they sought to make the most of it:

> You have to put 110% in. I always make sure things are done. I have learned – and it's quite a neat skill – to make the most of little pockets of time so I can rattle through stuff at an incredible pace, you know: I don't mess about when I'm at work . . . I don't hang around at *all* at work.
>
> (Eleanor, senior education manager)

> My experience is that actually you become a much, much more efficient worker as a parent because you just haven't got time to waste and your productivity actually is much better.
>
> (Estelle, psychotherapist)

This is at variance with the suggestion in Chapter 5 (Boase 2001; Yates 2001) that mothers regard the workplace as an opportunity for coffee breaks and light reading.

In contrast to some fathers, some mothers became excellent at compartmentalizing childcare and paid work. Sophie describes this phenomenon very clearly:

> I am very committed to my work. I don't think motherhood makes me any less committed other than the fact that I only do three days. But when I am there, I am at work. I have no photographs on my desk of my child. And people often say to me: 'Ooh, have you got a picture?' And I say: 'No, I haven't', and they think: 'Weird woman'. And I don't have a picture for one very good reason: if I had a picture I'd sit looking at it and be thinking, oh, you know, 'What is my baby doing?' And I don't want that. When I'm at work, I want to do my work, this is Sophie, lawyer, and that's it . . . I have a very good safety valve in that I work under a different name from that which I [use as]

> a mother so that helps me split it so I go to work and I am Sophie
> [maiden name] and I come home and I am Sophie [married name]
> and [that is my baby's time] because there has to be a cut-off point
> where that is the end of work. So my life is very definitely depart-
> mentalized and that allows me to step into work mode. And I am
> lucky, I have really good childcare and right from day one I have gone
> into the office and forgotten my home and my family and my child
> completely, even if he's ill sometimes, I can switch off to that extent
> . . . and when I'm there, that's how committed I am to my work.
>
> (Sophie, lawyer)

Eleven women believed their ability to get more done in less time
had made them better managers. In the case of four women who were in a
position to employ others, this had influenced their own approach to valuing
colleagues:

> I believe I am even more efficient because I am so focused, I have all
> these balls to juggle and I don't waste time. I aim to develop that
> positive approach in terms of recruitment. If any mother is returning
> to work then that sends out positive vibes to me, I know what *I* have
> to do to manage it, and if *they* are attempting to manage it they are
> good people to have on the team.
>
> (Louise, public sector manager)

All mothers considered that the continuation of their professional career
was a choice that they had undertaken willingly, despite pressures which
made this a difficult decision, because it answered a deep need within them.
All had been in paid work for an average of ten years before the arrival of a first
child and their wish to work was connected with the fact that they recognized
themselves, and their identity, through their profession as well as through
motherhood.

. . . and the pain of parting: The commitment of mothers to their children

The wish of mothers to maintain their paid work did not mean that they were
uncommitted to their children, but the reverse. With two possible exceptions,
all mothers – no matter how anxious they were to get back to work, or how
difficult they found it being at home with a baby – felt torn about leaving their
child in the care of someone else and worried about them if they were ill or
unhappy. This view was unaltered whether the mother was working full-time
or part-time. One mother noted:

> I remember very clearly the first day I went back after I'd had [my baby]. I went for a sandwich at lunchtime and I saw somebody pushing a pushchair and it nearly made me burst into tears. Because the emotional wrench of leaving them I think is really hard and even though you can steel yourself to it, with each of them the first time I've left them I've had tears running down my cheeks.
>
> (Suzanne, lawyer)

Another mother stated:

> The parting from my child at nursery was very hard at first. If she was under the weather or crying that would live with me and come back to haunt me. I once forgot when she was supposed to be in fancy dress and felt dreadful that I had not been a good mum ... but if everything is normal then I can concentrate at work and then back onto my daughter at the end of the day.
>
> (Victoria, academic)

Three women were so determined to combine paid work with continued breastfeeding that they somehow managed to make their bodies adapt and fed their babies at night-times only even though this was sometimes difficult and upsetting:

> There were instances in which, because of the way our courts are, you are at the whim of magistrates and so [if] they decided we were going to work until nine at night and I had left the house at eight in the morning I [would be] engorged, and yes, I could sort up express milk and use breast pads but it was more the emotional side. I felt upset that the baby wouldn't get his feed.
>
> (Pandora, lawyer)

'I want to spend more time with my kids than my Dad did': The commitment of fathers to paid work and children

All but one of the fathers who took part in the research indicated a change in his own attitude to paid work, once mothers were combining motherhood with career. This meant that their commitment to childcare increased – in direct proportion to the amount of time spent with their children (as argued by Lewis 1986). It has already been explained, in Chapter 7, that five men reduced the number of hours spent in paid work once their children arrived, two of them taking on the role of full-time childcarer and three in part-time paid work. With one exception, this was a choice made by the men because they wished to spend more time with their children, and has been recognized as such by both partners:

> What's quite clear is that my husband's attitude to work has changed since we have had children. So I think that he has become, not less focused, but it is inevitable that the time you can devote to your work has to change because you've got something else in your life . . . so he is going to take a back seat in terms of his career, go into teaching but on a part-time basis.
>
> (Eleanor, senior education manager)

Another father, who also changed his job to allow more time with his children, stated:

> I certainly want to spend more time with my kids than my Dad did. And as I make sacrifices – my Dad was a very successful business man – I'm sure I will be less successful in my job because of that but I would prefer that rather than the extra success I suppose I could take.
>
> (Chris, industrial chemist)

Once the men became involved in the day-to-day care of the children, they also felt torn about being parted from them, and often thought about them when they were at work:

> If I have been worried about one of the children it's with me constantly. At times of upset [nothing to do with children], work can help you forget about things, but I just can't forget about the children at all, but it's not always when they are unwell, you think about them through the day for nice reasons.
>
> (Sam, lawyer)

Twelve men worked full-time but nevertheless shared the task of taking children to and from nursery, meaning that they were obliged to establish clear boundaries regarding when they arrived at and left the workplace. To a greater or lesser extent, therefore, it was the case for all but one of the men that the amount of time devoted to the children lessened the amount of time given to work, though this was not necessarily seen as negative:

> I think you look on things differently and things that previously meant . . . all or nothing at work become more in perspective.
>
> (Sam, lawyer)

> Boy, for me, curiously I think there was quite a shift. Because [the birth of my children] just radically changed my priorities. I was just

not ... work just stopped being the number one thing in my life which in some ways it probably had been. Oh, dramatically so. It did mean that my hours dropped but ... my efficiency changed, my productivity went up ... I mean the amount of *time* I used to waste ... and I think, you know, other people see me as much more sensible and rounded and fun. So commitment's complex, isn't it?

(David, psychiatrist)

As I began to discuss in Chapter 7, it seemed that the fathers in this small sample 'may be starting to make choices between competing identities as "new man" father and the Parsonian model of "good provider" father' within the intimate relationship. This marks a departure from the literature as it has been described (by Smart and Neale 1999: 55) as a choice more commonly faced following divorce. It is probable that fathers had expected, in their youth, to be tied to the role of major breadwinner during their adulthood, because – as Potuchek's (1997) study demonstrates – this was the expectation of heterosexual males as they were growing up. If Potuchek's thesis can be extended to this group of men (who would have been of a similar age to Potuchek's research participants), it is likely that they regarded paid work as something they 'had' to do in order to fulfil the social roles expected of them. The experience of adulthood, however, and the fact that they are living with women earning professional salaries has meant that, for fathers, choices have not been as sharply circumscribed as they predicted. As a result of their wives/partners choosing to maintain their careers, the men concerned – in practice or in principle – have the option of reducing the amount of paid work they undertake because their partner is also earning money. It is arguable that the existence of this choice has caused all men in the research sample to reflect on their commitment to paid work. Consequently, in all but one case, fathers' attitudes regarding the importance of paid work, relative to the wish to spend time with their children, have changed. In my view, this may well reflect a change in attitude among the wider population – a change not reflected in the literature on commitment to paid work, which focuses almost exclusively on mothers.

Precious time

In accordance with the concept of mothers' high commitment to work, it was acknowledged by both male and female participants that mothers were prepared to give up a great deal, and to work to the point of exhaustion both in the workplace and the home, so as not to let any of their roles suffer. Without exception, the women interviewed did not sacrifice time spent on paid work to accommodate their children, but relinquished the time they had previously spent on themselves:

> Looking after a pre-school child and juggling a job ... my aim is trying to make that work successfully for me, but trying to balance all my roles ... you pinch hours from everywhere, particularly from your own time.
>
> (Louise, public sector manager)

Time, and the entitlement to some 'free time', was seen as a sacrifice that almost everyone interviewed had made in order to accommodate the needs of paid work and children. Personal time was seen as a valuable resource by some couples, and the right to this was sometimes a source of conflict. One couple admitted that the man had the 'lion's share' of time, both in terms of leisure and the opportunity to work at home, this reflecting a traditional view of women's poor access to quality leisure time (Sullivan 1997). However, in this instance the mother paid for the children to attend nursery for an additional morning to ensure some time for herself. One couple agreed that they each needed some free time to themselves and made a great effort to ensure that they managed this, even though it sometimes caused conflict between them. A further four of the women did manage to carve out small, clearly defined periods of personal time to enable them to pursue particular interests. This mirrors Deem's (1996) observation that working women believe they have, in the literal sense, earned the right to some protected personal time – in contrast, as Cusk (2001) argues, to full-time mothers who feel pressure to be with their children constantly. However, the remaining interviewees (both men and women) made it clear that they rarely (if ever) had any time to themselves as individuals:

> I've talked about having time with children which is precious. I've maintained my job and there's absolutely no space in that for me as an individual, I don't have time any more to do anything for myself and that's a problem.
>
> (Eleanor, senior education manager)

> It's very much feeling: do *you* have any life at all? And it's such an effort to actually do anything beyond work [and childcare].
>
> (Stephen, GP)

It was notable that spare time was even more pressured because, where research participants did undertake any 'extra-curricular' activities, these tended to involve studying and were connected with paid work. Seven women and four men were on courses of study linked to their careers in order to progress even further, this showing how ambitious they were. The combining of childcare with paid work restricted the social time that research participants spent as a couple (without the children). Two interviewees were explicit that they rarely went out without their child because they felt that any time when they were not at work 'belonged', as of right, to their daughter:

> We don't mind this, this is what we have chosen because [our daughter] is what it is all about, she is central, everything we have spare should be for, everything is for her.
>
> (Joseph, full-time childcarer)

> We have not had one night out in four years on our own ... we did not want to go out, we wanted to spend time with [our daughter], but it's a point to make that we are tied because I developed my career.
>
> (Louise, public sector manager)

The centrality of the child to the way this relationship was constructed reflected the observations of Beck and Beck-Gernsheim (1995). Another research participant stated:

> I think the thing that has suffered is not so much our work and not so much the children, it's our social life which has become non-existent almost, and we view that as a sacrifice we had to make, and our social life now revolves round children's parties. That's so sad! No, it's not sad really, it's nice.
>
> (Pandora, lawyer)

These findings reinforce the argument that the solutions advocated by early feminist writers, such as Firestone's (1970) and Valeska's (1984) assertions that mothers should not be obligated towards their children (this enabling them to focus on career), would be unattractive to many women. There is no doubt that, once they became mothers, women wanted to spend time with their children, which may have led them to change working practices. However, it did not appear to reduce their commitment or ambitions in relation to paid work. Indeed, given the personal sacrifices women had made in order to continue their careers, it could be argued that their commitment was greater than before motherhood. What is interesting in this context is the fact that many writers on women's work (such as Hakim 1996a; Tooley 2002; Hewlett 2002) fail to ask the next obvious question: What happens to the commitment of fathers towards paid employment, once children are born? This issue is now considered further.

Whose children? Power, the children and the intimate relationship

We have already seen that the maintenance of career, alongside involvement with children, was important to both women and men in relation to social identity and earned income. However, it appeared that mothers and fathers were aware of another kind of power which accompanied being at home with the children. This concerned the power of establishing a close relationship with children by being their principal carer, which (as noted in Chapters 3 and 4) has traditionally been regarded as the mother's territory. This power was seen to be under threat by some women – especially those who earned high salaries and left most of the childcare to their husbands. Some women, while ambitious, were careful not to hand over to their partners too much of their existing influence (Morgan 1986) as mothers. While maintaining their social identity as career woman, they were anxious that this should not erode their identity as mothers within the home. Lianne summed this up neatly, saying:

> Do I want a situation where I have to earn half the income (or more) and I have to abdicate the power that I've got at home? Because I have, I have a lot of power in the home.
>
> (Lianne, A-level teacher)

Suzanne expressed a similar view, arguing that she would reject any request by her husband to give up work and look after the children, even though this could have been afforded. She was honest about the fact that this would make her jealous and unhappy:

> I would have hated [my husband] to have stayed at home full-time. I'd have felt envious and anxious that he was spending all his time with the children. I would have felt really, really jealous of that, I wouldn't have liked it at all. So we never considered it that way around, that wasn't an option.
>
> (Suzanne, lawyer)

As noted earlier, it is my view (and that of Beck and Beck-Gernsheim 1995) that both mothers and fathers regarded children as central to their existence. For example, Nick described his relationship with his children as follows:

> the kids, they are my children, not *her* children, they are *our* children.
>
> (Nick, lawyer)

This is not an unusual statement in relation to mothers, as has been observed by Rich (1977), Oakley (1981) and O'Brien (1981), and it accords with the finding that mothers in this research valued highly their ability to bear and raise children (although they feared that this was not always recognized by society). It has been indicated in the literature that this level of commitment to children is becoming increasingly important for fathers, especially post-divorce (Smart and Neale 1999; Beck and Beck-Gernsheim 1995; Collier 1994). The discovery here that, to a varying extent, fathers were mediating their own relationships with children within the marriage/partnership, rather than relying on mothers to do this for them, reveals a departure from the past. This has implications for the mothers involved. As Maushart (2002: 138–9) points out, it is not unusual for women to limit fathers' involvement with their children if this poses a threat to their own territory as mothers. There is 'evidence of mothers' anxiety to retain their status as "parent of first contact" – as well as a . . . "sense of loss" when they took steps to establish greater equality of parenting . . .. There is no doubt that motherhood is far more central to most women's sense of identity than fatherhood is to most men's.' The issue of power in relation to the children (as in Lianne's quote above) was present in all the research interviews, though sometimes this was inferred rather than explicit. Seven of the women were comfortable with the situation where fathers mediated their own relationships with children and did not seem to consider their own situation to be under threat. Sonia stated:

> In terms of emotional stability within the home . . . well, the children, I would say we're pretty joint. We think similarly and there is no disagreement about whose role is what and what happens with the children. We're fairly equal in principles as regards the children.
>
> (Sonia, senior nurse)

However, some mothers appeared to feel territorial about relationships with their children, fearing that if fathers became too close, their own position as mothers might be threatened if things were to go wrong in the future. These worries may not have been misplaced. Although they did not state this in so many words, I inferred from the accounts of three fathers a suggestion that, should their marriage/partnership break down, they might not be prepared to concede residency to their wife/partner. For example, the account of one father seemed to imply a concern that his partner should not retain too much control of knowledge and information about the children's needs, in case he was exposed as 'secondary' parent if their relationship broke up (Morgan 1986). Another indicated that his career would accommodate the flexibility to care for children should the need arise. Some fathers were keen to establish 'ownership' of the children, which they regarded as being directly related to the amount of childcare work they undertook.

It has already been noted that five fathers rejected the traditional behaviours associated with fatherhood by voluntarily relinquishing or modifying their careers so that they could spend more time with their children, and that this marks a change from the patterns outlined by Dryden (1999) and Maushart (2002). Significantly, the wives of two of these men were conscious of the fact that, although this had allowed them to develop their careers to the point where both were very successful, they had paid a price for this because it meant that the scales had begun to shift in the other direction, with fathers acting as intermediary between mother and child. Louise and Eleanor, who worked full-time, reported mixed feelings about the close relationship between their children and the respective fathers:

> We went to the doctor's and my daughter sat on her daddy's knee, not mine. And the woman next to me said 'Is she a daddy's girl?'. And I said, 'Well he looks after her', and I suddenly realized, there is a growing special relationship there . . . I have noticed, it's daddy this, daddy that.
>
> (Louise, public sector manager)

> My husband has gone part-time and that has actually made life a lot easier for me because he's around a lot more. But there's a little bit of me, you know, if I'm honest (and I have said this to him), it's a peculiar one but although I'm doing this because I want to, I still feel a bit cheated because I wish it was *me* who was having a bit more time . . . time with the children is very precious, it's a very short time when kids are at the age where they really need you and that time is precious, and when I'm not there, it's him that is being needed.
>
> (Eleanor, senior education manager)

The opinions reported above suggest that both mothers and fathers had recognized that their children were a crucial source of power, and it is my view that both parents wanted a substantial stake in this. A 'post-modern' interpretation of power, such as that provided by Foucault (1990) or Latour (1986), would argue that, however powerful networks and social institutions may seem, these are intrinsically unstable and, if they are resisted by those whose compliance is needed to maintain the status quo, may falter. Within their own relationships, research participants were apparently trying to alter the status quo by sharing out the power related to paid work and childcare in a different manner than that which they believed was expected of them. This caused conflict because – as they were discovering – the redistribution of power threatened to shift the balance within marriage/partnership.

On an individual level this raises the interesting question of what will happen in the future if parents divorce or separate. It seems reasonable to suggest that a high proportion of fathers may wish to co-parent *post* divorce – which marks a departure from the findings of Smart and Neale (1999). Some men may even follow the trend outlined by Beck and Beck-Gernsheim (1995) and fight for sole residency of their children. This would mean that the career mothers paid a heavy price on divorce. It might also mean that the employers of these men cannot assume, *post*-divorce, that fathers' childcare responsibilities only extend to the weekend, as some may be full- or part-time carers for their children. This observation may be indicative of similar trends in the wider population, and suggests the need for further research. If considered in the wider context, the struggle of heterosexual parents between each having a career and a stake in children's everyday lives could be interpreted as a challenge on the part of research participants to resist attempts by the state to regulate behaviour through 'disciplinary coercions' (Foucault 1980: 11). For example, by making maternity rights available exclusively to women (while men receive only two weeks' paternity leave), it could be argued that the state aims to maintain the gendered notion of the 'institution of motherhood' (the 'domestic goddess') and also a patriarchal society, with the social identity of men grounded, in perpetuity, in their occupational status. These couples are challenging this situation because, even though paternity provision is not made for men, and even though higher-earning couples get no tax relief on childcare (an issue which is raised in the closing chapters of this book), the men and women who took part in this research are choosing to do things differently from what others seem to expect of them.

Summary

This chapter examined the commitment of mothers – and fathers – to their paid work. I offered explanations as to why career mothers of very young children are motivated to work, and what this means for their male partners. The key argument is that mothers in this study did not pursue their careers after childbirth simply to earn a pay cheque, but for personal satisfaction in order to maintain their social identity as career women and remain on equal terms with husbands/ partners. This was very wise of mothers, because fathers made it clear that if mothers relinquished their career, this would adversely affect the balance of power within the intimate relationship.

In my view – and in contrast to the views of Hakim (1995) and Tooley (2002) – mothers in the research sample were highly committed both to their children and to their paid work. They had raised their productivity and efficiency levels to accommodate the needs of both mothering and working, often sacrificing their own leisure time in the process. I have also asserted that the commitment to paid work among men changed as a result of close involvement with children, and speculated upon whether this may be applicable to a wider population of men. Additionally, I questioned assumptions, on the part of employers, about the respective childcare responsibilities of mothers and fathers *post*-divorce. Finally, I discussed the issue of power and small children, arguing that for mothers, in the event of relationship breakdown, there may be an element of high risk in 'handing over' their traditional carer role to fathers.

9 Everyone is equal . . .?
Parenthood and workplace discrimination

I feel short-changed. If the state wants to encourage people like me to work, then they need to recognize that equal opportunities is one of the most important aspects of life today. And oh, the *talk* is there about women and equal opportunities – but that is all it is. Just talk. And my God, you've got to *fight*, Caroline, really, you've got to push, push, *push* boundaries. And I *really* resent that, and I think 'Hey, come on a minute, I need a bit of support here!'

(Louise, public sector manager)

Just because I have a child doesn't mean that I'm less committed to my job than my husband is! When I'm there I give 100% if not more, and I certainly use lunch times and break times more effectively than he does. But the thing is, once you are a mother, the *minute* you ask for something from your employer – you know – just a bit of give and take, then there's just a change completely. From that minute onward, you're no longer the same person as far as they're concerned. And in a way people – and myself – used to think I was the golden girl there, at that school, but as soon as I had [my baby] I'm not anymore. It's like they rubbed the gold off and found I was tarnished underneath because I'm a mother. And it's like, well, we want the old Jane back, not this one. And yet I'm the same person . . . aren't I?

(Jane, A-level teacher)

Focus on:

'Fighting your own corner': Motherhood, discrimination and the workplace
During pregnancy
After childbirth – the link between flexible working and demotion
Being downgraded 'through the back door'

A paper tiger: 'Family-friendly' policies
The 'arduous battle': Who wants to go to court?
Support for mothers returning to work, and innovative practices
 'New' organizations and innovative practice
 Being assertive
Gendered approaches to returning mothers – and fathers!

Introduction

The resentment expressed by Louise and Jane neatly captures the main argument in this chapter, which is that equal opportunities policies and legislation are ineffective in protecting women (and men) who wish to combine mothering with paid work. Considering that the Sex Discrimination Act became law in Great Britain as long ago as 1975 (see Chapter 1), it might be anticipated that twenty-first-century mothers could expect equal treatment in the workplace as a matter of course. Furthermore, given that most traditional and public sector institutions have had equal opportunities polices in place for years, it might have been hoped that attitudes towards working mothers in these environments would be positive and supportive. One might also have supposed that, even if there were some small remaining 'pockets' of discriminatory practice in some of the more 'old-fashioned' institutions such as law, women with good qualifications and several years' work experience would be unlikely to be affected by these.

Unfortunately, the experiences of the mothers who took part in my research indicate that these hopes are unfounded. Explicit discrimination against working mothers remains a widespread and serious issue. As discussed in Chapter 5, this may occur whether or not women are mothers – their potential to bear children is enough. In the UK the Institute of Directors has argued that many employers and managers are resentful and suspicious of mothers' employment rights and may even be reluctant to employ women of childbearing age for this reason (Malthouse 1998). Padavic and Reskin (2002: 49) allege that employers in the USA are guilty of 'statistical discrimination' – preferring not to hire women because motherhood might make them more 'costly' than men. In this chapter it is argued that where mothers are concerned employers are free to defy the law, safe in the knowledge that they will probably never be challenged. This is because, although mothers may experience discrimination which appears to be barefaced and unjust (e.g. demotion), both individual women and employers are aware that the process of making a claim under equal opportunities legislation is cumbersome and stressful, meaning that few women will choose to take this route.

Thus, while it is acknowledged that some working practices (such as criteria for promotion) may *implicitly* be gendered (Halford *et al.* 1997), *explicit* discrimination against working mothers may often go unreported and undisputed, both in the UK and the USA (Padavic and Reskin 2002: 29), and thus it remains an extensive and hidden problem. Writers on motherhood and employment, both popular and academic (e.g. Tooley 2002; Hakim 1996a; Boase 2001; Knight 2002), have consistently underrated the commitment of mothers to their paid work. In the light of this, the assumption which many employers make – that women are even less valuable as employees (compared to men) once they have had children – is disappointing, but unsurprising. However, my research challenges the notion that mothers are less able and less motivated than their male, or childless, counterparts and argues that employers and colleagues are grossly underestimating the worth of a significant proportion of their 'human capital' if they take this view. In the cases of the mothers who took part in this research, existing policies and legislation offered little or no protection from discriminatory practice. It is also asserted here that arguments about flexible working practices being inconvenient and impractical are seriously flawed, since employers who hold these beliefs are unlikely to try out new ways of working, and as a result they risk losing experienced, committed and highly qualified personnel. Notably, as we will see in the stories that follow, all the women interviewed found that their maternal status changed the way they were viewed by employers, colleagues and clients. All but one woman discovered that, in a professional capacity, her 'value' had fallen. Eighteen out of 20 mothers experienced discrimination on returning to work, as well as finding it difficult to negotiate new ways of working with colleagues who had previously seemed supportive and reasonable. Significantly, those fathers in the sample who wished to change their working practices in order to accommodate childcare needs did not find employers/colleagues any more helpful than the mothers did – mostly because childcare is regarded as 'women's work', and employers saw no reason to provide help for fathers. Finally, it is particularly worrying that the open discrimination described below was experienced by a group of women who, with their high level of qualifications and relevant skills, might have been expected to experience this least (and who were, in fact, unaware that discrimination was such a serious problem until they became mothers). This is because of the implications that discrimination must have for those women who are poorly qualified and in low-paid, low-status jobs who may be suffering even worse treatment than those at the 'top' end of the job market.

'Fighting your own corner': Motherhood, discrimination and the workplace

Mothers who were struggling to manage their childcare responsibilities at the same time as re-establishing their status at work were offered little or no help from employers and colleagues. Instead, they were obliged to undertake a solitary and arduous battle to 'fight their own corner' if they wished to reclaim the position they had left when they began maternity leave, especially if they hoped to work more flexibly. Some women 'managed' their situations by being assertive and seeking alternative employment. Others were forced into a choice between continuing to work full-time and accepting (however reluctantly) being downgraded in status and pay.

During pregnancy

The literature suggests that discrimination against women in the workplace may occur, whether or not they have children (Cockburn 2002). However, for these women, the realization that their 'stock had plummeted' (Cusk 2001), and the recognition that they would not be treated on an equal basis with other staff, came as a shock and was directly linked to motherhood. This may be because their high level of qualifications and productivity had to some extent shielded them from 'unfair' treatment in a way that might not have applied to women in lower-status jobs. Thus, until they had experienced the return to work following a first period of maternity leave, most women had assumed that work would carry on exactly as before (perhaps with fewer paid hours) due to both their own previous 'track record' and the effective policies that would be in place to protect women's rights.

For almost all mothers, this presumption proved to be a serious miscalculation. In six cases, mothers reported that discriminatory attitudes became apparent even before they had given birth. From the moment their pregnancy was obvious, these women felt sidelined and stigmatized, due to an assumption on the part of others that motherhood would reduce their ability to perform well. Davidson (2001), writing about pregnancy and personal space, has noted that expectant women habitually find the attitudes of others to be patronizing and intrusive. Amanda, an established architect who runs her own business, reported her initial disbelief on discovering that excellent and long-standing relationships with clients were adversely affected by her pregnancy. Even though her smoothly organized working practices meant that she was well supported by her staff, and much of her work was with the public sector, she nevertheless found that:

> When I was obviously pregnant, I lost jobs. And I had *never* lost jobs before. I used to say I'd get 95% of what I went for. And I was effectively sacked from a project for no reason, no reasons were given, other than 'I don't particularly want you working with us any longer'. And I think there was a perception on their part that now I was having a child I shouldn't be working, or that I *couldn't* be working, or couldn't do their job effectively.

Also, when I was pregnant I did get fed up with people just raising the issue *all* the time . . . when is it due, etc. . . . I think people are surprised you are doing anything at all once you have a child. I got a letter from one client who said 'I am sorry to hear that you are still on maternity leave' as though this was an illness! So now I'm a bit careful with clients because of that attitude. Because I *did* lose jobs when I was pregnant and now I think, I shouldn't have gone along, I should have sent my [business] partner on her own. She should have gone on her own because I think, being pregnant, I gave people the wrong impression of how the job was going to be run and what might happen once I had the child; the fact that they could see I was pregnant put doubts in their minds.

(Amanda, architect)

Victoria, who works in a university setting, related a similar experience, having become pregnant during a research project. Because she had worked for the university for eight years (always on fixed-term contracts), Victoria was expecting that her contract would be extended and full maternity rights granted. When she broached this with the academic leading the research project, it was confirmed to Victoria that the intention had originally been to renew her contract. It was explained, however, that because of her pregnancy this offer would not now be made. Eventually, after a long battle, Victoria reached agreement with the university that her contract would be extended in the short term, but downgraded. She was told that she would be paid the standard 18 weeks' maternity leave. However, she was persuaded that this offer should be regarded as a special 'favour' for which she must pay a 'price'. Reluctantly, Victoria agreed that she would cut short her unpaid maternity leave, returning after only 24 weeks instead of the 40 weeks allowed in the university's 'official' policy:

When I was eight months pregnant they downgraded my contract and since then they have made it clear to me that I am not *entitled* to anything, so I feel powerless to kick back because they could take it all away from me. The employer uses a patronizing, grace-and-favour attitude so that pressure can be brought to bear.

(Victoria, academic)

After childbirth – the link between flexible working and demotion

For other women, the realization that mothers are held in low regard by employees and colleagues only began to dawn when they returned to their jobs. Until that point, mothers had assumed that they would be welcomed back, and imagined that those with whom they worked would make an effort to ease their re-entry to the work environment. What mothers found at the end of their maternity leave, however, was in complete contrast to this. As suggested by Beck and Beck-Gernsheim (1995), it would appear that mothers are neither regarded nor treated as equals within the workplace, and the level of discrimination experienced by mothers was extraordinary. Of the 20 women, all highly qualified, 18 experienced attitudes and practices which could be described as at best unhelpful and at worst openly discriminatory. This was particularly the case where mothers wished to change the way they managed their paid work – for example, if they wished to reduce their hours, even if only by a small amount. Some women were refused permission to make any changes to the work schedule they had followed before maternity leave. This accords with the literature on gender and the professions, which argues that working mothers suffer discrimination not only because of their gender but also because, if they wish to change working practices (by, for example, working part-time), they may also be changing accepted work patterns which have previously been beneficial to men (Pringle 1998). Sarah-Jane, the senior hospital doctor whose story I told in the Introduction, was forced, reluctantly, to accept a drop in status because it was argued that she could not maintain a consultant post unless she worked full-time. Thus, she was forced out of her position (which was given to a man working full-time) and formally demoted. This concurs with Pringle's (1998: 9) findings that, in the UK and Australia, 'lip-service' is paid to supporting women who wish to combine a medical career with motherhood because of a fear that allowing changes to working practices might threaten the male stranglehold on the senior areas of the medical profession. Thus, women who are not prepared to 'fit in' with the traditional career path of a male doctor must pay a heavy price – a downgrading of status from which they will never recover, even if they remain in work for another twenty-five years and even if, at some point, they wish to work full-time again. Sarah-Jane said:

> Someone who is very high up in [NHS] Human Resources said, 'We are absolutely crap at managing motherhood, absolutely awful'. And you know, that is something they are going to have to address. I mean they are miles behind, really. And when [my first baby] was born, that, for me, that was a huge thing because I knew that I would never work in that capacity [a hospital consultant] as a doctor again. Because to be a consultant in the Health Service you have to be able to commit yourself first to the service . . . I have worked 20 years to reach this level and I still have 20 years to work and I find it terrible, absolutely terrible that for this small break [working part-time] I am expected to sacrifice the rest of my career . . . I find that completely abhorrent.
>
> (Sarah-Jane, doctor)

In general, workplaces and colleagues were unreceptive to suggestions from mothers regarding new and innovative ways of working that might benefit all concerned. Several examples are given below, and these demonstrate the extent of the problem across a range of professions. Jane had been in her senior teaching job for seven years. She ran a large department and undertook evening and weekend work, and asked if she could do a job-share, or at least reduce her hours (even if this was only by one morning per week).

> The head teacher was very supportive initially and said she would advertise for a job-share. But months later, although I kept asking, she still had not got back to me. So I sort of had to be quite forceful and say 'What's going on?' and she said, well, to be honest she didn't want a part-timer or a job-share, it had to be full-time. So I made the decision to [seek alternative employment] very reluctantly and it's been a horrible decision because I love my job and the school and I thought I'd never leave. . . . I would have stayed if I could have even had just half a day off, 'cause I enjoyed the job so much. . . . I think job shares should be much more widely available. I really think you could end up with so much more benefit than having one person, there's so much potential there. I know some excellent people who could share my job and they would be getting two really good teachers for the price of one.
>
> (Jane, A-level teacher)

Jane was not prepared to back down on the issue of reduced working hours. She knew herself to be a good teacher and dealt with the situation by obtaining similar employment elsewhere, agreeing her new terms of work before accepting the post. In making this move, however, she was obliged to give up her status as head of department, and now finds herself working under someone less experienced and less effective than herself.

Suzanne, a lawyer who was refused permission to work part-time after the birth of her first child, was more successful in retaining her status. Like Jane, in the first instance she sought alternative employment. However, on gaining a job elsewhere, she used the threat of her resignation as a lever to persuade her firm to allow her to remain with them on her terms. Suzanne believes she was able to do this because she had concentrated on a specialist area of work which was important to her organization, meaning that she would have been very difficult to replace. Since then, Suzanne has progressed and (although she has had subsequent children and experienced similar problems) is now a very senior partner. However, she notes that this was the result of a long, hard fight on her part:

> When I went on maternity leave with [my second child] I took eight
> months' maternity leave and I had a battle then because I wanted to
> return to work part-time. And the person in charge was particularly
> obstructive and difficult. So during the negotiations I actually got a
> job [elsewhere] and the managing partner realized it would be bad
> news for the firm for me to leave because I had some unique
> knowledge. So I knew I was in a strong position really. So she basically
> forced [my head of department] into the deal which is still the deal I
> have now. And now I work part-time (80%) and I am pretty sure that
> I was the first part-time partner at any of this city's law firms. And
> eventually the chap who was head of department left but I was still
> there and they offered me an equity partnership.
>
> (Suzanne, lawyer)

Not surprisingly, although she has fought and won a series of battles, Suzanne
did not find this period in her life easy, having had to deal with the doubts of
others about her (very evident) competency at the same time as managing a
household and three very small children.

Lianne, a teacher, found herself the only person in her workplace to be
faced with redundancy on her return from maternity leave. However, rather
than fight a discrimination case, she sought and found appropriate alternative
employment:

> The previous head said that I was the 'weakest link' because I had
> asked for part-time. He said that meant I was not as committed as
> others in the department. And I could see that he saw this part-time
> thing as an easy way of easing me out. . . . And when you have just
> had a child – well, I had two small children – you just don't want that
> battle, do you? So even though I knew that the law was on my side,
> and I had been in touch with the union (and they had even sent the
> head a solicitor's letter), he was up for a fight and I just did not want
> that fight. So now I'm in a new job, and if I'm honest, I'm not as
> happy in the new job as I was in the old job. But just the same, I enjoy
> work and I feel like I'm giving something, I get a 'hit' from explaining
> to the children and I love it when they have understood something.
> And I took the new job on the basis of being part-time.
>
> (Lianne, A-level teacher)

Penelope, a social worker in a large department, had applied for and
obtained a new post in her field before she even became pregnant. An
ambitious and able woman who wanted to plan her career carefully, she chose
a job that was a 'step up' in career terms, but which was also more suited to the
needs of a breastfeeding mother than her previous work. Thus, she proposed

to combine professional progress with motherhood in a way that could be managed effectively, from both her own point of view and that of her employer. On her return from maternity leave, however, Penelope was dismayed to learn that her new post had been scrapped. Penelope had no alternative but to return to her previous job, which she had left due to its unsuitability in the first place:

> It was awful, just awful, because I had thought, 'Well I'm settled now, I've finally got a job where I can get on with the other side of my life, family', and then of course it was just sort of taken from me, it felt like completely beyond my control, it was just taken away from me. So then I had to go through it all again and reapply for jobs.
>
> (Penelope, social worker)

Some women who would have preferred to work fewer hours were forced to accept that this was not possible, either because their employers flatly refused to alter the terms and conditions of the respective jobs as they had existed before maternity leave, or because it was made plain to those requesting part-time work that if they chose this option, they would immediately be demoted. This is in keeping with the findings of Joshi *et al.* (1999) who demonstrated that motherhood has an immediate and detrimental effect on employment, especially where mothers return to work part-time. Eleanor related her own situation as follows:

> I've always worked full-time and that's an issue. I really resent that there hasn't been flexibility in my work to allow me to work part-time. Ideally I would have come back on, say, 75%, but it's not built into my level of position. I mean, I could go part-time if I took a drop in status, but I would have to resign from a position I don't want to leave, so really that isn't a choice. I was not allowed to continue to be the senior education manager on a part-time basis; the contract clearly lays down you have to be on site for a certain number of hours. But really, doing this job in a flexible way *wouldn't* be impossible, and there is no reason you couldn't have somebody sharing the responsibility [of senior manger] with someone else.
>
> (Eleanor, senior education manager)

Being downgraded 'through the back door'

In some cases, although discrimination was not quite as explicit as described above, employers nevertheless made it plain by their actions that mothers would be sidelined, especially if they worked part-time. Clear indications were given to some working mothers that promotion and prospects were privileges to which they would not be entitled, even if this was not stated in so many words. Jayne, an electronic engineer who chose to return to work part-time (80%), described this kind of downgrading as 'stealthy' because it occurred 'through the back door':

> I think working part-time mothers, you're not considered to be sort of the same as full-time staff. And I was shocked, I found I wasn't viewed in the same way, or given the same respect as when I was a childless full-time worker. I began to realize what was happening when they were doing the annual pay rounds – and I didn't get my pay review. Just nothing. And I mean, not to get *anything* when all of my peers at work did. That was awful. Because I was a lead engineer, and all the other lead engineers got something and I was the *only one* who didn't. So that's what introduced me to it. And you know I haven't had a personal development review since I started working part-time. And then I wasn't given the same responsibility in the big projects that, you know, all the other lead engineers were getting. Something new and exciting would come along and they'd get it, and I wouldn't get anything.
>
> (Jayne, electronic engineer)

A similar situation was experienced by Sophie, who was the only female partner in a large law firm. In Sophie's case, although she was not formally demoted, her colleagues offered her no support while she was bringing up her very young children, but pressured her instead, to the point where she gave up her partnership status and eventually moved to a different firm. Supposedly working part-time, and one of a group of seven partners, Sophie was allocated an impossible workload (greater than that undertaken by her full-time colleagues) which left her feeling increasingly frustrated and despondent:

> I'd come back [from work] steaming, you know, up on the ceiling. And administratively there was a *huge* amount of work pushed on to me, things would all be left to me to sort out. And then the other thing was that I was the only female partner . . . so I had all the staff problems, even though I was not supposed to be the staff partner. And I think [it didn't help that] I was blessed with male partners who probably did nothing at home, they were the sort of men whose wives did most of the stuff for them. And their wives didn't work . . . and I think these men tended to go home and their meal was on the table and so on. . . . And so [although I'd always thought] 'this is what you *do* as a professional, you become a *partner*', I gave up the partnership and went back as an employee. But then even when I gave *up* the partnership, they were *still* expecting me to do the things I had done

as a partner and I was so short of time. So now I am moving to another firm (as an employee) and I hope it will be . . . on the basis of what [I feel is appropriate] for an employee, rather than just having things dumped on me.

(Sophie, lawyer)

A paper tiger: 'Family-friendly' policies

It has been suggested (by Thair and Risdon 1999: 105) that professional women who return to work are likely to be working for 'public sector employers with "family-friendly" policies'. These and other writers (Dex *et al.* 1998) are assuming that public sector employers will offer support to working mothers. This did not prove to be the case in my research. Once mothers returned to work, it was notable that it was often the larger public sector 'institutions', such as universities and local government, that were most guilty of serious discrimination, for example, putting pressure on their staff to be available at all times, even when they were supposed to be in part-time employment. Mothers discovered that 'family-friendly' policies did not work in practice, and that they were continually obliged to 'fight their own corner' without support from their organizations. It was uniformly considered by those working for large institutions that these organizations would at best offer no support to career mothers, and at worst would expect more from women once they were mothers (and sometimes working part-time) than had been the case before. As argued by Freely (2000), there was constant pressure on mothers to 'prove' themselves as valuable employees. Although all the public sector organizations in question had 'family-friendly' policies in place, these were regarded by all female participants as nothing more than a 'paper exercise'. This is in keeping with the findings reported by Kvande and Rasmussen (1995) who, investigating opportunities for Norwegian managers, found bureaucratic institutions to be inflexible and static in their attitudes. It is notable in relation to Kvande and Rasmussen's arguments that, in this research, it was not perceived to be merely policy that was at fault, but attitudes towards working mothers. It has already been noted (in Chapter 6) that some women found friends and family disapproving of their decision to undertake paid work when children were small. Cockburn (2002: 186) argues that these opprobrious attitudes may spill over into the workplace, where individuals may resist 'family-friendly' policies due to a belief that mothers with small children should not be in the workplace at all: 'Underlying some of the resentment against maternity provision is a wide-spread view that mothers of young children morally ought to stay at home with them, should not attempt to "have their cake and eat it too".' Additionally, Cockburn has argued that often, even where family-friendly policies exist, they are resented because of the 'disturbance' that maternity rights cause in the workplace, meaning that those in charge are therefore unwilling to implement or to publicize them. Cockburn's views are consistent with the experiences described by Louise who, working for a county council at a senior level, cited several examples of organizational policy failing due to attitudes of colleagues who did not know about or disagreed with equal opportunities policies, possibly because, in Louise's view, they believed that mothers with very small children should remain in the home, providing the childcare themselves. Louise recalled an occasion when her baby was ill. Despite the fact that there were policies in place to cater for this eventuality, it was suggested to her that, if she needed to take time off work to care for her child, then she should not be in employment:

> We were entitled to one day to make arrangements for child sickness. This was never promoted in the organization. It was the policy, but it was not publicized, it was hidden. But I found out that it was policy, so I was then confident with where I stood, and I had a run-in with [an even more senior colleague] who said that taking the permitted day really was not acceptable under any circumstances. She said that if I wanted to be part of the working community then I had to 'get my childcare arrangements sorted'. That is another example of the organization having a policy but not being serious about it.
>
> (Louise, public sector manager)

The experiences of Louise and others indicate that (as Louise surmises) organizations which claim to have put 'family-friendly' policies in place may be paying lip-service to the idea, and might have no real intention of implementing or promoting the policies (and therefore are unlikely to discipline managers who refuse to apply them). This is in accordance with Finn's (1998) argument that employers are reluctant to back up paper policies with investment. However, the experiences of women like Louise might come as a shock to those policy makers who *believe* that they have put family-friendly policies into place, when in fact these are not working in practice. In support of her argument that 'family-friendly' principles are ineffective in practice, Louise went on to point out the fact that no attempt was made by her own employer (or any other in her experience) to address the practicalities of returning to work following childbirth. Louise cited as a key example the fact that although her (very large) employers professed to encourage women to return to work following maternity leave, they had no facilities for breast-feeding mothers, and nowhere for breast milk to be expressed or refrigerated. Significantly, Louise was one of ten mothers who were still breastfeeding on their return to work, and, notably, not one employer had made even the slightest attempt to accommodate this. Louise had been seriously ill when her baby was born, and unable to care for her until she was 2 months old, so her ability to breastfeed meant a great deal to her and she was determined to keep it up. Louise dealt with this problem by 'training' her body to adapt to the situation, arranging for her child to be bottle-fed on formula during the day, and breastfeeding at night.

> Initially I found it hard going back to work because I was still breastfeeding, in fact I continued to breastfeed every night for two years . . . It was hard at the beginning because I had been so ill and she was put on a bottle so when eventually I started breastfeeding I thought, 'Oh! I can do this!' So [I really did not want to give that up] so every night, even though I was working and therefore could not express, I breastfed [my daughter] and that was how she went to sleep.
>
> (Louise, public sector manager)

Penelope, who also worked for a large public sector employer, which might have been expected to put facilities in place, experienced a similar problem:

> I was coming home to feed him because he wouldn't take the bottle you see, he struggled with the feeder cup and so it was very hard and obviously worrying that he wasn't getting fed . . . it's your worst nightmare and I was filling up and I would have had to have expressed milk and there was nowhere, just *nowhere*, in my workplace to do that.
>
> (Penelope, social worker)

Victoria, the academic from a large research-based university, who has a doctorate, summed up the situation in relation to equal opportunities and 'family-friendly' policies as follows:

> There is an expectation that part-time mothers have 'spare' time which is available to the employer. You are sometimes expected to give extra for no pay. Oh, I know that the organization is *supposed* to have all these policies, but when it comes down to it they won't take *any* responsibility. It's up to you to fight your own corner. Their attitude is: 'if you want part-time then you have to manage the consequences of that'; that's it – *you* manage it.
>
> (Victoria, academic)

Although several mothers in the sample reported depression following childbirth, there were only two instances where mothers working for traditional employers reported receiving any practical support either from colleagues or their organization. In one of these instances, the interviewee (social worker Penelope, who needed to go home to feed her baby) made it clear that the organization should not receive credit for this help; it was due entirely to the assistance she received from one particular manager (a father with pre-school children). It has already been explained how, on her return to work, Penelope's employers were unhelpful in the extreme. However, her line manager made her situation 'bearable' by 'bending the rules' for her:

> He was very sympathetic, he just said 'Just do what you have to do, don't worry about it', 'cause he'd got a young family himself, his wife worked in the team and they'd got children under 5 so they knew what it was like. And sometimes he would even drop me off in his car and do some paperwork while he was waiting. But I was very fortunate to have that person who was understanding.
>
> (Penelope, social worker)

Only one mother working for a bureaucratic organization (a UK hospital) found her employers open to an innovative (temporary) solution to her need to work part-time. This was by persuading her employers to allow her to job-share with a colleague, a situation which worked well in practice, but which the job-sharers had had to organize and establish themselves:

> The difficulty is finding somebody who is at the [same] stage as you to do the job share, that's the difficulty. They will allow it if *you* put the work in. But it just depends if you can find somebody.
>
> (Elisabeth, doctor)

The unhelpful attitudes and discrimination experienced by mothers raise questions about the fairness of a society where women are often expected still to 'hand over control' of their bodies to the medical 'system' from the moment their pregnancy is confirmed (Miles 1992; Oakley 1984), but are offered little 'hands-on' support of any kind from the state after the child is born. This not only applies to basic rights to retain job and salary status on returning to work, but also is combined with additional issues such as flexibility for breastfeeding mothers and an appropriate space for expressing milk, a basic need for many mothers with small children which even large employers have apparently failed to recognize. Considering the level of poor health experienced by mothers in this research (discussed in Chapter 6), which is in keeping with research findings established over 20 years ago (Graham and McKee 1980), it does seem significant that nobody in any official capacity bothered to enquire how the mothers were managing or how they were feeling, let alone offer help on their return to work. Not one mother reported a visit from a health visitor, occupational health staff, personnel or any other similar body.

The 'arduous battle': Who wants to go to court?

From what was reported by the women in this research, it could be surmised that the organizations they worked for believed themselves to be above the law with regard to equal opportunities. It is also interesting that, although some research participants were aware they had suffered discrimination, none was willing to go to court over this, preferring (as in the case of teachers Jane and Lianne) to seek employment elsewhere rather than fight a legal battle. This may have been partly because they are well qualified, with easily transferable skills. It may also, however, highlight a deficiency in maternity rights legislation, which has been described as 'hazy' (Winston 1998) and is poorly promoted, meaning that employers' understanding of it is also conveniently 'hazy' (Malthouse 1998: 2). In addition, as noted in Chapter 5, equal opportunities laws in the UK still require individuals to make personal claims against employers, and this is a long, complicated process with no guarantee of success. Ironically, where the claims of individual women do succeed, individuals are likely to find themselves with monetary compensation but no job and, if the case is reported in the newspapers, limited prospects of future employment (Buckingham 2002: 3). Even if some mothers *were* prepared to face the prospect of a court battle, and managed to see it through without unwelcome publicity, in professions where the number of senior women is small (such as medicine or architecture) word would 'get around' and the knowledge that she was prepared to mount a legal challenge would probably render the woman unemployable in her field. The incentives for new mothers to fight discrimination are, therefore, limited as the winning of an anti-discrimination case would almost certainly be a pyrrhic victory, as noted by Gatrell and Turnbull (2003). Thus, in this sample, those who suffered discrimination decided that trying to fight their situation in court was not worth the heartache, and were obliged either (in some cases very reluctantly) to seek alternative employment or to put up with things as they were. As Penelope explained:

> I was actually put back into a job that didn't fit my job description at all, it was horrendous. And I looked at various ways I could try and change the situation. The best way really, apart from having the long, arduous battle with my employers, was to get another job.
>
> (Penelope, social worker)

Angela, who has a PhD and works in a traditional academic institution, seemed resigned to her situation, accepting it as the 'lot' of working mothers, and therefore not worth fighting. Angela described her situation as follows:

> And at the interview for this particular role, they offered me a permanent post and they put that in writing, but when the contract arrived through the post it was only temporary. And the attitude was, 'well yes, we know that is not what we agreed but we can't offer you a permanent post after all, so do you want this job or not?'. And at the time my baby was 6 months old and ill, and I suppose they just knew I wouldn't fight it. And I regret it bitterly now that I did not, but at the time I just wasn't up to it. *And* the woman who started on the same day as me . . . but works full-time, well she has been given a permanent post, whereas I am still struggling to manage a full-time workload on part-time pay, knowing all the while that the end of my contract hangs over me. And that means another battle I'll have to fight. And I do my research in my own time, paying for childcare so in effect I am subsidizing the university. Because as far as the university is concerned, they've put me where they think I belong – on the 'mummy track'.
>
> (Angela, academic)

In addition to the fact that 'protective' legislation was ignored by many employers, it was noted by some research participants that existing maternity laws and rights, such as they are, do not apply in certain circumstances. Thus, those working as partners in 'professional' businesses (such as lawyers and GPs) could not claim maternity 'rights' because they were employers, not employees – therefore they were obliged to negotiate with partners, which in some cases proved impossible. Other traditional institutions proved to be literally 'above the law'. One mother, working for the Crown in a legal capacity, explained:

> We are Crown servants so the employment legislation can't be enforced because of Crown immunity. And that's a real irony, isn't it – that the Crown is above the law.
>
> (Pandora, lawyer)

Support for mothers returning to work, and innovative practices

In the light of the experiences of those women working for 'traditional' or public sector employers, it is interesting to note that in some cases, where mothers were themselves employers, they had introduced new and innovative practices to the workplace to help other career mothers. These were found to be effective from the point of view of both the employer and the individual. Suzanne and some of her female partners, who ran a big law firm in a major city, had extended the number of weeks of paid maternity leave they offered to female staff at all levels from 18 to 26 weeks (before this step became mandatory, and before most other employers had introduced it). Not surprisingly, they found that those who had taken advantage of this were more relaxed and better able to readjust to the workplace than those who had previously returned after 18 weeks. Early signs showed that staff retention levels were also improving, an indication that the investment had paid off. Amanda, the mother who runs her own architectural practice, has revolutionized working practices in her firm. She employs mainly part-time female workers, whom she believes to be highly productive, and allows them to choose their own hours. All the women (who have worked closely as a team for years) are mothers and their work is organized around the needs of their own and one another's children. Nobody needs to be embarrassed about taking a day off because their child is ill, and at 'peak' times, such as school holidays, Amanda funds additional childcare costs. She is considering establishing a small workplace nursery so that people can bring their children to the office (even though she has less than 20 employees). With their agreement, instead of being paid a regular monthly salary, workers are paid an enhanced hourly rate for the work they do. As the employer, Amanda finds this an excellent arrangement and considers her colleagues to be loyal, hard-working and committed. Amanda's business is successful and clients and contracts are long-term – jobs often take up to three years. This small example raises a serious challenge to traditional institutions such as the medical profession, which has long argued that part-time or flexible working is not possible because it interferes with continuity of care (Pringle 1998).

'New' organizations and innovative practice

Significantly, in the case of a major television news network, where many of the journalists, producers and other staff had young children, it was notable that attitudes towards working mothers were more imaginative and more flexible than in more bureaucratic institutions (which had policies in place but failed to implement them). This is despite the fact that television news jobs are high-pressure, with tight deadlines. This finding concurs with those of Kvande and Rasmussen (1995), who observed that new industries in Norway, though demanding in some ways, could be more flexible and imaginative in their approach to working parents than 'traditional' organizations. One mother, Diana, who is a senior political producer at the news network, was offered the opportunity to return to work part-time without having to ask for it. She mentioned that this option was also on offer to male employees, and noted that one of her colleagues had taken it up because he wished to spend more time with his children. In the event, Diana elected to go back to work full-time. Part of the reason for her decision may have been the helpful attitude of her employer:

> [The television station] has been good about [family policies]. . . . There are an awful lot of family people here, men and women. So perhaps you would be thought more odd if you didn't have children or something. I mean it's accepted that if people have children then they have commitments and people will often leave because there is a school play on or something, people work round them . . . it's considered grown up to worry about the children.
>
> (Diana, television news producer)

Diana decided to give up breastfeeding on her return to work, as noted in Chapter 8. Although, unfortunately, this decision was partly due to the fact that there was no suitable space at work in which to express milk (as in the council offices described earlier), Diana nevertheless found employers and colleagues to be very supportive during the period while her baby daughter struggled to adjust to formula feeding and nursery:

> Other women at work who'd had children were lovely to me and I got so much support from the other women that had children. And [the employer] let me phone the nursery every hour saying 'has she drunk anything? Is she alright?' And I was allowed to be a worried mum by everybody. And finally it did work, it worked out, it was OK. And since then, I've been fine, no more depression, I'm very fit, but that was partly due to the support I got, you know, from [the employer] and the team at the time.
>
> (Diana, television news producer)

Although she had chosen not to take the option, Diana felt that going part-time would not have damaged her career prospects. Diana's experience is in contrast to the findings of Kvande and Rasmussen (1995), who worried that opportunities for women in new and non-traditional companies might be linked to spending longer hours at work:

> I think if you're good, you're good, so you can put restrictions on what you're prepared to do and they will go with that, they will work around you.
>
> (Diana, television news producer)

Being assertive

Where employers were not disposed to be helpful, those mothers who were most successful in achieving change were the ones who were most assertive, confident in their ability to do a good job and prepared to change jobs if existing employers were unhelpful. With the exception of Diana, the television news producer, all other women, to a greater or lesser degree, felt that the only way they could achieve a flexible work situation was to fight for it. Sophie described the situation thus:

> I think the only way there can be any benefits given to women is by *women* changing and becoming more assertive, which we don't like to do, but why should we kow-tow to them? I have had success with this with my new firm simply because you meet it head on . . . You've got to say, 'I am here, I have a child, my child is not going to come to the office and I don't expect you to give him a crèche, I have set up my childcare, *but* . . . There *are* going to be times when I do have to go. Is that OK?' And if the answer is 'No' then I think you have to [think] very carefully.
>
> (Sophie, lawyer)

However, although the need to be assertive was recognized by all the mothers who were employed (as opposed to those who were partners in their own businesses), it was also acknowledged by five mothers that this was not always easy. For example:

> It's as if I have to do something to appease. 'You should be grateful' is their attitude, and it's always me who has to compromise. After a while you begin to accept that as the way it is and you see yourself as this downtrodden person – it's OK to be so burnt out and I can't expect any better, because I'm a mother. There is a real pressure to fit a full-time workload into 2.5 days. I think I have become less assertive since I had children but I am aware that there is a need for mothers to be more assertive and manage the boundaries.
>
> (Victoria, academic)

Six women who had forged their way ahead in spite of attempts to demote them or 'ease them out' of their jobs, found that developing specialist skills in an area of value to clients or employers was a useful way of retaining job status and providing leverage for negotiation. Amanda explained:

> I think you have to target work, go for a particular market, which is what I've managed to do. And now people recognize me as a specialist

in the area [of historic buildings]. And you become more noticeable as a woman in a male profession if you specialize – people remember you better, and for women in the business (which is very much the 'old boys' club') the specialism, for me, has led to a springboard, its been an enormous springboard because there isn't anyone else who does quite what I do. So I did a master's thesis in it, and people still borrow it sometimes and the lecturer, she says 'you should try and publish from this'. People know that if they need that kind of work doing, there aren't many others with as much experience as me.

(Amanda, architect)

Gendered approaches to returning mothers – and fathers!

For all but two mothers, working practices were explicitly gendered and women found themselves disadvantaged in the workplace from the minute they returned after maternity leave (particularly if they wanted to work less than full-time). This is consistent with Cockburn's (2002) argument that organizations resent mothers in the workplace and actively resist implementing equal opportunities policies. It would be easy to assume, therefore, that workplace discrimination is gendered and applies only to mothers. My research would certainly appear to support the hypothesis that mothers experience discrimination, and that this is exacerbated if they wish to work part-time. However, fathers who chose to work part-time, or who attempted to change their work patterns to accommodate childcare responsibilities, also experienced unhelpful and discriminatory attitudes from employers and colleagues. Men who wished to downshift their career in order to care for their own children were accused by others of being 'weak' or 'odd', concurring with Durham's (2002) views that fathers who undertake childcaring duties more commonly associated with women are 'invisible' in the eyes of society. In contrast to prior expectations, it transpired that, for nine fathers who wished to include childcare commitments as part of their daily routine, no concessions at all were made at work. This was apparently due to a presumption that, after fatherhood, everything should continue as before and that support or flexibility would not and should not be needed by anyone.

As noted in the previous chapter, it is almost 50 years since Parsons, writing in the USA but highly influential in British politics and sociology (Robertson and Turner 1991), described the institutionalized roles of mothers as carers and fathers as economic providers. Nevertheless, despite significant changes in the demographic pattern from the days when mothers who could afford it stayed at home and fathers went out to work, the attitude of some employers remains firmly embedded in the past. The behaviour towards both working mothers *and* fathers who wished to combine work with childcare responsibilities suggests a belief on the part of employers (especially in the 'traditional' professions) that the best way of dealing with unpalatable changes is to ignore them. Thus, although working parents and some sociologists have acknowledged the need for the labour market to take account of more fluid and diverse family practices (Morgan 1996; Smart and Neale 1999), some employers prefer to cling to the Parsonian notion of the 'institutionalized' family which constitutes a male economic provider and a female 'domestic goddess'. It has been argued in Chapter 4 that recent changes in the law, which apply to fathers *post*-divorce, and which emphasize their financial responsibilities (Collier 2001), only serve to validate this approach. In my research, employers managed to ignore changing social structures by, where possible, disregarding equal opportunities legislation and making it difficult for women to maintain their careers while children were very small, knowing full well that in some cases (like Sarah-Jane's) this may damage career progression in perpetuity.

Where fathers are concerned, as we will see below, it was made clear that 'family-friendly' policies (which are often supposed to be in place for men as well as women, both in the UK and the USA) did not apply at all and, as a result, men were offered virtually no help at all. Charles, a scientist working in a large institution, described things from his perspective:

> For men it is acceptable in the first month after having a child to come in looking bleary-eyed, but if that was to go on for longer than this, which of course it does, then there would be big problems. After those first few weeks that man is expected to carry on 'as normal' . . . 'it's your choice to have a child, you didn't have to have one, so don't let it interfere with your work!' And its bad enough for mothers who ask for flexibility in their work, they will sense a whiff of disapproval, but for a *man* to do this – well, that is completely beyond the pale.
>
> (Charles, scientist)

Jack, a GP, was refused support from his partners when he needed to take time off to care for a very sick child. He subsequently changed his job because of this and recalled:

> My previous partners' attitudes were appalling. My little daughter was taken seriously ill that night and [my wife] spent the night with her in hospital. But [my wife] had to go to court next day and if she *hadn't* gone to court she would have been held in contempt of court. So unfortunately my job had to forfeit and I didn't go in. And my partners at that stage were quite appalled that that was my attitude. They were all clubbed together in like a kind of 'non-egalitarian' protest . . . they could not or would not understand, because they felt the woman

should have had to give up her job or her hours to look after the sick child.

(Jack, GP)

Three men had been obliged to change their jobs in order to give themselves the opportunity to work part-time. In Jack's case, his partners in the GP practice had made it clear that part-time work was 'not an option for a man'. In the second case, the father had left a research-based university to teach part-time at a local college, and in the third case, Tony, a computer programmer, had left a firm of inflexible financial consultants to undertake a lesser-paid job which allowed greater flexibility and shorter hours:

> I changed my job and things are much better ... my previous job caused terrible stress. I suddenly thought: 'I can't be accepting things this way ...' In the previous job, I had to leave because of the stress and suffering years of anger because I missed out on [my son's baby-hood]. I mean, they knew I had a child and I was studying, and just occasionally [I felt] my boss could have said things like: 'Well, it's time for you to go home ... but she assumed because I was the man that [my life] wouldn't change.
>
> (Tony, computer programmer)

Peter, a social worker, managed to negotiate part-time hours within his existing paid work, but felt that there were tensions because his employers could not handle the concept of fathers (as opposed to mothers) reducing their hours of paid work to accommodate childcare:

> [Part-time] becomes an issue for a man because it's not as acceptable for a man to be taking that time off work as it is for a woman. And although in the work setting they like to sort of promote equality, *underneath* that you get a very strong feeling that you've not got a right to go part-time, it's down to your partner to actually do that. That was not actually verbalized to me because they know that I have got an understanding as to my rights. So consequently it was a very silent 'no' but without a doubt it was there, and it's up to you whether you choose to ignore that, as I did, or do what's expected of you.
>
> (Peter, social worker)

Men who appeared to manage the situation most effectively were those who, like Peter, were assertive and determined about what they were going to do, regardless of what colleagues thought of them. It helped if, like Sam and Nick (lawyers) and Jeremy (an academic), they were sufficiently senior to be able to organize their own schedules and were firm about sticking to these:

The fortunate thing is, I am partner now, so I am an employer. So I don't have to tell or ask anyone what I intend to do, I just do it.

(Sam, lawyer)

I work very, very long hours, often late into the night, but I am also lucky to have the kind of full-time job where I can pretty much choose how and when I do things. So I can collect children and do all that, then begin work again at eight or nine in the evening.

(Jeremy, academic)

Summary

In this chapter I have explained how mothers experienced explicit discrimination and received little or no support from their workplace. Fathers who attempted to change working practices fared even worse. This must have put additional strain on working mothers, because if inflexibility on the part of employers limited the freedom that fathers had to arrange their hours around childcare, mothers would inevitably be left with an even greater share of the responsibility. In both this chapter and the previous one I argued that the 'institution of motherhood' and the traditional view of fathers as 'economic providers' still exert a powerful influence on parents. This is because this was what they believed others (employers, friends and relatives) expected of them, meaning that they had to 'fight their corner' if they wanted to live their lives differently. Attitudes regarding what couples *ought to be* doing were in conflict with what couples were *actually* doing, which meant career mothers putting paid work at the forefront of some of their daily activities but still wishing to spend time with their children, and some fathers choosing to combine paid work with childcare. Both mothers and fathers were explicit about the difficulties they faced as they struggled to reconcile their various roles, given what was also expected of them by others in their circle.

10 '*My* children must become *our* children'

I think there needs to be a cultural change that actually recognizes that if people don't have children we don't have a future . . . it's about valuing the creation of a new generation.

(Estelle, psychotherapist)

Focus on:
Practical help
Challenging 'Parsonian' attitudes
Changing social attitudes to family practices
Conclusions

Introduction

In each interview, the last question I put to mothers and fathers was: 'What practical steps do you think could be taken by society to improve things for career couples?' In this final chapter, recommendations are made for changes to family policy – but not only by me. In keeping with earlier chapters, the answers to the above question are presented in research partici-pants' own words, allowing them as far as possible to take a direct role in the dialogue. Although some practical changes were called for (such as tax relief on childcare), a change in social attitudes was seen as the key to improving things for families where mothers work.

Practical help

As noted in earlier chapters, there was a clear view that parents did not wish to go to the extreme of abrogating responsibility for their children, as advocated by Firestone (1970) and Valeska (1984), because both fathers and mothers gave a high priority to the parent–child relationship. I have already observed that mothers valued their maternity in the manner described by O'Brien (1981), and most fathers welcomed the chance to mediate their own relationships with children in accordance with descriptions by Dienhart (1998) and Durham (2002). I have also noted that, in some situations where fathers were principal carers, the mothers concerned found it difficult when this threatened their status as parent of first contact (Maushart 2002: 138–9). Despite their commitment to their children, however, all parents took the view espoused by both Firestone and Valeska that parents bringing up children should be offered greater support by the rest of society. Many were explicit that those who had children were benefiting others because they were providing the next generation, and they criticized the 'child-free' lobby (e.g. Boase 2001) for wishing to deny financial and other benefits to parents, because of antagonistic attitudes to working mothers:

> I think it should be taken on board as a society responsibility to raise children rather than just parents' responsibility. Sure, those parents have decided to have children but the people who aren't having children are depending on those people as well, I don't think they have realized that.
>
> (Andy, hospital pharmacist)

> I think this backlash is just horrendous, you know, the child-free lobby, the fact that ... people who choose not to have children think they are carrying people who have children. And I think, in my experience of working whilst having children or having employees who have children, mothers overcompensate for having children by working differently, more efficiently, using their resources far better, their time management's better, their whole approach is different. And that is what people who don't have children can never understand because they've got all the time in the world.
>
> (Amanda, architect)

> You look at your children growing up, and if they are well adapted and happy, that's a massive achievement. I look at them and feel that myself, but you don't know if anyone else in society feels that. I've only done it for three years but to get [my son] to where he is, is no

mean feat – we've been through an awful lot to get there. So I think if anyone has children they know what that's like. But for these young singletons, they don't know what that's like. I saw something on a documentary and it interviewed some single girls. And they were really having a go at working women with children, saying they're not committed and they shouldn't get promoted – and they were really, *really* horrible. And I don't know who they thought were going to be their GPs and things when they were infirm in later life in a wheelchair in a nursing home. And if these women don't have any children there will be no one to provide for pensions, or look after them when they are older.

(Lucy, hospital pharmacist)

All participants held strong views on the practical steps which could be taken by society to improve matters for career mothers and their families, though there was a concern that increased benefits for parents of young children should be a 'free good', not a trade-off. In other words, help for career mothers and fathers should not reduce the amount of assistance available for single mothers or families in deprived areas. The most commonly cited request was for tax relief on childcare (or subsidized nursery places from babyhood). Crèches as a regular feature in the workplace were also mentioned, as this was an advantage from which only two couples in the sample benefited. Those without a workplace nursery were often involved in long and arduous journeys (in one case 40 minutes' drive in the wrong direction) to get their children to day-care before even beginning the journey to work, due to the paucity of provision in their area. Twelve research participants expressed a wish for longer maternity and paternity leave. The general consensus seemed to be that this should be paid for up to one year. Three interviewees argued that parents should have the option to share this, for example, by taking six months each away from the workplace. As noted in Chapter 8, four women, each of whom had two or more children under school age, would have liked the option of a longer career break (unpaid, for between one and four years after the paid maternity leave) with no loss of status:

The freedom not to work when your children were very small with the guarantee that your job was there at the end . . . I think ideally that what I would like is for someone to say to me 'Right, for the next five years you can come back and pick up where you let off. And then that's your job for the next 20 years. But that doesn't exist'. And I do think actually, I have worked 20 years . . . and I still have 25 years left to work! And if I have five years off now, I will never work again, for the rest of those years. And I find that terrible, absolutely *terrible,* that for this small break I am punished, I am expected to sacrifice the rest of my career.

(Sarah-Jane, hospital doctor)

A desire was expressed by 17 women and 10 men for formal strategies to be put in place to facilitate a smooth and gradual return to the workplace for both men and women after maternity leave. This was linked to flexibility in terms of part-time work, job-sharing and non-standard working hours.

There should be flexibility of hours so that the day does not have to start at eight or nine and you could perhaps go in in the evenings, to sort of work in the evening. I mean, I could do lab work in the evening and in fact probably get a lot done because there wouldn't be a lot of the day-to-day interruptions going on.

(Elisabeth, doctor)

It has already been observed that not only did parents have to negotiate post-childbirth working arrangements on their own, but also mothers and fathers received little support on their return to employment. Fourteen women and four men suggested that proactive support from the workplace and 'official' agencies such as local health and social care services to help ease the transition back to work would have been helpful. Some interviewees regarded the lack of this as a fact of life, and appeared resigned to it. Others, however, regarded it as a glaring omission and felt angry that no one had bothered to talk to them about their situation. Participants considered that employers should ensure that existing policies were well publicized, and accessible to all in practice, not just on paper. As Eleanor and others explain:

On a personal level it's a very simple, practical thing: nobody took the time to talk to me about what I wanted to do when I came back to work. I mean, I knew my rights in terms of maternity leave and unpaid leave (I had up to 40 weeks) . . . so I had already made a decision to come back, but had somebody, for example in personnel, said 'Let's have a chat about this, let's have a look at the terms and conditions on which you want to come back, can we make it any easier for you?', that would have made a tremendous difference for me. And actually as far as [the employer] is concerned it wouldn't have made an awful lot of difference had they said, for example, 'Why don't you look at more flexible hours, why don't we have a look at you starting at 9 a.m. and finishing at such a time?'. But because it wasn't ever broached, I felt very uncomfortable raising it with my line manager on my own. I felt there was a tremendous responsibility on me to come back full-time and give the impression that I was this sort of super-mum. And it never occurred to them it might be a problem, they assumed I'd had a baby and I'd come back full-time and I'd just have to cope.

(Eleanor, Senior education manager)

For men you have to cover up the difficulties you might be having at home because you've got a new child, that is what is expected of men. And it's an attitudinal thing, but . . . just the fact that fathers could be *invited* to sit down with [personnel] and their boss and work out a strategy for a year or two, a time frame, how I'm going to *manage* these things – a shared responsibility and some commitment from the workplace that they would actually take that into account, that you've had a baby. But look, I could never see that happening. But it would be nice, it would make a difference.

(Charles, academic)

I think that employers should actually ask women, I think there should be somewhere for me to say where I had problems, maybe within occupational therapy. And also care and quality of care [for children], information on what's available – and it's not a question of me saying well, I expect someone to lay it out on a plate, I'm quite a good resource investigator, so I can find out the agencies who provide this information, but the information available is not really helpful, not really what I want. There is talk about equal opportunities but as a mother I don't see any results on the table.

(Louise, public sector manager)

Challenging 'Parsonian' attitudes

In accordance with the opinion of Silva and Smart (1999: 2–3), parents considered the views of government, media and society regarding family practices to be hopelessly outdated. Thus, although mothers and fathers sought practical changes to improve things for working parents, they also felt that these would be difficult to implement and access without changes in attitude. Some parents cited 'attitudes' as more important than 'practical steps' because they feared that cultural shifts were harder to achieve than pragmatic ones. As Lianne put it:

It's a society thing, not a work thing, and how do you change that?

(Lianne, teacher)

Significantly, almost 50 years ago, Parsons and Bales (1956) argued that social roles were 'learned' and that those playing them were influenced by what they believed to be expected of them by society. In more recent times, as noted in Chapter 2, Parsons has been criticized for focusing on the significance of 'social institutions' at the expense of individual agency (e.g. by Robertson and Turner 1991; Giddens 1984). His sociological beliefs have also been described by some writers (such as Porter 1998) as less relevant now than when they were written because of changes in society, such as equal opportunities legislation. In relation to the experiences of the mothers and fathers who took part in this research, however, it would appear (even if the laws have changed), that attitudes described by Parsons have undergone remarkably little adjustment since the 1950s. It would still appear, at the beginning of the twenty-first century, that fathers are '*expected* to be a good provider, to be able to secure for the couple a "good position in the community" ' (Parsons and Bales 1956: 173; emphasis in original), while mothers shop, care for children and 'make the home harmonious' (Parsons and Bales 1956: 163). As this book has established, the demographic pattern has changed significantly since the 1950s when Parsons was writing and when mothers, if this could be afforded, were at home while fathers went out to work. However, the attitude of some employers and agencies towards the parents in this research suggests that, even though this is now no longer the case, there remains a belief that this is how it 'ought' to be. This is perhaps because, instead of recognizing that family practices are now more fluid and diverse than when Parsons wrote in the 1950s, opinion formers are still clinging desperately to the Parsonian notion of an 'institutionalized' family which constitutes a male economic provider and an 'angel in the house'. As recently as July 2002, *The Sunday Times* (Dobson and Chittenden 2002) reported on a study which claimed to prove that 'Working mothers' children lag behind in tests', in which the authors constructed stay-at-home mothers as virtuous and successful, while working mothers were seen to be failing their children. The authors provided a 'glowing' example of a mother who had given up her job on childbirth, and, while they urged working mothers 'not to panic', argued that 'nothing fully compensates for a mother's absence' (Dobson and Chittenden 2002). It is interesting that the writers do not make the link between working fathers and failing children, presumably because men are expected to focus on their role as economic provider – just as Parsons and Bales described in 1956.

Research participants accused organizations and the professions of failing to appreciate that (for them at least) the 1950s model of a family with a female full-time mother and a male provider no longer existed. Four participants referred to a BBC *Panorama* programme screened in the UK in 2000 which examined the situation of career couples and took a disparaging approach to the working mothers:

I think people so often kick back into the idea of [child-rearing] being the mother's job. Because that's where I think there's this vacuum about how do you create a cultural shift that creates a very positive paternal model in a way that opens up egalitarianism. And I'm at a bit of a loss . . . There is something about the way we value autonomy but assume autonomy as a male prerogative.

(David, psychiatrist)

You should be given every support in your choice, you shouldn't feel in any way disadvantaged because you've chosen to be a full-time mother or a working mother, or a full-time father for that matter. Men who are doing that are not respected. I know [someone] who picks his children up from school with all the other mothers and they think there must be something wrong with the family if the father comes to always drop the kids off and pick them up from school. And he feels slightly ostracized and they think, 'Oh, he's not working, maybe he can't get a job'.

(James, electronic engineer)

I think the main help from society as a whole really is the change in the thought process about what is the man's role and what is the woman's role, that seems to me to be the most significant thing.

(Peter, social worker)

I think society has to recognize that men have children too and it's still all the emphasis on women. There was this *Panorama* programme that was on fairly recently and it was a terrible missed opportunity to look at the situation of men. The whole emphasis was on women and how these 'bad' mothers were managing their careers and children. But men have children, too. I think what the shame is, there isn't anything written or policy for men and there needs to be. I mean, I've interviewed four men in the last couple of weeks for teaching jobs and every single one of them – and this has *astounded* me – had given up a full-time job to go into part-time work. And all of them said quite unashamedly, 'I've got young children and I just didn't see them, I was working away all the time' or 'I was so busy and I miss them'. A deputy head was one and the other was just working all over the country. So they have all given up well-paid, high-powered jobs to spend more time with their family.

(Eleanor, senior education manager)

In relation to this, mothers (and fathers) noted that there were two areas in which they could improve their own situation in relation to work. The first of these was in developing assertiveness and being firm about work–life boundaries. The second was in developing expertise or specialist skills in a 'niche' area, which was useful in safeguarding one's position and providing levers for negotiation. Nine women found their 'specialist' skills helpful, either in agreeing better working conditions within their existing employment, or in enabling them to move to a new post on their own terms. (These mothers observed that the job market was favourable to highly qualified women, meaning that their skills were highly transferable, should employers operate discriminatory practices.)

Changing social attitudes to family practices

As I noted in the Introduction, Giddens has written of his belief that social structure and human agency are interdependent, that social rules are developed as a result of human activity and that consequently 'the most rigid of social institutions' can be changed by the actions we take in our day-to-day lives: 'all routines, all the time are contingent and potentially fragile accomplishments' (Giddens 1993: 6). As Giddens points out, 'To speak of an individual is to speak not just of a "subject" but also of an agent' (Giddens, 1993: 5). Giddens has also noted that human beings are conscious of the social norms and routines which constrain them and, as active agents, may try to resist these. In the context of Giddens's assertions, one of the most important themes to arise from my research was a belief among participants that they *were* challenging the 'social rules' with which they grew up (Giddens 1979: 66). Parents saw themselves as acutely aware of the social structures which oppressed them and were anxious to achieve change. As I have already established, parents regarded children as central to their lives and, in all but one case, wished to invest time in their day-to-day upbringing. This led to an explicit desire to challenge the institutionalized roles of mother–childcarer and father–provider, and most parents were prepared to defy the social expectations of others in order to follow a new course of action. Mothers actively resisted the pressure to relinquish their jobs by rejecting the institution of motherhood (even if this made them feel guilty) and acknowledging the powerful work orientation they still felt after giving birth. They asserted their rights to love and nurture their children without sacrificing careers they had spent many years building up. At the same time, most fathers regarded their partners' decision to combine mothering with career as an opportunity for greater involvement with their children. As observed in Chapter 7, some fathers also saw this as a chance to shake off the constraints of the provider–father role, and five challenged the institution of fatherhood in the most literal sense by choosing to reduce or give up their paid work altogether. This is in contrast to social expectations which, as recently as 1999, were seen to demonstrate the 'belief that material provision is intrinsic to fathering and shows the centrality of the provider role for fathers' (Warin *et al.* 1999: 9).

The work of Giddens helps in understanding the behaviour of this group of research participants in the context of the wider social setting. Although, at a micro level, parents were operating as individuals within a household, negotiating roles and relationships with one another and their children, they were also consciously challenging perceived existing paradigms by choosing, as far as possible, to alter the 'regulative (sanctioning)' aspects of social rules through their own day-to-day behaviour (Giddens 1979: 66). It is worth pointing out, however, that change was much easier to achieve if *both* partners had an interest in challenging the traditional way of doing things. For example, the strong work orientation among the women, combined with the desire to increase childcare involvement on the part of fathers, meant that couples were jointly prepared to step outside convention, even if this meant social embarrassment (such as being asked to leave Mothercare, as described in Chapter 7). Where it was not seen to be in the interest of both partners, however (i.e. in the division of domestic labour), social change was slower. Even the angriest mothers in the sample were obliged to deal with housework by either resigning themselves to doing it or (if they could afford it) paying someone else to do it. It seems significant to note, at this point, that none of those interviewed reported actively 'campaigning' for what they believed – for example, nobody mentioned being part of a specific action group for parental rights. Nevertheless, however, all those interviewed indicated a sense that they were part of a significant social change, and 37 of the 38 interviewees indicated a firm hope that their individual contribution to this changing paradigm would help change existing social conventions. Some had made real sacrifices to achieve this. One mother noted:

> If I had stayed with my first marriage, my first husband expected me to stop working and have babies and go back to work when they went to school. I mean he actually said that, which was the point at which I said: 'Goodbye, I don't want to stay with you.' Because I mean he was absolutely institutionalized and he subsequently remarried and that's exactly what his wife did. And I just laughed. So at that point I thought, 'No', even after only two years, I thought 'this is *not* going to happen like that' so right at that stage it was there, in me, saying 'No, you've *got* to keep going with [your career].
>
> (Sophie, lawyer)

Finally, one father suggested another means through which the attitudes of society might change. David argued that those in single-sex partnerships challenged traditional gendered parenting stereotypes. He regarded this as a major step forward to the benefit of all parents because it validated the concept that men and women should not need to take up institutionalized roles once they became parents:

> Maybe it's the old thing about valuing diversity and two of our friends are lesbian, a lesbian couple, and I have a weird feeling that we're going to have to piggy-back real cultural shifts on the back of quite radical things like single-sex parenting and . . . taking the gay male world as an identity shift for *all* men, *all* males. And I think it's quite interesting how much fascination there has been with those two gay millionaire businessmen who adopted the twins, you know, . . . the fact that they were gay had a lot of 'rightness' about it. And then it was also on the radio and quite a few of the men who phoned in were saying the same thing. And they didn't sound like your reconstructed image of 'new man', they were people who in some ways came across as quite conventional in their view of what a 'man' should do.
>
> (David, psychiatrist)

This is consistent with Giddens' (1992) theory that same-sex couples will be the catalyst for social change because, having faced discrimination by exclusion in many areas (including in the legal sense that they may not marry), they have the opportunity to invent new ways of doing things, this in itself creating new social norms.

Conclusions

The purpose of this book has been to understand what life is like, at the turn of the century, for professional mothers of babies and pre-school children, and for the fathers of these children within marriage/partnership. The objective has been to explore the lived experiences of mothers and fathers and to understand what they are *actually* doing, as opposed to what others might think they *ought* to do. I have attempted to understand how mothers and fathers are managing their day-to-day lives, to explain why mothers are committed to their professional status and to consider the implications this has for family policy and employment. In doing so, I have built upon existing literature on the sociology of parenthood and paid work, contesting assertions that well-qualified mothers should choose between paid work and children (a nonsense in any case, since 452,000 such women in Britain are already combining motherhood with career). Additionally, I have provided a challenge to arguments put forward by writers such as Hakim (1996a, 1996b), Knight (2002) and Tooley (2002) that women are uncommitted to their work, and that they regret the opportunities afforded to them as a result of education and anti-discrimination laws, because they would rather be at home doing wifework. As I have shown, mothers demonstrated that they were deeply committed to their professions, going to great lengths to enable them to continue in employment. Women carried on with their paid work despite ill health, public criticism (Carvel 2001), discriminatory practices in the workplace, and the guilt they felt about leaving children in the care of others. Furthermore, men, as well as women, valued the parent–child relationship to the extent that they were prepared to invest time and hard work in their children. The implication of this was that, in contrast to the findings of Ribbens (1994) and Lewis (1986), fathers were responsible for mediating their own relationships with children, rather than leaving this task to mothers. This meant not merely spending time playing with them but undertaking practical hard work. This is a major, new finding in terms of the existing literature, where it is argued that fathers rarely undertake emotional labour in relation to children unless this is *post*-divorce. This has implications for family practices and family policy in the future, as it implies that employers and government agencies cannot assume that only employed women might be involved in caring for their children.

Finally, I have shown that many mothers and some fathers experienced discrimination from employers and colleagues in relation to their children and childcare responsibilities. Given that equal opportunities legislation and local employers' policies are supposed to protect parents from unfair treatment at work, the inference is that, over 25 years since the Sex Discrimination Act became law, policies are still ineffective. This problem might apply to a much wider population, including those who are in low-paid jobs with no qualifications and without transferable skills upon which to draw when attempting to negotiate flexible working. The provision by society of better assistance and protection for working parents is key if mothers and fathers of all socio-economic levels are to continue combining parenting with paid work because, as McDowell (2001: 460) notes, unless 'care-giving becomes universal', women will be for ever trapped in their institutionalized roles. While mothers and fathers are more than willing to take responsibility for parenting their small children, they are calling for a more supportive attitude from society. Parents contend that they are raising the next generation of adults who will teach in schools, run our state systems and care for us when we are ill. Today's children will also be contributing to a future economy which will be funding our pensions – an important issue for all members of society. Thus, the parents who took part in this research are seeking better support from society in the broadest sense. As Valeska (1984) argued: '*My* children must become *our* children'.

References

Achilles Heel (1994) The radical men's magazine, *Families need Fathers*, issue 17, http://home.freeuk.net/achillesheel/article 17–2.html (last accessed 5 July 2002).

Adkins, L. (1995) *Gendered Work, Sexuality, Family and the Labour Market*. Buckingham: Open University Press.

Aiken, O. (1998) Back into the fold, *People Management*, 4: 7.

Allen, S. and Hawkins, A. (1999) Maternal gatekeeping: mothers' beliefs and behaviours that inhibit greater father involvement in family work, *Journal of Marriage and the Family*, 61: 199–212.

Ananova (2004) Children raised by lesbian couples 'aren't disadvantaged'. http://www.ananova.com/news/story/sm-482039.html (last accessed 5 April 2004).

Appleyard, D. (2000) Motherhood, the next generation, *Daily Mail*, 3 August: 41–8.

Appleyard, D. (2003) Meet the REAL Stepford Wives! *Daily Mail*, 3 November: 28–9.

Armistead, L. (2002) Trouble with women. Why can't more women do as well in business as Barbara Cassani? *Sunday Times, Business Focus*, 28 April: 5.

Audit Commission (1997) *First Class Delivery: Improving Maternity Services in England and Wales*. London: Audit Commission.

Backett-Milburn, K., Cunningham-Burley, S. and Kemmer, D. (2001) *Caring and Providing: Lone and Partnered Working Mothers in Scotland*. Bristol: Family Policy Studies Centre.

Baxter, S. (2002) Flying solo: Almost half of all powerful career women are childless – but only a few through choice, *Sunday Times News Review*, 7 April: 8.

Beasley, C. (1999) *What is Feminism? An Introduction to Feminist Theory*. London: Sage.

Beck, U. (1992) *Risk Society: Towards a New Modernity*, London: Sage.

Beck, U. and Beck-Gernsheim, E. (1995) *The Normal Chaos of Love*. Cambridge: Polity Press.

Beck-Gernsheim, E. (2002) *Reinventing the Family: In Search of New Lifestyles*. Cambridge: Polity Press.

Bernardes, J. (1997) *Family Studies, An Introduction*. London: Routledge.

Boase, T. (2001) The baby war, *Sunday Times News Review*, 11 November: 1–2.

Bostock, L. (1998) 'It's Catch 22 all the time'. Mothers' experiences of caring on low incomes in the 1990s. Unpublished PhD thesis, Lancaster University.

Bowlby, J. (1965) *Child Care and the Growth of Love*, 2nd edition. Harmondsworth: Penguin.

Brannen, J. and Moss, P. (1991) *Managing Mothers: Dual Earner Households after Maternity Leave*. London: Unwin Hyman.

Brannen, J., Meszaros, G., Moss, P. and Poland, G. (1994) *Employment and Family Life: A Review of Research in the UK (1980–1994)*. Research Series no. 41. Centre for Research on Family Life and Employment, Thomas Coram Research Unit, University of London, Employment Department.

Buckingham, L. (2002) Afraid to tackle the sexists in the city? *Financial Mail on Sunday*, 23 June: 3.

Burghes, L., Clarke, C. and Cronin, N. (1997) *Fathers and Fatherhood in Britain*. London: Family Policy Studies Centre.

Buxton, J. (1998) *Ending the Mother War, Starting the Workplace Revolution*. London: Macmillan.

Carvel, J. (2001) Children of working mothers 'at risk', *The Guardian*, 14 March: 6.

Chira, S. (1998) *A Mother's Place: Choosing Work and Family without Guilt or Blame*. New York: Harper Perennial.

Cockburn, C. (2002) Resisting equal opportunities: the issue of maternity, in S. Jackson and S. Scott (eds) *Gender: A Sociological Reader*. London: Routledge.

Collier, R. (1994) The campaign against the Child Support Act: errant fathers and family men, *Family Law*, July: 384–7.

Collier, R. (1995) *Masculinity, Law and the Family*. London: Routledge.

Collier, R. (2001) A hard time to be a father? Reassessing the relationship between laws, policy, and family (practices), *Journal of Law and Society*, 28: 520–45.

Cosslett, T. (1994) *Women Writing Childbirth: Modern Discourses of Motherhood*. Manchester: Manchester University Press.

Cottee, A. (2001) No more Mrs Superwoman, *Daily Mail*, 27 February: 34–5.

Crompton, R. (1997) *Women and Work in Modern Britain*. Oxford: Oxford University Press.

Cusk, R. (2001) *A Life's Work: On Becoming a Mother*. London: Fourth Estate.

Davidson, J. (2001) Pregnant pauses: agoraphobic embodiment and the limits of (im)pregnability, *Gender, Place and Culture*, 1: 283–97.

Davies, H., Joshi, H. and Peronaci, R. (2000) Forgone income and motherhood: what do recent British data tell us? *Population Studies*, 54: 293–305.

Daycare Trust (2002) News from Daycare Trust. http://www.daycaretrust.org.uk (last accessed 5 July 2002).

Deem, R. (1996) No time for a rest? An exploration of women's work, engendered leisure and holidays, *Time and Society*, 5: 5–25.

Delphy, C. and Leonard, D. (1992) *Familiar Exploitation: A New Analysis of Marriage in Contemporary Western Societies*. Oxford: Polity Press, in association with Blackwell Publishers.

Department of Health (1993) *Changing Childbirth, Report of the Expert Maternity Group*. London: HMSO.

Department of Trade and Industry (2002) *Employment, Work and Parents: Competitiveness and Choice*. http://www.dti.gov.uk/er/workparents.

Dex, S., Joshi, H., Macran, S. and McCulloch, A. (1998) Women's employment transitions around childbearing, *Oxford Bulletin of Economics and Statistics*, 60: 79.

Dienhart, A. (1998) *Reshaping Fatherhood: The Social Construction of Shared Parenting*. Thousand Oaks, CA: Sage.

Dobson, R. and Chittenden, M. (2002) Working mothers' children lag behind in tests, *Sunday Times*, 28 July: 10.

Doucet, A. (1995) Gender equality and gender differences in household work and parenting, *Women's Studies International Forum*, 18: 271–84.

Driscoll, M. (2002) Can Superwoman still fly? *Sunday Times Focus*, 16 June: 19.

Driscoll, M. (2003) Selling out, *Sunday Times News Review*, 14 September: 1–2.

Driscoll, M. and Waterhouse, R. (2002) Some mothers can't 'ave 'em, *Sunday Times*, 27 January: 14.

Dryden, C. (1999) *Being Married, Doing Gender*. London: Routledge.

Duncombe, J. and Marsden, D. (1993) Love and intimacy: the gender division of emotion and emotion work, a neglected aspect of sociological discussion of heterosexual relationships, *Sociology*, 27: 221–41.

Duncombe, J. and Marsden, D. (2002) Whose orgasm is this anyway? 'Sex work' in long term heterosexual relationships, in S. Jackson and S. Scott (eds) *Gender: A Sociological Reader*. London: Routledge.

Dunne, G. (1999) A passion for 'sameness?' Sexuality and gender accountability, in E. Silva and C. Smart (eds) *The New Family?* London: Sage.

Durham, M. (2002) Stand up, you wimpy invisible fathers, *Sunday Times News Review*, 16 June: 6.

Dyck I. (1990) Space, time, and renegotiating motherhood: an exploration of the domestic workplace, *Environment and Planning D: Society and Space*, 8: 459–83.

Eastham, P. (2002) 'Train more male GPs', *Daily Mail*, 10 April: 30.

Ehrenreich, B. and Hochschild, A. (eds) (2003) *Global Woman: Nannies, Maids and Sex Workers in the New Economy*. London: Granta.

Eichler, M. (1997) *Family Shifts, Families, Policies, and Gender Equality*. Oxford: Oxford University Press.

Etzioni, A. (1993) *The Parenting Deficit*. London: Demos.

Families Need Fathers (2002) *Founding Fathers*. http://ww.fnf.org.uk/history.htm (last accessed 5 July 2002).

Figes, K. (1998a) *Life after Birth*. London: Viking.

Figes, K. (1988b) Mother heroine of work culture, *The Guardian*, 12 December: 12.

Figes, K. (2001) Home rules? *The Guardian G2*, 14 March: 9.

Finch, J. (1989) *Family Obligations and Social Change*. Cambridge: Polity Press.

Finn, W. (1998) Pass the parcel, *Director*, 52: 33–7.

Firestone, S. (1970) *The Dialectic of Sex*. New York: William Morrow and Co.

Foucault, M. (1990) *Politics, Philosophy, Culture: Interviews and Other Writings 1977–1984*. New York: Routledge.

Franks, S. (1999) *Having None of It: Women, Men and the Future of Work*. London: Granta.

Freely, M. (2000) *The Parent Trap: Children, Families and the New Morality*. London: Virago Press.

Friedan, B. (1965) *The Feminine Mystique*. Harmondsworth: Penguin.

Gaillie, D., White, M., Cheng, Y. and Tomlinson, M. (1998) *Restructuring the Employment Relationship*. Oxford: Clarendon Press.

Gatrell, C. and Turnbull, S., (2003) *Your MBA with Distinction: A System for Succeeding in Your Business Degree*. London: FT/Prentice Hall.

Giddens, A. (1979) *Central Problems in Social Theory: Action, Structure and Contradiction in Social Analysis*. London: Macmillan.

Giddens, A. (1984) *The Constitution of Society*. Cambridge: Polity Press.

Giddens, A. (1992) *Transformation of Intimacy, Sexuality, Love and Eroticism in Modern Societies*. Cambridge: Polity Press.

Giddens, A. (1993) *New Rules of Sociological Method*. Cambridge: Polity Press.

Gilman, C.P. (1998) *Women and Economics*. Mineola, N.Y.: Dover Publications. First published in 1898.

Gilman, C.P. (2002) *The Home: Its Work and Influence*. Walnut Creek, CA: AltaMira Press. First published in 1903.

Ginn, J., Arber, S., Brannen, J., Dale, A., Dex, S., Elias, P., Moss, P., Pahl, J., Roberts, C. and Rubery, J. (1996) Feminist fallacies: a reply to Hakim on women's employment, *British Journal of Sociology*, 47: 167–74.

Goldbeck-Wood, S. (1997) Women's autonomy in childbirth, *British Medical Journal*, 314: 1143.

Graham, H. (1983) Do her answers fit his questions? Women and the survey method, in E. Gamarnikow, D. Morgan, J. Purvis and D. Taylorson (eds) *The Public and the Private*. London: Heinemann.

Graham, H. (1993) *Hardship and Health in Women's Lives*. Hemel Hempstead: Harvester Wheatsheaf.

Graham, H. and McKee, L. (1980) *The First Months of Motherhood*. Summary Report. Health Education Council Monograph Series (No. 3), London.

Greer, G. (1970) *The Female Eunuch*. London: MacGibbon and Kee.

Gregson, N. and Lowe, M. (1994) *Servicing the Middle Classes: Class Gender and Waged Domestic Labour in Contemporary Britain*. London: Routledge.

Grief, G. and De Maris, A. (1995) Single fathers with custody: Do they change over time?, in M. Marsiglio (ed.) *Fatherhood: Contemporary Theory, Research and Social Policy*. Thousand Oaks, CA: Sage.

Grint, K. (1998) *The Sociology of Work*. Cambridge: Polity Press.

Hakim, C. (1995) Five feminist myths about women's employment, *British Journal of Sociology*, 46: 429–55.

Hakim, C. (1996a) *Key Issues in Women's Work: Female Heterogeneity and the Polarisation of Women's Employment*. London: Athlone.

Hakim, C. (1996b) The sexual division of labour and women's heterogeneity, *British Journal of Sociology*, 47: 178–88.

Hakim, C. (2000) *Work-Lifestyle Choices in the 21st Century: Preference Theory*. Oxford: Oxford University Press.

Hakim, C. (2003) *Models of the Family in Modern Societies, Ideals and Realities*. Aldershot: Ashgate.

Halford, S., Savage, M. and Witz, A. (1997) *Gender, Careers and Organisation: Current Developments in Banking, Nursing and Local Government*. London: Macmillan.

Harding, S. (ed.) (1987) *Feminism and Methodology*. Milton Keynes: Open University Press.

Haywood, C. and Mac an Ghaill, M. (2003) *Men and Masculinities*. Buckingham: Open University Press.

Hewlett, S. (2002) *Baby Hunger: The New Battle for Motherhood*. London: Atlantic Books.

Hitchens, P. (2002) Why can't we free our wage-slave mothers? *The Mail on Sunday*, 7 April: 29.

Hochschild, A. (1983) *The Managed Heart*. Berkeley: University of California Press.

Hochschild, A. (1997) *The Time Bind: When Work Becomes Home and Home Becomes Work*. New York: Henry Holt.

Horna, J. and Lupri, E. (1987) Father's participation in work, family life and leisure: a Canadian experience, in C. Lewis and M. O'Brien (eds) *Reassessing Fatherhood*. London: Sage.

Howlings, J. (1998) Expecting dismissal? *People Management*, 4: 23.

Hughes, D. and Dean, J. (2001) Firms' alarm as mothers are offered a year off with baby, *Daily Mail*, 2 May: 15.

HRM Guide Canada (2004) http://www.hrmguide.net/canada/diversity/ gender_gap.htm (last accessed 18 February 2004).

Jackson, J. (2002) Letter of the week, Letters, *The Mail on Sunday*, 16 June: 80.

Jackson, S. and Jones, J. (1998) *Contemporary Feminist Theories*. Edinburgh: Edinburgh University Press.

Joshi, H. and Paci, P. (1998) *Unequal Pay for Women and Men: Evidence from the British Birth Cohort Studies*. Cambridge, MA: MIT Press.

Joshi, H., Paci, P. and Waldfogel, J. (1999) The wages of motherhood: better or worse? *Cambridge Journal of Economics*, 23: 534–64.

Kaplan, M.M. (1992) *Mothers' Images of Motherhood*. London: Routledge.

Kaufmann, J.-C. (1998) *Dirty Linen: Couples and their Laundry*. London: Middlesex University Press.

Kitzinger, S. (1984) *The Experience of Childbirth*. London: Penguin.

Kitzinger, S. (1992a) Birth and violence against women: generating hypotheses from women's accounts of unhappiness after childbirth, in H. Roberts (ed.) *Women's Health Matters*. London: Routledge.

Kitzinger, S. (1992b) Childbirth and Society, in I. Chelmers, M. Enkin and M. Keirse (eds) *Effective Care in Pregnancy and Childbirth*. Oxford: Oxford University Press.

Knight, I. (2002) The role models we love to hate, *Sunday Times News Review*, 16 June: 4.

Kvande, E. and Rasmussen, B. (1995) Women's careers in static and dynamic organizations, *Acta Sociologica*, 38: 115–30.

Latour, B. (1986) The powers of association, in J. Law (ed.) *Power, Action and Belief: a New Sociology of Knowledge*. Sociological Review Monograph 32. London: Routledge & Kegan Paul.

Law, J. (1992) Notes on the theory of the actor-network: Ordering, strategy and heterogeneity, *Systems Practice*, 5: 379–93.

Law, J. (1994) *Organizing Modernity*. Oxford: Blackwell.

Lawlor, J. (1998) The benefits of companies that care, *Sales and Marketing Management*, 2: 51.

Lawson, N. (2000) *How to Be a Domestic Goddess: Baking and the Art of Comfort Cooking*. London: Chatto and Windus.

Lea, R., (2001) *The Work–Life Balance and All That. The Re-regulation of the Labour Market*. IoD Policy Paper. London: Institute of Directors.

Lewis, C. (1986) *Becoming a Father*. Milton Keynes: Open University Press.

Lewis, P. (2000) Pregnancy and maternity leave: employment law as a family friend? *Industrial Relations Journal*, 31(2): 130–43.

Lupton, D. and Barclay, L. (1997) *Constructing Fatherhood: Discourses and Experiences*. London: Sage.

MacMillan, I.C. and Jones, P. (1986) *Strategy Formulation*. St Paul, MN: West.

Macran, S., Joshi, H. and Dex, S. (1996) Employment after childbearing: a survival analysis, *Work, Employment and Society*, 10: 273–96.

Malthouse, T.-J. (1997) *Childcare, Business and Social Change*. London: Institute of Directors.

Malthouse, T.-J. (1998) *Maternity: Institute of Directors Employment Comment*. London: Institute of Directors.

Marshall, H. (1991) The social construction of motherhood: an analysis of childcare and parenting manuals, in A. Phoenix, A. Woollett and E. Lloyd (eds) *Motherhood: Meanings, Practices and Ideologies*. London: Sage.

Marshall, H. and Wetherall, M. (1989) Talking about career and gender identities: a discourse analysis perspective, in S. Skevington and D. Baker (eds) *The Social Identity of Women*. London: Sage.

Maushart, S. (2002) *Wifework: What Marriage Really Means for Women*. London: Bloomsbury.

McDowell, L. (2001) Father and Ford revisited: Gender, class and employment change in the new millennium, *Transactions of the Institute of British Geographers*, 26: 448–65.

McIntyre, S. (2002) Babies turn women into jelly-heads, *Daily Mail*, 10 August: 15.

McMullen, J. (1999) Ignorance is no defence, *British Journal of Administrative Management*, May/June: 19.

McNay, L. (1992) *Foucault and Feminism: Power, Gender and the Self*. Cambridge: Polity Press.

Miles, A. (1992) *Women, Health and Medicine*. Buckingham: Open University Press.

Millar, J. (1998) Policy and changing family forms: placing lone motherhood in context, in *Proceedings from Seminar 'Current Research on Lone Mothers'*. Centre for the Analysis of Social Policy, University of Bath.

Morgan, D. (1975) *Social Theory and the Family*. London: Routledge & Kegan Paul.

Morgan, D. (1985) *The Family, Politics and Social Theory*. London: Routledge & Kegan Paul.

Morgan, D. (1992) *Discovering Men*. London: Routledge.

Morgan, D. (1996) *Family Connections: An Introduction to Family Studies*. Oxford: Polity Press, in association with Blackwell Publishers Ltd.

Morgan, D. (2002) You too can have a body like mine, in S. Jackson and S. Scott (eds) *Gender: A Sociological Reader*. London: Routledge.

Morgan, G. (1986) *Images of Organisation*. London: Sage.

Morgan, P. (1999) *Farewell to the Family? Public Policy and Family Breakdown in Britain and the USA*. London: IEA Health and Welfare Unit.

Morris, L. (1990) *The Workings of the Household*. Cambridge: Polity Press.

Oakley, A. (1976) *Housewife: High Value, Low Cost*. London: Penguin.

Oakley, A. (1981) *From Here to Maternity: Becoming a Mother*. Harmondsworth: Penguin.

Oakley, A. (1984) *The Captured Womb*. Oxford: Blackwell.

Oakley, A. (1993) *Essays on Women, Medicine and Health*. Edinburgh: Edinburgh University Press.

Oakley, A. (2000) *Experiments in Knowing: Gender and Method in the Social Sciences*. Cambridge: Polity Press.

Oakley, A. (2002) *Gender on Planet Earth*. Cambridge: Polity Press.

O'Brien, M. (1981) *The Politics of Reproduction*. London: Routledge & Kegan Paul.

Padavic, I. and Reskin, B. (2002) *Women and Men at Work*. Thousand Oaks, CA: Pine Forge Press.

Pahl, J. (1989) *Money and Marriage*. Basingstoke: Macmillan.

Pahl, R. (1993) Rigid flexibilities? Work between women and men, *Work, Employment and Society*, 7: 629–42.

Parsons, T. (1971) The normal American family, in B. Adams and T. Weirath (eds) *Readings on the Sociology of the Family*. Chicago: Markham.

Parsons, T. and Bales, R. (1956) *Family and Socialization and Interaction Process*. London: Routledge & Kegan Paul.

Pasley, K., Futris, T. and Skinner, M. (2002) Effects of commitment and psychological centrality of fathering, *Journal of Marriage and the Family*, 643: 130–8.

Patmore, C. (1856) *The Angel in the House*. London: Boston, Ticknor and Fields.

Pearson, A. (2003) *I Don't Know How She Does It*. London: Chatto and Windus.

Phillips, M. (1999) Women want the right to work – and not to work, *The Sunday Times*, 11 November: 17.

Phoenix, A., Woollett, A. and Lloyd, E. (eds) (1991) *Motherhood: Meanings, Practices and Ideologies*. London: Sage.

Poovey, M. (1986) The medical treatment of Victorian women, in C. Gallagher and T. Laquer (eds) *The Making of the Modern Body*. London: University of California Press.

Popay, J. (1992) 'My health is all right, but I'm just tired all the time': women's experiences of ill-health, in H. Roberts (ed.) *Women's Health Matters*. London: Routledge.

Porter, S. (1998) *Social Theory and Nursing Practice*. London: Macmillan Press.

Potuchek, J.L. (1997) *Who Supports the Family? Gender and Breadwinning in Dual Earner Marriages*. Stanford, CA: Stanford University Press.

Pringle, R. (1998) *Sex and Medicine*. Cambridge: Cambridge University Press.

Pullinger, J. and Summerfield, C. (1998) *Social Focus on Women and Men*. Office for National Statistics. London: The Stationery Office.

Quigg, M.R. (2001) *Mary Rose's 1001 Country Household Hints*. Devizes: Selectabook.

Rhoades, H. (2002) The 'no contact mother': reconstructions of motherhood in the era of the 'new father', *International Journal of Law, Policy and the Family*, 16: 71–94.

Ribbens, J. (1994) *Mothers and Their Children: A Feminist Sociology of Child-rearing*. London: Sage.

Rich, A. (1977) *Of Woman Born: Motherhood as Experience and Institution*. London: Virago.

Robertson, R. and Turner, B. (1991) An introduction to Talcott Parsons: theory, politics and humanity, in R. Robertson and B. Turner (eds) *Talcott Parsons: Theorist of Modernity*. London: Sage.

Rothman, B.K. (1982) *In Labor: Women, and Power in the Birthplace*. New York: W.W. Norton.

Rowbotham, S. (1997) *A Century of Women: The History of Women in Britain and the United States*. London: Penguin.

Scott, J. (1999) Family change: revolution or backlash? in S. McRae (ed.) *Changing Britain, Families and Households in the 1990s*. Oxford: Oxford University Press.

Scott, J. and Duncombe, J. (1991) *A Cross-National Comparison of Gender-Role Attitudes: Is the Working Mother Selfish?* Paper Number 9, Working Papers of the ESRC Centre on Micro-social Change.

Seltzer, J. and Brandreth, Y. (1995) What fathers say about involvement with children after separation, in W. Marsiglio (ed.) *Fatherhood: Contemporary Theory, Research and Social Policy*. Thousand Oaks, CA: Sage.

Silva, E.B. (1996) *Good Enough Mothering? Feminist Perspectives on Lone Motherhood*. London: Routledge.

Silva, E. (1999) Transforming housewifery: dispositions, practices and technologies, in E. Silva and C. Smart (eds) *The New Family?* London: Sage.

Silva, E.B. and Smart, C. (eds) (1999) *The New Family?* London: Sage.

Silver, R. (1985) *Health Service Public Relations: A Guide to Good Practice*. London: King Edward's Hospital Fund.

Skevington, S. and Baker, D. (eds) (1989) *The Social Identity of Women*. London: Sage.

Smart, C. and Neale, B. (1999) *Family Fragments?* Cambridge: Polity Press.

Somerville, J. (2000) *Feminism and the Family: Politics and Society in the UK and the USA*. Basingstoke: Macmillan Press.

Spender, D. (1982) *Invisible Women: The Schooling Scandal*. London: Writers and Readers.

Stanley, L. and Wise, S. (1993) *Breaking Out Again: Feminist Ontology and Epistemology*. London: Routledge.

Stoffman, J. (2002) Working Mom's Oscar Wilde, *The Toronto Star*, Sunday Entertainment, Books: 1.

Sullivan, O. (1997) Time waits for no (wo)man: an investigation of the gendered experience of domestic time, *Sociology*, 31: 221–39.

Summerfield, P. (1998) *Reconstructing Women's Wartime Lives*. Manchester: Manchester University Press.

Taylor, D. (2001) The question: US research suggests that toddlers who spend more time in childcare are . . . 'smart and nasty', *The Guardian G2*, 25 April: 11.

Thair, T. and Risdon, A. (1999) Women in the labour market: Results from the Spring 1998 Labour Force Survey, *Labour Market Trends*, 107: 103–28.

Tooley, J. (2002) *The Miseducation of Women*. London: Continuum.

Top Santé (1999) Worked up and worn out, *Top Santé*, April: 94–5.

Towers, S. (2001) Equal? *Sunday Times*, 18 November: 4 (letters).

Valeska, L. (1984) If all else fails I'm still a mother, in J. Trebilcot (ed.) *Mothering: Essays in Feminist Theory*. Totowa, NJ: Rowman and Allanheld. Essay first published in 1975.

Van Every, J. (1995) De/Reconstructing gender: women in anti-sexist living arrangements, *Women's Studies International Forum*, 18: 259–69.

Vogler, C. and Pahl, J. (1993) Social and economic change and the organisation of money within marriage, *Work, Employment and Society*, 7: 71–95.

Vogler, C. and Pahl, J. (1994) Money, power and inequality within marriage, *Sociological Review*, 42: 263–88.

Walby, S. (1990) *Theorising Patriarchy*. Oxford: Blackwell.

Walsh, J. (1998) Sex discrimination claims put EOC on the defensive, *People Management*, 4: 12–13.

Walters, J., Tasker, F. and Bichard, S. (2001) 'Too busy?' Fathers' attendance for family appointments, *Journal of Family Therapy*, 23: 3–20.

Walzer, S. (1996) Thinking about the baby: gender and divisions of infant care, *Social Problems*, 43(2): 219–34.

Warin, J., Solomon, Y., Lewis, C. and Langford, W. (1999) *Fathers, Work and Family Life*. London: Family Policy Studies Centre.

Waters, J. (1999) Prejudice is right on – the men are the victims, *Irish Times*, 12 January: 14.

Welch, J. (1997) Parents' rights still in infancy, firms admit, *People Management*, 3: 11.

Whitehead, S. (2002) *Men and Masculinities*. Cambridge: Polity Press.

Winston, P. (1998) It's time to clarify UK workers' rights, *Business Insurance*, 32: 41.

Wishart, H. (2002) No shades of grey in a two tone world, *Times Higher Educational Supplement*, 6 September: 32.

Woolf, V. (1979) *Women and Writing*. London: Women's Press.

Yates, A. (2001) Are working mothers cheats? *Sunday Times*, 18 November: 4 (letters).

Yudovin, S., Eldridge, H., Maher, A. and Madell, R. (1999) The power study, *Pharmaceutical Executive*, 19: 122–42.

Index

Page references in italics refer to tables

WORK, CONSUMERISM AND THE NEW POOR
SECOND EDITION

Zygmunt Bauman

Reviewers' comments on the first edition:

> Zygmunt Bauman presents a cogently argued and compelling thesis . . . an important book from a distinguished scholar that adds a new dimension to the poverty debate.
>
> *British Journal of Sociology*

> It will be of great interest and value to students, teachers and researchers in sociology and social policy . . . [Bauman] provides a very forceful and sophisticated statement of the case; and a very well written one too. As a wide ranging analysis of our present discontents it is an admirable example of the sort of challenge which sociology at its best can offer to us and our fellow citizens to re-assess and re-think our current social arrangements.
>
> *Work, Employment and Society*

> This is a stylish and persuasive analysis of the transition between the age of the 'society of producers' to that of the 'society of consumers'.
>
> *Political Studies*

It is one thing to be poor in a society of producers and universal employment; it is quite a different thing to be poor in a society of consumers, in which life projects are built around consumer choices rather than on work, professional skills or jobs. Where 'being poor' was once linked to being unemployed, today it draws its meaning primarily from the plight of a flawed consumer. This has a significant effect on the way living in poverty is experienced and on the prospects for redeeming its misery.

Work, Consumerism and the New Poor traces this change over the duration of modern history. It makes an inventory of its social consequences, and considers how effective different ways of fighting poverty and relieving its hardships are.

The new edition of this seminal work features:

- Updated coverage of key thinkers in the field
- Discussion of recent work on redundancy, disposability and exclusion
- Current thinking on the effects of capital flows on different countries and the changes on the shop floor through, for example, business process re-engineering
- New material on security and vulnerability

Key reading for students and lecturers in sociology, politics and social policy, and those with an interest in contemporary social issues.

Contents:
*Series editor's foreword – Introduction – **Part one:** The meaning of work: producing the work ethic – From the work ethic to the aesthetic of consumption – **Part two:** The rise and fall of the welfare state – The work ethic and the new poor – Work and redundancy in the globalized world – **Part three:** Prospects for the new poor – Notes – Index.*

144pp   0 335 21598 X (Paperback)   0 335 21599 8 (Hardback)

SOCIAL EXCLUSION
SECOND EDITION

David Byrne

Social exclusion' is the buzz phrase in social policy and social politics across most of contemporary Europe. It is a description of the condition of individuals, households, neighbourhoods, ethnic and other 'identity' groups, who can be identified as socially excluded.

The second edition of this widely read book returns to these issues at the beginning of the twenty-first century. It explores developments in social theory, social experience and social policy in relation to social exclusion. The first part examines the origins of the term and implications of the difference between the ideas of 'exclusion', 'underclass', 'residuum' and related concepts. The discussion is informed by the application of 'Complexity Theory'. In the updated second part, the theoretical account is developed through a detailed review of the dynamics of individual lives in a changing social order. Income equality, spatial division, and exclusion in relation to health, education and cultural provision and processes are examined in a range of societies in Europe, North America and 'the South'.

The last part contains a new chapter outlining the content and impact of national and international policies which have been specifically developed to address issues of exclusion. These approaches are tested against a proposed 'radical alternative', based on an integration of the participatory programme best known through the work of Paulo Freire and the complexity based approach which informs the books as a whole.

Contents

204pp   0 335 21594 7 (Paperback)   0 335 21595 5 (Hardback)

GENDER AND SOCIAL THEORY

Mary Evans

- What is the most significant aspect of current literature on gender?
- How does this literature engage with social theory?
- How does the recognition of gender shift the central arguments of social theory?

We know that gender defines and shapes our lives. The question addressed by *Gender and Social Theory* is that of exactly how this process occurs, and what the social consequences, and the consequences for social theory, might be. The emergence of feminist theory has enriched our understanding of the impact of gender on our individual lives and the contemporary social sciences all recognise gender differentiation in the social world. The issue, however, which this book discusses is the more complex question of the extent to which social theory is significantly disrupted, disturbed or devalued by the fuller recognition of gender difference.

Mary Evans examines whether social theory is as blind to gender as is sometimes argued and considers the extent to which a greater awareness of gender truly shifts the concerns and conclusions of social theory. Written by an author with an international reputation, this is an invaluable text for students and an essential reference in the field.

Contents
Series foreword – Acknowledgements – Introduction – Enter women – The meaning of work – The world of intimacy – The gendered self – The real world – Now you see it, now you don't – Notes – Bibliography – Index.

160pp   0 335 20864 9 (Paperback)   0 335 20865 7 (Hardback)

TRANSITIONS IN CONTEXT
LEAVING HOME, INDEPENDENCE AND ADULTHOOD

Clare Holdsworth and David Morgan

This book addresses important aspects of youth transitions, by considering cross-cultural differences in leaving home experiences and the inter-relationships between transitions to adulthood, the achievement of independence and leaving home. It places the processes of leaving the parental home in a wider perspective, theoretically and in terms of policy concerns. There is a comparative emphasis throughout the text.

Drawing on a broad range of disciplines including sociology, social policy, geography, youth studies and cultural studies, this is a key text for researchers, post-graduate students and final year undergraduates interested in issues related to the family, youth studies and comparative sociology.

Contents
Introduction – Trends and Comparisons – Methodological Issues and Theoretical Approaches – Time, Process and The Life Course – Space, Place and Home – Independence – Adulthood – Social Embeddedness: Family, State and Social Networks – Conclusion – Index.

192pp   0 335 21538 6 (Paperback)   0 335 21539 4 (Hardback)

FEMINIST RESEARCH IN THEORY AND PRACTICE

Gayle Letherby

This is a clear and accessible exploration of feminist method, methodology and epistemology. After situating herself and her work, Gayle Letherby charts the debates concerned with the epistemological, political and practical issues involved in doing feminist research, and places the debates within a wider consideration of the status of knowledge. The main focus of the book is then the particular and practical issues for feminist researchers. It examines how the process of research affects the results of that research and explores the relation between politics and practice in terms of research and knowledge production. Throughout the book there is a practical emphasis on specific examples of feminist research in action and, as well as summarizing current theoretical debates, Gayle Letherby adds to them.

Feminist Research in Theory and Practice is designed and written as a textbook for students (at advanced undergraduate and postgraduate level) but will be a valuable resource for any researcher or individual interested in women's studies, feminism and in researching in the social sciences.

Contents
Acknowledgements – Introduction – Educating Rita revisited: knowledge and language in the 'male' academy – United we stand? The feminist reconstruction of knowledge – Doing it for ourselves: feminist research as feminist theory in action – Quoting and counting: the qualitative/quantitative divide – Whose life is it anyway? Issues of power, empowerment, ethics and responsibility – Texts of many lives: the implications for feminist research – Close encounters: presentations and audiences – Reflections – References – Index.

208pp   0 335 20028 1 (Paperback)   0 335 21464 9 (Hardback)

ENGENDERING THE SOCIAL
FEMINIST ENCOUNTERS WITH SOCIOLOGICAL THEORY

Barbara L. Marshall and Anne Witz (eds)

- How were the foundations of sociological theory shaped by an implicit masculinity?
- Did classical sociology simply reflect or actively construct theories of sexual difference?
- How were alternative accounts of the social suppressed in sociology's founding moments?
- Does the masculine subject still lurk beneath the allegedly generic individual in modern sociological theory?

The focus of this edited volume is on the problematic engendering of classical and contemporary sociological theory. Feminist interventions in sociology continue to be regarded as marginal to the enterprise of sociological theorizing, resulting in a truncated vision of the scope and concerns of sociological theory. This collection challenges this narrow vision, and contributes to expanding the conventional diet of sociological theory. In part one, contributors interrogate the classical canon, exposing the masculinist assumptions that saturate the conceptual scaffolding of sociology. In part two, contributors consider the long-standing and problematic relation between sociology and feminism, retrieving voices marginalized within or excluded from canonical constructions of sociological theory. In part three, contributors engage with key contemporary debates, explicitly engendering ostensibly gender-neutral accounts of the social. This collection is unique in that it goes beyond a critical feminist interrogation of sociological theory to develop a politics of reconstruction, working creatively with the sociological heritage to induce a more adequate conceptualisation of the social.

Contents

192pp   0335 21269 7 (Paperback)   0335 21270 0 (Hardback)

FAMILIES, VIOLENCE AND SOCIAL CHANGE

Linda McKie

An exciting new addition to the series, this book tackles assumptions surrounding the family as a changing institution and supposed haven from the public sphere of life. It considers families and social change in terms of concepts of power, inequality, gender, generations, sexuality and ethnicity.

Some commentators suggest the family is threatened by increasing economic and social uncertainties and an enhanced focus upon the individual. This book provides a resume of these debates, as well as a critical review of the theories of family and social change:

- Charts social and economic changes and their impact on the family
- Considers the prevalence and nature of abuse within families
- Explores the relationship between social theory, families and changing issues in familial relationships
- Develops a theory of social change and families through a critical and pragmatic stance

Key reading for undergraduate students of sociology reading courses such as family, gender, health, criminology and social change.

Contents

*Series editor's foreword – Acknowledgements – Introduction – **Part one:** Families, violence and society – Your family, my family, their family – Identifying and explaining violence in families – Families: Fusion and fission – **Part two:** Gender, age and violence – Embodiment, gender and violence – The ambiguities of elder abuse: Older women and domestic violence – **Part three:** Towards a critical theory – Unpalatable truths: Recognizing and challenging myths – A critical social theory of families, violence and social change – Conclusions – References – Index*

c.192pp   0 335 21158 5 (Paperback)   0 335 21159 3 (Hardback)